# Understanding Post-Communist Transformation

The fall of the Berlin Wall launched the transformation of government, economy and society across half of Europe and the former Soviet Union. This text deals with the process of change in former Communist bloc countries, ten of which have become new European Union (EU) democracies while Russia and her neighbours remain burdened by their Soviet legacy.

Drawing on more than one hundred public-opinion surveys from the New Europe Barometer, the text compares how ordinary people have coped with the stresses and opportunities of transforming Communist societies into post-Communist societies and the resulting differences between peoples in the new EU member states and Russia.

Subjects covered by *Understanding Post-Communist Transformation* include:

- Stresses and opportunities of economic transformation
- Social capital and the development of civil society
- Elections and the complexities of party politics
- The challenges for the EU of raising standards of democratic governance
- Differences between Russia's and the West's interpretations of political life.

Written by one of the world's most renowned authorities on this subject, this text is ideal for courses on transition, post-Communism, democratizations and Russian and Eastern European history and politics.

**Richard Rose** is the Director of the Centre for the Study of Public Policy, University of Aberdeen. A fellow of the British Academy and of the American Academy of Arts and Sciences, he has published over 40 books translated into 18 languages.

# Understanding Post-Communist Transformation

## A bottom up approach

**Richard Rose**

LONDON AND NEW YORK

First published 2009 by Routledge
2 Park Square, Milton Park, Abingdon, Oxon, OX14 4RN

Simultaneously published in the USA and Canada
by Routledge
270 Madison Avenue, New York, NY 10016

*Routledge is an imprint of the Taylor & Francis Group, an informa business*

Typeset in 10/12pt Times NR MT by Graphicraft Limited, Hong Kong
Printed and bound in Great Britain by TJ International Ltd, Padstow,
Cornwall

*British Library Cataloguing in Publication Data*
A catalogue record for this book is available from the British Library

*Library of Congress Cataloging-in-Publication Data*
Rose, Richard, 1933–
  Understanding post-communist transformation : a bottom up approach /
Richard Rose.
  p. cm.
  Includes bibliographical references.
  1. Europe, Central—Social conditions—1989– 2. Europe, Eastern—Social
conditions—1989– 3. Post-communism—Europe, Central. 4. Post-
communism—Europe, Eastern. 5. Civil society—Europe, Central. 6. Civil
society—Europe, Eastern. 7. European Union—Membership. I. Title.
  HN380.7.A8R64 2008
  306.09171′709049—dc22
                              2008026699

ISBN13: 978-0-415-48218-9 (hbk)
ISBN13: 978-0-415-48219-6 (pbk)

ISBN10: 0-415-48218-6 (hbk)
ISBN10: 0-415-48219-4 (pbk)

**To Bill Mishler**
**Scholar, gentleman of the old school, friend**

No decade in the history of politics, religion, technology, painting, poetry and what not ever contains its own explanation. In order to understand the religious events from 1520 to 1530 or the political events from 1790 to 1800 or the developments in painting from 1900 to 1910, you must survey a period of much wider span.

(Joseph Schumpeter)

# Contents

# Figures and tables

## Figures

**Tables**

# Introduction

## Transformation and its aftermath

> We are making such a large turn that it is beyond anyone's dreams. No other people has experienced what has happened to us.
>
> (Mikhail Gorbachev, speech at Khabarovsk, 1991)

While every society is in transition, few have experienced transformation as abruptly and pervasively as nations once in the Communist bloc. Transformation is different in kind from the adaptation that established political systems periodically engage in to maintain their stability. Transformation is abnormal; it starts with the disruption of a steady state. It is a relatively short phase in a country's history, an interlude between a way of life that has been upset and the establishment of a new way of governing society. In the case of the Communist bloc, it was more than a political revolution. There was the treble transformation of the economy, society and the political regime – and often of the boundaries of the state as well.

Understanding post-Communist transformation is important because the bloc that Moscow dominated had upwards of 400 million subjects. Moreover, substantial elements of Communist practice, such as using a party as an organizational weapon and a state-controlled economy, have appeared in dozens of countries across Asia, Latin America and Africa. From a changing China to Cuba, more than 1.5 billion people have been or are now under Communist rule.

The actions of charismatic leaders such as Boris Yeltsin and Lech Walesa could disrupt a Communist regime; doing so left a wreckage as the starting point for building a replacement. It was politically convenient to describe what was happening as transition. Doing so implied predictability: we not only knew where a country was coming from but also knew where it was going. Many transition studies assumed that even if transformation was not literally the end of history, it would lead to the creation of societies from East Berlin to Vladivostok that would become 'just like us'.

In the midst of transformation, it was clear what was being left behind, but it was not clear what lay ahead. As the Soviet Union was sliding toward the political abyss, no one, including its leader, Mikhail Gorbachev, knew what would fill the void created by its collapse. At the time, the only thing we could be sure of was that our knowledge of how a Communist system worked was no longer adequate to understand new regimes that were holding free elections in order to demonstrate their break with it. It quickly became evident that our knowledge of how a neo-classical economic system works in theory was inadequate to understand how economies in transformation were working in reality. As a Russian central banker subsequently reflected, 'Life has proved to be richer and more complex than the theoretical notions that all of us were guided by' (Johnson, 2001: 253).

The collapse of the Berlin Wall was an event, while transformation and its aftermath is a process of learning. This book's purpose is to understand that process from the bottom up, that is, from the point of view of ordinary people. Whereas many political events happen 'over the heads' of ordinary people, the upheavals and opportunities of transformation immediately affected everyone's daily life. How did ordinary people respond to the collapse of the institutions that had been the framework of their lives? This book shows how the skills that ordinary people developed to get around the old regime could be used to cope with the shocks of transformation; it also shows whether two decades later they are still in use or fading into the distant past. It also highlights the benefits and opportunities that freedom has brought to people, especially in Central and Eastern European countries that are now member states of the European Union (EU).

*Beliefs about how the world works.* Beliefs about how the world works are the basis for economic and political understanding. When people live in different 'worlds', then their beliefs ought to be different. Notwithstanding differences in national histories, the peoples of Central and Eastern Europe and the former Soviet Union had been governed for generations by Communist party-states with institutions very different from those of Western societies. While the ideology of Marxism-Leninism was capable of multiple interpretations, the operation of Communist regimes was distinctive: the dismissal of the rule of law and individual freedom as signs of bourgeois 'false' consciousness, the rejection of private property and market mechanisms, the creation of a dictatorship of the proletariat with the Communist Party mobilizing people to conform to its doctrines. The means used to pursue totalitarian goals were unconstrained by Western institutions and values.

Amidst the confusion of transformation, what you see depends on when you look. Since the world of Western societies was very different from that of the Communist bloc, its collapse was a test of the extent to which theories based on Western behaviour are equally relevant in unfamiliar circumstances. Many succumbed to the temptation first identified by Leon Trotsky, who characterized such observers as 'seeking salvation from unfamiliar phenomena in familiar terms' (Jowitt, 1992: 124). Lawrence Summers (1991), then chief economist of the World Bank, confidently prescribed that the way to deal with transformation was: 'Spread the truth – the laws of economics are like the laws of engineering. One set of laws works everywhere'. In Russia Summers's approach was characterized as 'market Bolshevism'. Such naive views could not be ignored and they could be exploited by those who understood their limitations.

Historians tend to generalize from the past to the present and in a steady-state society this may be appropriate for a period of time. However, in a society such as Germany, with very different twentieth-century experiences, this leaves open which past is chosen. Because transformation is about discontinuities, it implies that the past is an inadequate guide to the present. The dramatic events that followed the fall of the Berlin Wall and the break-up of the Soviet Union encouraged a focus on the present, for example, the first free elections in Central and Eastern Europe in 1990 and Boris Yeltsin's televised defiance of an attempted counter-coup in Russia in August 1991. However, since Communism collapsed, more than 6,000 evening news bulletins have been televised and most days have been without dramatic news in Eastern Europe or in Russia.

Whereas journalists err in overreacting to what has happened in the last 24 hours, academics can err in thinking that a newly published book based on fieldwork undertaken some years previously is sufficient to understand the ongoing process of transformation and its aftermath. Studies may be an account of past events that stop before the present or a snapshot of a particular event, for example, voting in an election in which major parties have since ceased to exist. To avoid these traps, this book adopts a dynamic approach. It starts with the world of the Communist bloc as it was when it appeared as solid as the concrete of the Berlin Wall. It continues to the world as it is two decades later.

The actions of governments during transformation and its aftermath have led to divergences between peoples once subject to Moscow. Ten Central and Eastern European (CEE) countries – Bulgaria, the Czech Republic, Estonia, Hungary, Latvia, Lithuania, Poland, Romania, Slovakia and Slovenia – are now member states of the European Union. By contrast, Russia and other successor states of the Soviet Union have gone in another direction. The Russian Federation has been transformed into what Vladimir Putin calls a 'sovereign democracy' rather than a European democracy and economic activity is affected by the rule of the *siloviki* (security agents) as well as by the rule of law. The institutions that are visible from the bottom-up view of post-Soviet citizens are different from those in new European democracies.

*Approach of the book.* Transformation is unsettling, because it introduces unpredictability. Thus, any theory used to understand it should be sufficiently open to learn from the existential problems of post-Communist societies. Like policymakers proceeding by trial and error to cope with these problems, social scientists should look out for ideas and evidence that fit the problems at hand. Since transformation disrupted the official sources of information that Communist systems used to portray progress, to understand how ordinary people have responded we need unofficial as well as official data.

The most straightforward way to understand how people have coped with transformation is to ask them. Social science offers a familiar methodology for doing so, the nationwide sample survey. This book draws on a unique resource: a programme of surveys that the Centre for the Study of Public Policy began in 1991 to monitor mass behaviour and attitudes from the bottom up. Since then, in collaboration with researchers from Vienna to Moscow, I have directed more than 100 surveys interviewing 120,000 people in 20 countries of Central and Eastern Europe and the former Soviet Union from 1991 to 2008 (see Appendix A). In order to understand important differences in national contexts, this book compares the results of two parallel sets of long-term surveys. The New Europe Barometer (NEB) covers the ten Central and East European countries now in the European Union. The New Russia Barometer (NRB) has completed 17 surveys since it was launched in January 1992, the first month of the Russian Federation and, to test the generalizability of the Soviet legacy, Belarus and Ukraine have been frequently surveyed too.

To construct a questionnaire requires observation of the realities of everyday life. Questions should follow the KISS principle – Keep It Simple, Stupid. But what is talked about in colloquial language must also be related to abstract concepts such as support for democracy and national economic data. Observation calls attention to the importance in transformation societies of concepts taken for granted by contemporary Western social scientists, such as the rule of law and freedom from the state. It also turns other concepts inside out because of the importance of the legacy of an anti-modern society, and democratization backwards, and substitutes the idea of an hour-glass society for the concept of civil society.

A questionnaire that asks questions relevant to respondents in their everyday life and to seminars of academics is a pre-condition of meaningful statistical analysis. Doing so integrates evidence of what people say and do with theories of behaviour consistent with Herbert Simon's theory of bounded rationality (1978) and Max Weber's (1947: 8f, 94ff) idea of *verstehen Soziologie* (sociology for understanding). It avoids the photocopying of questionnaires based on alien theories, a practice that can lead to *missverstehen Soziologie* (a sociology based on misunderstanding).

This book is written for a broad audience of people who are not only interested in understanding how ordinary people have reacted to upheavals that are now becoming part of the past but also what it means for their lives today – and for the lives of their fellow Europeans. Readers familiar with top-down accounts of transformation will find this book adds to their understanding by showing how people behaved outside the beltways of capital cities and out of sight of diplomats and inside dopesters. Not least, this book can show people who have lived through transformation and its aftermath how their own experiences may compare with those of others in their own and neighbouring societies.

In writing this book I have had the advantage of experiencing history forwards rather than backwards; this makes one aware of the contingencies of history (Rose, 1997). I saw my first Soviet troops in Vienna when Austria was then under four-power occupation pending the negotiation of a Cold War peace treaty. I first experienced the absence of a market in Moscow during the premiership of Leonid Brezhnev. I experienced the *nomenklatura* class system at the 1979 International Political Science Association convention in Moscow, when the same hotel served me differently on three different occasions, depending on the rank of the person accompanying me. I first saw the Berlin Wall in 1968 and visited Dresden, an example of the contradictions of European culture and Soviet controls, half a dozen years before Vladimir Putin went there to control the *Stasi* (security police) that spied on Germans. The Saturday before the Wall came down, I did not attend the demonstration in Alexanderplatz, East Berlin, because I had a cold – and because I did not know whether the East German police would shoot. I sat in a flat in suburban Moscow working on the first New Russia Barometer questionnaire in autumn 1991 as the snow and the Soviet Union were falling and we did not know what would be there when the snow melted in spring.

The head of a British university once asked me: How do you study post-Communist countries? My answer was simple: I work with people who live there. Over the years many individuals and institutions have contributed to this book. Co-authors of materials used here are named in full in the Acknowledgements (see Appendix B). They have come from countries on three continents – including Austria, Germany, Hungary, Russia, Sweden, the United States and Australia as well as the United Kingdom. Results of research in progress have been presented to interested and interesting audiences in Russia and all 10 Central and East European countries that were once part of the Communist bloc; across almost all old member states of the European Union; the United States, Canada, and places as far afield as Beijing, Cape Town, Mexico City, Tbilisi and Tokyo.

*Plan of the book.* Part I shows how the division of Europe came about and how people living in hour-glass societies kept their private opinions separate from opinions that they had to endorse in public. Soviet society appeared modern, because it could produce steel and put a man in space, but was in fact anti-modern, rejecting the values and institutions of modern European states. Subjects of Communist regimes had the bittersweet reward of seeing their societies make progress while simultaneously falling behind countries of Western Europe. Given no choice, people patiently endured what seemed to be a system built to last, only to have it collapse in a matter of months.

The starting point for transformation was the ruins of a Communist system. Part II shows how the distinctive forms of social capital that people had developed to cope with its pathologies were useful in dealing with the immediate shock of economic transformation. In the absence of a civil economy, people turned to uncivil economies or grew food on urban plots to eke out what could be bought with depreciated currency at inflated prices. Juggling multiple economies enabled households to avoid destitution. In the aftermath of transformation, people have taken advantage of new opportunities to buy consumer goods and enjoy better health than under the old regime.

The collapse of Communist regimes has given ordinary people freedom from the state. However, as Part III shows, the legacy of the past means that democratization began backwards, for free elections were introduced before the rule of law was properly established. With different degrees of success, politicians have sought to replace or adapt the institutions they inherited. East Germans have had a unique experience. Instead of being compelled to create new institutions from scratch, they have benefited by becoming part of a ready-made state, the enlarged Federal Republic. Elsewhere, many ex-Communists have shown that they have not changed – 'Once an opportunist, always an opportunist' – and used their old networks to create social democratic and populist parties.

Competitive elections have now been held in Central and Eastern Europe for almost two decades. Instead of voting as government commands, citizens have often exercised their democratic right to turn the government out. However, as Part IV shows, this has yet to create a properly accountable party system. In the absence of civil-society institutions, parties that politicians have launched often sink after one or two elections. The result is a floating system of parties. Electors are forced to become floating voters when the party they voted for at the last election does not appear on the ballot at the next. The problems of volatility are compounded by popular distrust of parties, which results in individuals with political values often being unsure whether any party on the ballot represents their views.

While the shocks of transformation are large and pervasive, they are short, whereas the aftermath of transformation is long. Part V shows how time matters. The period since transformation now spans more years than that from the final battles of the Second World War to the time when six participants in that war banded together to form the European Community. For young voters in the European Parliament election of 2009, the Communist era is becoming like centuries of kingdoms and wars, something that happened before they were born. The aftermath of transformation has given ordinary citizens time to learn what their new political, economic and social institutions are like, and to adapt to them. This has been for the better in Central and Eastern Europe. In successor states of the Soviet Union the passage of time has created something that people now recognise as *normalno*.

Even though what were once Communist systems may claim to be stable states, they are not static states. There is unfinished business from the past, such as the problem of low standards of governance and corruption in some old as well as new EU member states. There are opportunities arising from the emergence of a European public space with the free movement of people, goods and ideas across a continent. The heterogeneity of a Europe with some 30-odd states challenges West European as well as post-European societies to adapt to a re-made continent and to a transformed Russia.

Every chapter in this book is freshly written and freshly thought, while each draws on one or more of the many studies that I have written since the early 1990s. Whereas an article must focus narrowly on a single topic, a book can link major political, economic and social themes arising from transformation. Although Russia is referred to more often than any other country, within a book there is scope to show that transformation is a process in which the outcome has differed between individuals within a country and between countries. In the course of writing a book for a wide audience, I have left out reviews of academic literature and statistical analyses more appropriate to specialist journals. They can be found in publications referenced in the Acknowledgements (Appendix B). This makes it possible to begin to do justice to the experiences of ordinary people during the great transformation of Europe and beyond.

# Part I
# The legacy

# 1 The Iron Curtain falls

> The current dramatic economic and social situation in our country is the price we have to pay for the economy we inherited from the Soviet Union. But then, what else could we inherit?
>
> (Vladimir Putin, Millennium address to the Russian people, 31 December 1999)

Ignoring the past encourages a misunderstanding of the present. Today's political institutions were not chosen by today's governors; they are, as Vladimir Putin has recognized, an inescapable legacy of the past. At the start of transformation, there was much talk about societies being in transition, but less was said about where they were coming from. In Central and Eastern Europe the past was what people were trying to escape from. However, in most successor states of the Soviet Union new institutions were viewed as the problem, because they supplanted what was familiar in the past. To understand what the consequences of transformation are, we first need to understand the system that was in place before transformation.

The answer to the question 'What is Europe?' is 'When?' (Rose, 1996). The history of twentieth-century European states has been an account of successive transformations. Pre-1914 states were undemocratic multinational empires. States were properties that monarchs acquired by inheritance, marriages of political convenience, or conquest. In Central and Eastern Europe the Habsburg, the Prussian and the Tsarist empires were neither democratic nor democratizing. The typical European state was a constitutional oligarchy in which power was in the hands of the few. The rule of law was upheld – but it was a system of law in which the state's authority was far more important than the rights of individuals. When war broke out in Europe in August 1914, the belligerents assumed that it would be no different from wars that had gone before. But it was.

By the time the First World War ended, the map of Europe had been transformed. The Tsarist empire was the first to disappear. The Prussian, Austro-Hungarian and Ottoman empires collapsed as a result of military defeat. In Central and Eastern Europe Woodrow Wilson's goal of applying the principle of national self-determination to create new democracies was partially realized. Multinational empires were broken up and their lands were transformed into what were described as nation-states. However, many had ethnic minorities within their boundaries. For example, the population of Poland was one-fifth German and one-tenth Jewish. Of the dozen-plus countries of Central and Eastern Europe, by the late 1930s only Czechoslovakia was democratic.

A distinctive feature of the interwar period was the emergence of totalitarian regimes in the Soviet Union and Nazi Germany. Although nineteenth-century autocracies did not hold democratic elections, many could claim to be governing by the rule of law. By contrast, totalitarian regimes rejected any limit to the state's power to command individuals and institutions of civil society. Their goal was total control of what people said and did. The Soviet regime described itself as a dictatorship of the proletariat with the Communist Party monopolizing power. It used schools, the media and the workplace to propagate its views and security services to coerce its subjects. In Adolf Hitler's Germany the Nazi Party mobilized supporters and intimidated critics; it proscribed art and music that it defined as degenerate; and persecuted and then murdered millions of Jews.

Whereas the First World War broke up empires, the Second World War broke up Europe. Soviet troops advancing from the east and Allied troops advancing from the west met in Central Europe. The result was the disappearance of Central Europe. Parts of Romania, Poland and East Prussia were annexed by the USSR, adding to Stalin's earlier annexation of Estonia, Latvia and Lithuania. Hungary, Poland, Czechoslovakia and the eastern part of Germany were incorporated into the Moscow-oriented Communist bloc. On the other hand, Austria and the Federal Republic of Germany became part of Western Europe. The labels had nothing to do with geography, for Prague was west of Berlin and Vienna was east of it; they had everything to do with politics. In Western Europe countries that had been dictatorships between the wars turned into democracies.

The Soviet Union imposed Communist regimes in the countries it controlled. Stalinism purged social democrats, liberals and other opposition groups. Barbed-wire fences and well-armed border guards prevented unwilling subjects from leaving. In spring 1946, Winston Churchill warned of an Iron Curtain falling across Europe from the Baltic to the Adriatic, separating countries in the Soviet sphere of influence from European countries to the west. The Atlantic Ocean became a link between Western Europe and the United States. Ties were embodied in Marshall Plan economic aid and in the North Atlantic Treaty Organization (NATO). By 1949 the division of Europe was complete.

## I Behind the Iron Curtain

From 1949 to 1989 politics transformed geography (cf. Figure 1.1). Warsaw is as close to Zurich as it is to Moscow, Budapest closer to Paris than to Moscow, and Prague is actually closer to Dublin. Soviet troops and the national Communist leaders they backed forced Iron Curtain countries to look to Moscow for leadership. However, as post-1989 events demonstrated, the apparent stability of Communist regimes was not a sign of consent but of coercion.

Marxist-Leninist ideology emphasized that Central and East Europeans were living in a different world than people in Western Europe. Within the Communist bloc of states there was no freedom of speech and no choice about which party should govern. Communist regimes insulated their citizens from contact with other Europeans by censoring the media, prohibiting travel outside the Communist bloc and controlling visitors from abroad. Schools gave priority to teaching Russian and limited the teaching of 'subversive' languages such as English.

Politics not the market was the foundation of the command economy. Decisions about the production and consumption of goods were made by ministries of the party-state. Instead of consumer demand stimulating the supply of goods and services, the government made an annual plan setting out what industries should produce. Military

*Figure 1.1* A map of contemporary Europe.
Source: About.com, 2008, Free Blank Outline Map of Europe, http://geography.about.com/library/blank/blxeurope.htm. Accessed 10 June 2008.

defence and investment in the military-industrial sector had first claim on the budget. Public spending on the theatre, music and art was generous – as long as they were consistent with the party line. Shortages controlled consumption. Ordinary people had to use connections to get 'shortage goods' out the back door of shops and enterprise managers did the same to get supplies to meet their targets under the plan. In extreme cases, factories were not adding but subtracting value, as their output was worth less than the materials, labour and equipment used to produce it. Whereas before the Second World War most Central and East European countries had traded principally with capitalist nations such as Germany, afterwards trade was concentrated within the Communist bloc through the Council of Mutual Economic Assistance, also known as COMECON.

Moscow's ideologues described the Communist bloc as 'the socialist, peace-loving camp'. The Warsaw Pact organized the camp into a military alliance under the control of the Soviet high command. It enabled the Soviet Union to station troops as far west as Berlin and Prague. For the Soviet Union, which had twice been invaded by Germany in the twentieth century, this enhanced its defence. However, for countries that had protest demonstrations crushed by a show of force, such as Hungary, Poland and Czechoslovakia, the presence of Soviet troops was a sign of subjugation. After the Iron Curtain fell, the states of Central and Eastern Europe showed their preferences by joining NATO in order to secure protection against the threat of another Russian invasion.

The goal of the Soviet Union was to dominate half of a divided Europe. How this was done differed from one country to another. Communist regimes had to conform to a template imposed by Moscow, but the degree of political repression varied. Two years before the fall of the Berlin Wall, the international non-governmental organization Freedom House rated Bulgaria, Romania and the Soviet Union as just as unfree as Iraq and Saudi Arabia; Czechoslovakia as on the same level of repression as Iran; and Hungary and Poland as just as unfree as Jordan and Tunisia.

East Germany was proclaimed as a separate state, the German Democratic Republic, under the control of Communist leaders. During the 1950s East Germans dissatisfied with the regime could leave by taking a subway or bus from East to West Berlin, where they were accepted as citizens of the Federal Republic. The construction of the Berlin Wall in August 1961 closed this exit route. East Germans were trapped in a Communist system, which repressed dissent and killed persons trying to flee across the Berlin Wall.

Czechoslovakia, unique in having had an interwar democratic regime, was subject to particularly harsh repression. Immediately after the end of the war it had a coalition government of democratic and Communist parties but in 1948 it was forced to become a Communist party-state. A series of Stalinist trials with overtones of anti-Semitism purged Czechs accused of being 'home Communists', that is, more loyal to their own country than to Moscow. In 1968 there was a brief Prague spring, as a new party leader, Alexander Dubcek, introduced measures promoting individual freedom. Warsaw Pact troops invaded Czechoslovakia and Dubcek was arrested and taken to Moscow. A new leadership was imposed and it actively suppressed dissent until the collapse of Communism.

Poland has historically been anti-Russian and its invasion from the east as well as the west following the Nazi–Soviet Pact of August 1939 re-inforced that enmity. The political fate of postwar Poland was decided in the closing months of the Second World War when Soviet troops refused to come to the aid of Polish underground forces seeking to liberate Warsaw from the Nazis. By 1948 a Soviet-backed regime had taken control. The fiercely nationalist Catholic Church was a focal point of resistance to Soviet domination. A series of popular demonstrations against the regime began in 1956. In 1980, following demonstrations in Gdansk led by Lech Walesa, the Polish government recognized the right of protesters to organize in trade unions such as Solidarity. In 1981 this was revoked and martial law proclaimed under General Jaruzelski.

After being on the losing side in the Second World War, Hungarians established a regime with competitive elections and the Communist Party won less than one-fifth of the vote. However, in 1948 Communists used control of the Ministry of Interior and police to arrest their opponents and seize control. Following a period of intense repression, there was a popular uprising against Communist rule in Budapest in 1956, a new coalition government was formed and Hungary announced its intention to withdraw from the Warsaw Pact. Soviet troops crushed the new government, executed its leaders and installed Janos Kadar in power. An understanding was reached that if Hungarians did not openly challenge the Communist system, repression would be relaxed. It was summed up in the cynical maxim: 'Those who are not against us are with us'. The economy was modified to benefit consumers, a policy described as 'Goulash Socialism' and Hungary became the least repressive of Communist regimes.

Caught between the Ottoman Empire and Tsarist Russia, Bulgaria had traditionally sought alliances with Russia. However, in the Second World War the monarchist regime sided with Hitler to advance territorial claims against its Balkan neighbours. Following defeat, it became a Communist party-state closely linked with Moscow under the leadership of Georgi Dimitrov. In 1954 Todor Zhivkov became general secretary; he held this post without any visible challenge until 1989.

Romania was a monarchy that attacked the Soviet Union during the Second World War but then changed sides. In 1947 the king was forced to abdicate and a Communist party-state established. Although poor by European standards, because of its oil fields Romania had a major economic resource lacking in most Communist states. In 1965 Nicolae Ceausescu became Communist leader and initiated an increasingly independent foreign policy, which won some favour with Western leaders. Domestically, the Ceausescu regime ruled by terror through police institutions loyal to the ruler.

Estonia, Latvia and Lithuania were independent Baltic states until the Nazi–Soviet Pact of August 1939 led to their occupation by German and Soviet forces and their subsequent incorporation as republics of the Soviet Union. The movement of Russian speakers into the Baltic region, especially in Estonia and Latvia, reduced Estonian and Latvian speakers to a bare majority but did not lead to their Russification. The federal structure of the Soviet Union was consistent with republic-level institutions of party and state offering opportunities for bilingual Estonians, Latvians and Lithuanians to gain high posts there, and those who wanted could seek positions in Moscow or other parts of the Soviet Union. Nonetheless, the Baltic peoples retained a strong sense of their national identity and kinsmen abroad lobbied to keep alive the hope of regaining their interwar dependence. In these nations, the idea of *perestroika* meant more than restructuring; it meant independence.

Unlike other East European countries, Yugoslavia did not rely on Russian troops to gain liberation from German occupation. Partisan armies that were divided along ethnic and political lines fought the occupiers and each other. The forces of Marshal Tito triumphed and Yugoslavia was established as a Communist state with six republics. Initially, Tito aligned the country with Moscow. However, in 1948 he broke with Moscow, while maintaining a one-party state and an economy different from Western Europe. Following the death of Tito in 1980 ethnic differences between its heterogeneous republics increasingly became sources of friction.

Criticism of strategies existed within the higher echelons of Communist parties, but the doctrine of democratic centralism meant that it should not spread outside the party. Opposition to Communist rule existed, but critics were intimidated. Dissidents were tolerated as long as they were small groups that did not organize public demonstrations. If demonstrations were organized, they were suppressed by police strength or, if necessary, gunfire and tanks.

## II The fall of the Berlin Wall – and much else

After becoming general secretary of the Communist Party of the Soviet Union in 1985, Mikhail Gorbachev decided that major changes were needed to preserve and strengthen the Communist system. The key themes were *glasnost* (openness) and *perestroika* (reform or restructuring). The Soviet leader did not anticipate that Central and East Europeans would interpret reform as meaning the removal of Communist political, economic and military control. The proclamation of the 'Sinatra doctrine' granted Central and East European governments the right to introduce reforms on a 'do-it-your-way' basis. The logic of Gorbachev's position made it difficult for him to crush dissenters with tanks, since his critics within the Communist Party would seize on this as evidence that his reform strategy was a failure. The result was the peaceful collapse of the Communist bloc. The dissolution of the Warsaw Pact in 1991 freed Central and East European states from being military allies of the Soviet Union and removed the justification for stationing Soviet troops there. In the same year, the trade bloc, COMECON was dissolved as part of the transformation of a command into a market economy.

*Central and Eastern Europe.* The start of transformation differed with national circumstances. In October 1989, hundreds of thousands of East Germans began weekly candlelit street protests. These demonstrations were the more impressive because East Germans had previously been the most submissive of Communist subjects. A regime that had previously shot and killed individuals trying to escape from East Germany no longer had the political will to shoot. The opening of the gates in the Berlin Wall in November 1989 was the beginning of the end of the Cold War division of Europe. In the absence of Soviet backing, the East German state disappeared. The re-unification of Germany occurred in October 1990 by the five East German *Länder* becoming additional regions of the Federal Republic of Germany.

In Hungary, opposition groups were allowed to organize in 1987. When Hungary opened its border with Austria in May 1989, this enabled other nationalities, such as East Germans, to flee to West Germany by travelling via Hungary to Austria. Big changes in Poland commenced in April 1989, when the Communist regime granted legal recognition to the anti-Communist trade union Solidarity. In June, National Assembly elections were held; Solidarity swept the popular vote. By January 1990, Lech Walesa, the Solidarity leader, had become president. In Czechoslovakia the transition between regimes was described as the Velvet Revolution, because of its smoothness. In Bulgaria change began with a *coup* of reform Communists, backed by the army, deposing Zhivkov in November 1989. Under pressure from demonstrators in Sofia, the Communist regime agreed a new constitution and free elections were held in June 1990. In Romania demonstrations led to bloodshed in Hungarian-speaking areas of western Romania. Military dissidents and Communists in favour of reform revolted against the Ceausescu regime; an estimated 8,000 died in the fighting that followed. Ceausescu and his wife were tried by a military court on charges of genocide, embezzlement and perverting the authority of the state and summarily executed.

Although Yugoslavia was not directly involved in changes in the Soviet bloc, its leaders were challenged by demands for independence from the six constituent republics of the federal state. In 1990 the federal government abolished the Communist Party's monopoly of power and held free elections in all of its republics. The governments that were elected sought independence from the federal government in Belgrade. In June 1991 Slovenia and Croatia declared independence. Concurrently, there were conflicts within republics containing more than one ethnic group. Fighting broke out between Serbia and Croatia and spread to Bosnia and the paths of successor states diverged. Slovenia, the one Yugoslav successor state to join the European Union in 2004, is included as one of 10 Central and East European countries analyzed in this book.

When a 1991 opinion poll asked Central Europeans which country they would like to emulate, the replies showed the rejection of the way of life that respondents knew best, the Communist way. Of Czechs and Slovaks, Hungarians and Poles 1 per cent

*Table 1.1* Country Central Europeans want to emulate

|  | Czechoslovakia % | Hungary % | Poland % | Average % |
|---|---|---|---|---|
| Germany | 31 | 38 | 37 | 35 |
| Sweden | 32 | 34 | 21 | 29 |
| United States | 14 | 10 | 30 | 18 |
| Italy | 9 | 9 | 0 | 6 |
| France | 5 | 2 | 7 | 5 |
| Britain | 3 | 3 | 3 | 3 |
| Other | 6 | 2 | 2 | 3 |
| Soviet Union | 0 | 1 | 0 | 0.3 |

Source: Freedom House, *Democracy, Economic Reform and Western Assistance: Data Tables*, 1991, p. 154. Due to rounding, here and elsewhere percentages may not add up to exactly 100.

or less said that they wanted their country to emulate the Soviet Union (Table 1.1). The countries most admired were two Central European countries, social market Germany and social democratic Sweden. The Soviet arch enemy, the United States, came third.

*The Soviet break-up.* The creation of the Russian Federation by the break-up of the Union of Soviet Socialist Republics (USSR) was an unintended consequence of the Gorbachev initiatives. Elections at the republic level gave Boris Yeltsin, a renegade Communist Party apparatchik, a platform as president of the Russian republic of the Soviet Union. In an ironic turn of fate, the August 1991 coup attempt by hardline Communists to restore the old Soviet system ended in failure and the outlawing of the Communist Party of the Soviet Union (CPSU). A coalition of major republics took advantage of the disarray within the all-Union Communist Party to engineer the peaceful dissolution of the USSR in December 1991. The Russian Federation, the dominant republic of the USSR, is the primary basis here for comparing and contrasting post-Soviet states with CEE countries. Estonia, Latvia and Lithuania, independent states until forcibly annexed by the Soviet Union, had their status as CEE countries confirmed by admission to the European Union in 2004.

The collapse of the Soviet Union made it possible for Russians to voice in public opinions that were previously kept very private. When the first New Russia Barometer survey went in the field in January 1992, it asked about eight symbols relevant to different Russian regimes (Figure 1.2). The replies showed that, notwithstanding a lifetime of indoctrination into Marxist-Leninist ideology, there was indifference or hostility to Communist values: only one-sixth were positive. Although every Russian had been taught that socialism was what people ought to want and capitalism was bad for society, only 24 per cent showed positive attachment to socialism, 1 per cent less than those who viewed capitalism positively. Only 7 per cent reflected the traditional party line of being positive about socialism and negative about capitalism; 12 per cent were consistently negative about socialism and Marxism-Leninism and positive about capitalism.

The values that most Russians endorsed were those that were inimical to the principles and practices of the Soviet Union. The most frequently endorsed value was freedom (*svoboda*). Russians could differentiate the meaning of openness (glasnost), which was widely supported, from Gorbachev's efforts to reform the Soviet system (perestroika), which had little support among the mass of Russians. Communist

Q. We often hear the following words.  What feelings do they evoke?

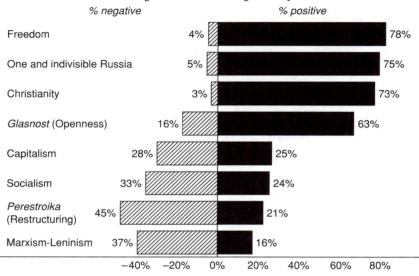

*Figure 1.2* Russian values at the start of transformation.
Source:  Centre for the Study of Public Policy, New Russia Barometer, 1992.

Note: Those saying 'difficult to answer' are not shown.

campaigning against religion and the promotion of a materialist approach to life was counter-productive. Even though few Russians are churchgoers, almost three-quarters reported feeling positive about Christianity, more than four times the percentage feeling positive about Marxism-Leninism. The nationalist slogan – 'one and indivisible Russia' (*Edinaya i nedelimaya Rossiya*) – was denounced as counter-revolutionary by Stalin and Trotsky. However, it was viewed positively by three-quarters of Russians.

Consigning Communist values to what Marxists described as 'the ash can of history' was easy for people who had never believed these doctrines in the first place and had only given them lip service when it was required to gain entrance to university or promotion at work. However, the legacy of four decades or more of Communist rule could not be disposed of so easily. In the prescient words of a Hungarian sociologist, Elemer Hankiss (1990: 7):

> People will have to realize that the fight for a free and prosperous society is a much more difficult and complex task than they had imagined in the years and decades of despair and servitude. The golden age of innocence and simplicity has passed.

## III  Escaping absolute dissatisfaction

At the start of transformation, it was much easier to describe societies by what they had been than by where they were going. In a worst-case analysis, history could be cited to argue that they would default into nationalist or fascist dictatorships. Conventional economic prescriptions could hardly be applied in the absence of statistics about how ordinary people and their employers were meeting their everyday needs in the interlude between a command and market economy. In the unprecedented circumstances of introducing a market economy in the ruins of a non-market economy, there were no precedents to indicate what should be done or how.

*Satisficing as a goal.* Dissatisfaction was the starting point for Central and East European societies that rejected government by a single party and centralized control of a non-market economy (Rose, 1992). The repudiation of the one-party state and centrally planned economic systems was an extreme expression of dissatisfaction. In Herbert Simon's theory of satisficing (1978), dissatisfaction stimulates a search for a means of dispelling it. Unlike most conventional political and economic theories, a satisficing model does not identify a unique outcome, whether democracy or dictatorship. Satisfaction is arrived at by a process of trial and error. Such a model is appropriate to understand transformation because it not only emphasizes that countries were trying to get away from the legacy of Communist rule but also that their leaders faced great uncertainties about how to deal with the problems that transformation forced on them.

The Latin root of the word satisfaction means 'enough'; hence, a satisficing political strategy does not pursue a distant, unattainable ideal such as complete democracy or perfect market competition. The objective is to achieve enough to end dissatisfaction. The aim of ordinary people was not to become millionaires but to get enough to live on each week. When the first free elections were held it was not necessary to know who to vote for but who to vote against. Insofar as dissatisfaction with the past is absolute, then almost any alternative will be preferable as a lesser evil. The basic principle was enunciated by Winston Churchill (1947):

> Many forms of government have been tried and will be tried in this world of sin and woe. No one pretends that democracy is perfect or all wise. Indeed, it has been said that democracy is the worst form of government, except all those other forms that have been tried.

The Churchill hypothesis not only justifies people preferring life in Sweden to that in Romania, but also preferring any Romanian government, whatever its faults to the known evils of the Ceausescu regime.

Because of the critical importance of *dis*satisfaction, measures of public opinion should not be confined to asking people how much they approve of a given system of government, whether real (e.g. a newly elected government trying to cope with the challenges of transformation) or ideal (democracy or socialism in the abstract). It should also offer people the opportunity to register how much they dislike a given system. Thus, the New Europe Barometer asks people to evaluate political and economic systems on scales running from +100, total satisfaction, to −100, total dissatisfaction. There is also a midpoint, 0, to register uncertainty or indifference.

*Modelling the search.* In a society in transformation, everyone has lived in at least two regimes; therefore, it is meaningful and necessary to compare popular evaluations of the new regime with its predecessor. Insofar as the past is assessed as absolutely unsatisfactory, then dissatisfaction with the present regime makes it appear as a lesser evil. The difference between a rating of −100 for the old regime and −25 for a fledgeling democracy is more a difference in kind than in degree, an indication that even though errors are being made, so too is progress in escaping from absolute dissatisfaction. An assessment of a new system also gains significance when it is compared with expectations of the future. This is true whether present difficulties appear as a prelude to a brighter future or as a foretoken of conditions getting worse. In the early years of transformation, many Central and East European citizens were uncertain how or whether the new political system would work and gave negative evaluations of the new as well as the old system. They were not anti-democrats but sceptical about what the outcome of transformation would be.

In Central and Eastern Europe the benefits of transformation were immediately made evident by the first free elections of 1990. Ordinary people were no longer subjects ordered to vote for a regime they disliked; instead, they were citizens who could express their views, negatively or positively, about who should govern. Just as the Communist practice of erecting statues of the patron saints of Communism gave public evidence of the power of Moscow, the removal of these statues gave tangible evidence that Communism was no more. At Lubyanka station in Moscow, where once a massive statute of the founder of the KGB stood in front of its notorious prison, the plinth was taken away too.

Victory in the first free election landed the winners in trouble. New governors faced the responsibility of doing something about an official economy that appeared to be in free fall and the introduction of a market economy was sending prices into orbit. Coalition governments of inexperienced politicians often quarrelled with their colleagues or helped themselves in ways that ordinary people viewed as corrupt. At the second free election, governments were often voted out of office. However, dissatisfaction with the government of the day did not reflect dissatisfaction with representative government. It was the continuation of a trial-and-error search for governors that could make the new system work better.

At the start of transformation, a host of alternative scenarios could be envisioned (Rose, 1992: 380ff). The most optimistic assumed that there would be uninterrupted progress toward the establishment of a democratic polity and a prosperous market economy. This was quickly found to be unrealistic. New governors turned to a trial-and-error search for ways to reduce dissatisfaction. Insofar as they could institutionalize successes and remedy errors, the result would be a gradual amelioration of the worst effects of transformation and the establishment of foundations for a stable post-transformation regime.

In the early years of transformation many feared that the costs of transformation were not temporary but long term, and would thus undermine fledgeling democratic institutions and a market economy. Developments in the successor states of the Soviet Union showed that while those who seized power in the chaos of 1991 were no longer Communists, they were also not democrats. Where transformation led to disorder, as in parts of the former Soviet Union and Yugoslavia, undemocratic political leaders could promise to replace the disorderliness that accompanied freedom with a regime that offered order without freedom.

Governors could blame the legacy of an anti-modern regime for the inability of the new regime to achieve a satisfactory way of life in the duration of a single parliament. Even if ordinary people had difficulties in coping with the costs of transformation, that did not mean that they wanted to return to a past that was viewed as even worse. If people expected conditions to worsen and they remained the same, this was a better-than-expected performance and offered governors a reprieve from popular dissatisfaction. Moreover, when expectations of a brighter future were not promptly met, governors of a new regime could ask citizens to be patient.

# 2  Living in an anti-modern society

All animals are equal, but some animals are more equal than others.

George Orwell, *Animal Farm*, 1945

The starting point for post-Communist societies was not a modern society. Marxist-Leninist analysis had 'proven' that capitalist societies were not modern but decadent; the more they developed, the closer they approached the imminent collapse of capitalism. Nor had Communist systems modernized in the manner of a third-world society. In a developing country, modernization starts with the population divided into three sectors – a relatively small modern sector, a sector of first-generation residents of urban shanty towns wanting themselves or their children to become modern and a backward rural population living as their ancestors had. In such circumstances, modernization is a gradual process of people progressing from one to another sector until the modern sector becomes dominant.

Communist rulers rejected incremental change. They promoted a fourth-world totalitarian goal of pervasively transforming every aspect of society. The method was that of the 'big bang'. It started by imprisoning, exiling or shooting members of the scientific elite who were deemed a threat to the party's way of thinking and acting. It treated similarly capitalists and enterprise managers who had previously been in the forefront of modernizing the national economy. In rural areas, those peasants who had been most successful in adapting to modern agriculture lost their land; in the collectivization of agriculture under Stalin, millions lost their lives too. The consequence was that Communist transformation exterminated whatever modern sector had previously existed.

Ordinary people were expected to behave in accordance with the totalitarian aspirations of their leaders and do whatever was commanded, such as 'spontaneously' demonstrating in favour of the regime or 'volunteering' to do extra work. The intrusive top-down pressure to conform to the party's dictates had lessened prior to the system's collapse, but the experience of being socialized into a totalitarian regime could last a lifetime. Whereas pre-industrial institutions of West European societies had provided a solid foundation for political and economic modernization, the legacy of Communism did not.

Believers in the power of institutions did not always agree on which Western institutions would best achieve rapid modernization but they shared the expectation that citizens would respond to new incentives and constraints as in Western societies. Political parties were created as readily as a budding entrepreneur might print designer T-shirts

– and with as little concern about what the logo on the T-shirt represented. The idea of 'plugging in' the market assumed that if one only followed the appropriate macro-economic policies, individuals would become profit-maximizers and new businesses blossom.

## I  The character of an anti-modern society

Theories of political and economic development emphasize that history is about change; however, there is a big difference between the incremental changes that occur within a democratic political system with a modern market economy and the 'creative destruction' that occurs when one regime abruptly replaces another or an economy is transformed. In Western Europe the process of replacing peasant and household production with modern enterprises trading in national and international markets took more than a century. In Central and Eastern Europe industrialization began later and initial attempts at democratization involved more destruction than creative benefits (Chapter 11).

*Modernization – Communist-style*. The goal of Communist transformation was a new civilization that would be based on the principles of Marxism-Leninism rather than those of decadent (that is, modern) Western societies. In order to achieve this goal, the Communist party-state claimed total ownership of all the resources of society, including the lives and minds of its subjects. The party sought to remould the thoughts and actions of its subjects in order to create Soviet man. It was never a woman. Moreover, the men depicted in striking posters were normally blond, blue-eyed Slavs rather than representative of the multi-ethnic population of the Soviet Union. The Stalinist promoter of a form of biology that rejected genetic science, Trofim Lysenko, proclaimed: 'In our Soviet Union people are not born. What are born are organisms. We turn them into people – tractor drivers, engine drivers, academicians, scholars and so forth' (quoted in Heller, 1988: 8).

Ideological pronouncements in forms immortalized by George Orwell substituted for scientific observation. To doubt this aspiration, for example, by telling jokes, risked being charged with committing a crime against the Soviet state. A Soviet satirist, Mikhail Koltsov, challenged this view at the 1934 Soviet Writers' Congress on the grounds that 'in the history of the class struggle, the working class will have the last laugh'. The claim was rejected on the grounds that:

> In the land of the Soviets a new type of comedy is being created – a comedy of heroes. A comedy that does not mock its heroes but depicts them so cheerfully, emphasizes their positive qualities with such love and sympathy that the laughter of the audience is joyful and the members of the audience will want to emulate the heroes of the comedy to tackle life's problems with equal ease and optimism.
> (quoted in Lewis, 2008)

When statements of the party line were insufficient to control behaviour, the party-state resorted to the use of fear and terror. In 1939 Koltsov's satires were cut short by his arrest and the following year he was executed.

The challenge facing the founding generation of Soviet rulers was to create a new civilization in the backward conditions of post-Tsarist Russia rather than in a capitalist society such as Germany, where the institutions of a modern society were already in place. In Central and Eastern Europe, Communist-style modernization occurred in societies that had been more developed than Tsarist Russia, but the ravages of the Second World War had left a legacy of destruction to which Communist commissars added.

Communist-style modernization was effective both politically and economically. It succeeded in mobilizing its subjects to give public demonstrations of support and in preventing the organization of political opposition. The party-state's economic plan decided what would be produced. It not only produced statistics showing the fulfilment of plans but also products that met the demands of the military-industrial complex. The Communist system did not fail because it was ineffective, but because of how it achieved its effects. It did not operate as a modern society; it was anti-modern and operated at a great cost. For example, satellite regimes were so distrusted by Moscow that not only did the East German regime have a massive state security service, the Stasi, to spy on its populace but the Soviet KGB also sent operatives to East Germany to control the Stasi. Among those tasked to do so was a young KGB recruit from Leningrad, Vladimir Putin.

To academics who relied on official statistics to chart modernization, Communist regimes appeared to have succeeded in their efforts to modernize. Economic statistics showed high levels of investment and economic growth, full employment and little or no inflation. Social statistics showed the spread of secondary and university education, implying that the peoples of Communist societies were increasingly learning to view the world in modern, scientific ways rather than in terms of ideology. The success of Soviet space exploration supported this belief. Increasing numbers of cars on the streets and television sets in high-rise flats made the Communist system appear successful in spreading material benefits. However, the presence of some attributes of a modern Western society, such as colour television and engineering graduates, was not proof that life in a Communist society was just like that in the West. In a narrow sense, a Communist economy could be described as functional, but it did not function as a modern economy does.

*The anti-modern result.* Communist societies were not modern in the European sense. Even though they had mass education, big cities and jet aeroplanes, the harsh application of Marxist-Leninist principles created something different, an anti-modern society (Table 2.1).

The Communist system was founded on the power of the party-state. The Soviet Constitution stated that its aim was to achieve 'the dictatorship of the proletariat' and the Communist Party provided the dictators. The most powerful office was not that of president or prime minister but the general secretaryship of the Communist Party. Within the Party, the doctrine of democratic centralism was used to maintain control

*Table 2.1* Modern and anti-modern societies compared

|  | *Modern* | *Anti-modern* |
| --- | --- | --- |
| *Rule of law* | Yes, bureaucratic | Arbitrary, political |
| *Openness* | Transparent | Opaque |
| *Signals* | Prices, laws | False accounts, bribes, personal contacts |
| *Cause and effect* | Predictable | Uncertain |
| *Output* | Efficient | Inefficient |

of the organization. Marxist-Leninist ideology was used as a framework for interpreting how the economy and polity should be governed, and for prescribing policies. At the higher levels of the party there could be debate about the application of ideology, but once a decision was taken, to question the party line was to risk expulsion from the party as a deviationist or even being branded an enemy of the state. In the succinct phrase of Koestler's (1940) inquisitor in *Darkness at Noon*, 'There is no salvation outside the party'.

A modern state is a *Rechtsstaat*, in which the rule of law not only controls what governors may do but also what they may *not* do. It is a regime in which right rather than might prevails, because it 'avoids capriciousness, arbitrariness and unreliability in political rule' (Freddi, 1986: 158). The Communist system was the opposite; it was unconstrained by laws or concepts of human rights. In the succinct words of Leonid Brezhnev, 'In our society whatever serves the interests of communism is moral' (quoted in Heller, 1988: 23).

A modern state is a bureaucratic state, in which the laws enacted by governors predictably control the actions of the many bureaucrats who carry out the routine tasks of government. The great scope of the party-state's activities required many rules and regulations, but the control of their interpretation by the Party meant that their enforcement by bureaucrats was often arbitrary. In Central and East European societies where bureaucratic norms had been established prior to Communist rule, the result was de-bureaucratization.

In the absence of the rule of law, subjects could not rely on bureaucrats to deliver services to which they were entitled by law. To get things done required much more time and energy than when dealing with a modern bureaucracy working with the predictability of a vending machine. People who wanted to benefit from what the planners decided turned to an economy of favours in which *blat* (that is, connections) counted more than rules. The Communist system was a perverse example of Weber's (1973: 126) dictum that 'power is in the administration of everyday things'. The power of the Communist party-state was evident in the maladministration of everyday things.

A surfeit of rules imposes delays. Individuals are forced to invest an unreasonable amount of time in pleading with and pushing bureaucrats to compensate for organizational inefficiencies. If bureaucrats offered to waive obstructive regulations in return for a side payment, this delivers a service – but in an anti-modern way. The result is popular ambivalence about the rule of law (Table 2.2). A New Russia Barometer survey found that more than two-thirds consider their government fell far short of being a law-governed state (*pravovoye gosudarstvo*) and almost as many thought that the way laws were administered was often very hard on ordinary people. There is little demand for a law-governed state: most Russians hope that harsh laws will be softened by their non-enforcement.

A modern society is transparent: everyone can observe what is happening and make rational calculations about what to do. There is a continuing feedback between governors and governed and between producers and consumers in the marketplace. However, the Communist system was opaque. For all the Soviet prattle about cybernetics, rulers ignored or repressed feedback. Neither votes nor prices were used to determine what people wanted. Instead, the Party decided what the people were supposed to want.

Unfree elections were held without risk of popular dissatisfaction being expressed at the ballot box. The 99.99 per cent vote for the party was a public demonstration

*Table 2.2* Low supply and demand for the rule of law

| Q. How closely do you think the national government comes to the idea of the law-governed state (pravovoye gosudarstvo)? | % |
|---|---|
| Very close; to some extent | 29 |
| Not very close; not at all | 71 |
| Q. Some people say that laws in this country are often very hard on ordinary people? | |
| Agree | 61 |
| Disagree | 39 |
| Q. A writer once said: 'The harshness of Russian laws is softened by non-enforcement'. Do you think this is true? | |
| Agree | 73 |
| Disagree | 27 |

Source: Centre for the Study of Public Policy, New Russia Barometer, 1998.

that, whatever people thought privately, everyone was willing to endorse the regime publicly. Power and ideology determined economic plans and bureaucrats and Party officials rather than prices allocated goods and services. The unrealistic targets of five-year plans encouraged factory managers to practise deceit and exaggeration in order to make it appear that everything was working all right – at least on paper. The contrast between reality and what ideology said was happening created what one critic characterized as a 'surreal' society (Z, 1990: 298ff) and a Polish economist (Winiecki, 1988) described as 'pseudo-modern'.

The Communist Party claimed credit for such modern values as full employment and human rights in order to impress Westerners who wanted to believe that the Soviet Union was building a new society and who could not or would not see that modern forms could hide anti-modern practices. For example, Beatrice and Sidney Webb, co-founders of the London School of Economics, visited the Soviet Union in the 1930s and wrote up what they were told. At the end of the title of the first edition of *Soviet Communism: A New Civilization*, published in 1935, there was a question mark. It was dropped when the second edition was printed (Webb and Webb, 1937). Communists cynically regarded those who gave such support as 'useful idiots'.

Subjects of Communist regimes were under no illusion about what their rulers had created. A joke current in Czechoslovakia summed up the situation thus:

> The first peculiarity of socialism: everybody is employed and nobody works. The second peculiarity: nobody works and the plan gets fulfilled 100 per cent. The third peculiarity: the plan is fulfilled and there is nothing to be had in the shops. The fourth peculiarity: there is nothing to be had in the shops and people have every-thing. The fifth peculiarity: people have everything and everybody grumbles about the regime from morning until night. The sixth peculiarity: everybody grumbles about the regime all the time and in the election everybody votes for it.
>
> (quoted in Tworzecki, 2003: 37)

## II An hour-glass existence

The relationship between individuals and institutions is central to governance. In a modern society there is a two-way exchange of information and influence through representative institutions of civil society. Governors listen to those they are meant to serve and citizens accept that they should obey laws and pay taxes as well as receive benefits. In an anti-modern society, the state creates uncivil institutions that it uses to make subjects do what it wants. In response, ordinary people try to insulate themselves from contact with government by living an hour-glass existence in which they carry on their lives at the bottom of society with as little contact as possible with elites at the top.

*Civil society*. The institutions of a civil society include small-scale, face-to-face associations of such groups as sports enthusiasts, bird watchers and choral singers, and large, formal organizations, such as universities, television companies, business organizations and federations of trade unions. In a modern society, civil-society institutions are important not only for the direct benefits they offer members but also as intermediaries that relate the concerns of their members to government and the activities of government to their members.

The paradox of civil-society institutions is that they ought to be independent of government yet relate to public policy. In Anglo-American thinking, civil society organizations operate in the public interest but free of public (that is, state) control. In Robert Putnam's (1993) theory of civic democracy, individuals actively participate in a variety of social institutions, many of which are non-political, such as hobby groups or bowling leagues. Participation in such groups is assumed to spill over into politics when groups represent their views to government locally and, indirectly, through national organizations. The continental tradition of the public interest is rather different. In the nineteenth century, states licensed which groups were recognized as civil society institutions and regulated what they could do. For example, newspapers and theatres were censored. Public opinion was not what individuals would voice to a stranger who knocked on their door to conduct an interview for an opinion poll. It was what the state allowed groups to say; individuals often had to confine their political opinions to private conversations.

*Uncivil society*. The idea of civil society giving direction to government by aggregating popular views from the bottom was contrary to Communist practice and ideology. Civil society institutions were not only weak; they were illegal. Communist ideology did not allow for the expression of diverse opinions. At any given moment there was only one opinion, the 'correct' opinion, as expressed in the party line of the day. To disagree with that opinion could be labelled an 'anti-state' activity and invite punishment.

A Communist regime created an uncivil society, in which the Party sponsored intermediary organizations to regulate the behaviour and opinions of their members. The function of these uncivil institutions was to instruct individuals what was required of them, whether it was a factory workers' union urging workers to meet higher production quotas or a guild of musicians directing composers not to write 'bourgeois' symphonies but symphonies that glorified workers. To encourage people to join these organizations, Communist regimes used a mixture of incentives and sanctions, such as making membership compulsory in order to hold a given job or gain promotion.

The totalitarian ideology of the Communist Party meant that there was no distinction between political and non-political organizations. Margaret Thatcher's assertion that there is no such thing as society was inverted to state that there was no such thing as individuals. People were simply productive units that could be used (or sacrificed) to build a new society. The family was seen as the lowest (and potentially subversive) unit. It was meant to be integrated in the Communist system by mobilization that extended from the top of government through the schools and Party-controlled youth organizations. Children who reported their parents to the security services for anti-state behaviour were held up as role models for Communist youths.

The Party's aspiration for the total control of society meant that it had to mete out punishments to those who deviated. A 'soft' punishment for an intellectual would be the denial of the right to publication or as in the case of a Polish friend, a forced career shift from sociology to the safe field of Renaissance musicology, or for a Russian friend, from applied economics to pure maths. The next level of punishment was to lose one's job. Being sent to prison or the gulag, the fate of millions of ordinary people as well as of intellectuals, was a more severe punishment. Political purges ended in death for those who fell out with the party. Beyond that, the KGB pursued widows and children of the 'class traitor', making them cut out the faces of the 'traitor' from family photo albums and wedding pictures (King, 1997: 7).

The suppression of freedom of speech and civil-society organizations, combined with the threat of being punished as an enemy of the state, led to the silent and often sullen subjugation of the people. Individuals cultivated what a Hungarian sociologist, Elemer Hankiss (1990: 7; italics in the original), called 'ironic freedom', that is, 'the freedom of *living outside the system in which they lived*; the freedom of not identifying themselves with the system'.

The reaction against totalitarian attempts to mobilize citizens created an hour-glass society. At the top of the hour-glass there is a rich political and social life, in which elites could compete for power, wealth and prestige as representatives of different interests within the party-state, such as the army, the security services, energy, agriculture or industry. Yet from the 'under-all' view of the ordinary individual, this did not create a civil society because those who debated did not represent them.

Instead of being positively integrated in the party-state, many subjects preferred to be negatively integrated. The narrow mid-point of the hour-glass reduced the influence of repressive top-down institutions. At the bottom there was a dense network of connections on which individuals could rely. These informal networks depended upon diffuse, face-to-face ties between friends and relatives. The networks could extend to friends of friends too. As the Russian proverb puts it, 'A hundred friends are worth more than a hundred roubles'. The Bulgarian version was more pointed, 'Without friends you are dead'.

Up to a point the hour-glass society encouraged 'idiotization', that is, 'the conscious rejection of the obligations of a citizen' (Nodia, 1996: 26). Insofar as contacts with the state were necessary, for example, to get special medical treatment for a family member or to get a place in a good school for a child, the aim was to exploit the exploiters. Ordinary people developed what Poles called *srodowisko*, a social circle of those they could rely on to offer help when needed (Wedel, 1992: 12). The circles could be used to permeate institutions of the party-state, since many public officials wanted to have friends who were normal people rather than dedicated Communist apparatchiks.

The party-state tolerated informal networks as long as activities were confined to looking after small-scale, individual concerns and did not affect activities that were affairs of state. However, any attempt to mobilize networks for a public challenge to the regime was treated as a crime against the state. And the political police watched people who *might* transgress the line between what could be said among friends and what could be said in public. Moreover, 'friends' with whom one shared conversations could be agents of the political police. For example, after the fall of Communism gave access to secret police reports, the Hungarian economist Janos Kornai (2006: 163ff) found out to his surprise who reported on him and who had betrayed his friendship.

Anti-modern societies were caught in a low-level equilibrium trap. At the top of the hour-glass, governors avoided problems that ideology denied the existence of. At the bottom, subjects sought to avoid the party-state and evade the production targets of the command economy. Transformation voided the institutions of uncivil society but could not provide civil institutions overnight. At the bottom of the hour-glass, ordinary people continued to rely on informal networks to cope with the stresses of transformation (see Chapters 6 to 8). When the New Europe Barometer asks whether people like themselves have more influence on government today than under the former Communist regime, the majority see no difference. The good news is that while citizens do not believe that they can influence the state, big majorities also believe that the state is now unable to control their lives.

# 3 Making progress and falling behind

> For most of the twentieth century Russia lived under the Communist doctrine. It would be a mistake not to recognize the unquestionable achievements of those times. But it would be an even bigger mistake not to realize the outrageous price our country and its people had to pay for that social experiment.
>
> What is more, it would be a mistake not to understand its historic futility. Communism did not make Russia a prosperous country with a free people. Communism doomed our country to lagging steadily behind economically advanced countries. It was a blind alley, far away from the mainstream of civilization.
>
> (Vladimir Putin, Millennium address to the Russian people, 31 December 1999)

Across a long span of time, economic and social progress has everywhere been the norm. Every country of Central and Eastern Europe and the former Soviet Union made great progress in improving their living conditions between the end of the Second World War in 1945 and the fall of the Berlin Wall in 1989. Even if Europeans regard current living standards as less than ideal, they are invariably better than those of parents or grandparents who grew up during depression or war. Communist societies were no exception to this rule.

When comparisons are made within a country, ordinary people have grounds to be satisfied if conditions today are better than yesterday. This also offers hope that tomorrow will be better than today. However, when comparisons are made between countries, the evidence shows that Communist systems paid what Vladimir Putin describes as an 'outrageous' price for making progress in an anti-modern way. Communist societies had simultaneously been making progress and falling behind neighbouring countries of Western Europe (Rose, 1995a).

With hindsight it appears obvious that modern democratic market systems are far better placed to make progress than a society burdened with the pathologies of an anti-modern party-state. However, the point was not so obvious at the end of the Second World War. Both Western as well as East German cities had been bombed flat. German food rations were at subsistence levels and there was no assurance that people could obtain the calories they needed. Vienna suffered much more from bombing than did Prague. Austria, like Germany, was under four-power military occupation and only escaped German-style partition by the 1955 Peace Treaty.

The offer of economic assistance through the Marshall Plan was open to all the countries of Central Europe. The government of Czechoslovakia initially sought to participate, only to have its hopes of doing so vetoed by Moscow. The Soviet regime promoted development through the institutions of the command economy and the party-state and it did so with great confidence. At a Kremlin reception for Western diplomats in 1956, Soviet leader Nikita Khrushchev boasted, 'Whether you like it or not, history is on our side. We will bury you.'

The Communist-bloc countries with the best chance of matching the performance of modern societies were those of Central Europe, where populations separated by the Iron Curtain had previously lived together for centuries. To see what difference living in a modern or anti-modern society made, this chapter compares social, economic and political progress in two groups of countries, the Communist-bloc regimes of Czechoslovakia, East Germany, Hungary and Poland, and West Germany and Austria from 1949, when the two Germanies were formally separated, to the fall of the Berlin Wall four decades later.

## I Matters of life and death

Regardless of the flag that flies over their country, life and death are important to everyone. Moreover, public policies directly affect health, whether they are promulgated by a modern or anti-modern regime. In the first half of the twentieth century the demography of Central Europe was altered for the worse by war and for the better by improvements in public health. The Second World War led to the death or forced emigration of millions of people as Nazi and then Soviet troops moved across the region and the Holocaust led to the extermination of millions of Jews. However, since 1945 there has been an era of peace not war, removing a major determinant of life and death, and thus leading to improvements in health throughout Europe.

*Infant mortality* is a classic indicator of health care. The ability of an infant to survive for a year after birth reflects the health of the mother, the quality of health services and the more general conditions of society. In the immediate aftermath of the Second World War, infant mortality was high across Central Europe. It ranged between 108 deaths per 1,000 in Poland and 92 deaths in Austria to 75 deaths per 1,000 in the Federal Republic of Germany and 72 deaths in East Germany.

In the decades after the Second World War, every country made great progress in reducing infant mortality. It fell at least 64 deaths per 1,000 in East Germany and by as much as 92 deaths per 1,000 in Poland (Table 3.1). There was also a substantial

*Table 3.1* Infant mortality trends in Central Europe, 1949–1989

|  | 1949 | 1960 | 1970 | 1980 | 1989 | Change |
|---|---|---|---|---|---|---|
|  | *Infant mortality (deaths per 1,000)* | | | | | |
| Germany: East | 72 | 39 | 19 | 12 | 8 | −64 |
| Germany: West | 75 | 34 | 24 | 13 | 8 | −67 |
| Czechoslovakia | 78 | 24 | 22 | 18 | 12 | −66 |
| Austria | 92 | 38 | 26 | 14 | 8 | −84 |
| Hungary | 91 | 48 | 36 | 23 | 16 | −75 |
| Poland | 108 | 57 | 33 | 21 | 16 | −92 |

Sources: Germany (East and West) and Austria: UN and OECD health statistics; Communist countries: United Nations and World Bank statistics; UNICEF International Child Development Centre, *Children at Risk in Central and Eastern Europe*, 1997, p. 155.

reduction in difference between the best and the worst infant mortality rate. In 1949 there was a difference of 36 deaths per 1,000 between Poland and East Germany. In 1989 there were eight deaths per 1,000 in the two Germanies and Austria as against 16 deaths per 1,000 in Poland.

The reduction in infant mortality did not mean that Communist-bloc countries were catching up with countries the other side of the Iron Curtain; instead, the reverse was happening. In 1949 Czechoslovakia and Hungary had lower mortality rates than neighbouring Austria. However, following the withdrawal of Soviet troops from Lower Austria and Vienna, health conditions there began improving and by 1989 infant mortality in Austria was significantly lower than in Czechoslovakia and Hungary. Similarly, East Germany had a lower level of infant mortality than West Germany in 1949. However, four decades later mortality there was no better than in its two neighbouring states, because West Germany and Austria had made greater progress. In relative terms, the difference in infant mortality had actually increased between three of the four Communist-bloc countries – Czechoslovakia, Hungary and Poland – and Austria and West Germany.

When comparison is extended to Western Europe and a wider range of Communist-bloc countries, the result is the same: on both sides of the Iron Curtain there was absolute progress in reducing infant mortality but, contrary to the aspirations of believers in a society moulded in accord with the ideal of new Soviet men and women, the Communist bloc had not caught up with modern societies (Rose, 1994: Chapter 2).

*Life expectancy* has been rising from one decade to the next everywhere in Europe. The chief difference is the extent to which life expectancy has improved. In an advanced industrial society the normal pattern is that life expectancy increases by a seemingly small rate from one year to the next. Cumulatively, this produces a substantial increase in longevity from one decade to the next. A second common feature of life expectancy is that it tends to be higher for women than for men; the achievement of longer life does not alter the gender gap in favour of women.

In 1949 life expectancy for women was highest in East Germany, followed closely by the Federal Republic and Austria. It was lowest in Poland and only slightly better in Hungary (Table 3.2). In the four decades since, the life expectancy of women has risen everywhere. It went up most in Austria and in West Germany and least in East

*Table 3.2* Life expectancy trends in Central Europe, 1949–1989

|  | 1949 | 1960 | 1970 | 1980 | 1989 | Change |
|---|---|---|---|---|---|---|
|  | *Female life expectancy (years)* | | | | | |
| Germany: East | 69 | 72 | 72 | 75 | 76 | 7 |
| Germany: West | 67 | 72 | 73 | 76 | 79 | 12 |
| Austria | 67 | 72 | 73 | 76 | 79 | 12 |
| Czechoslovakia | 65 | 73 | 73 | 74 | 75 | 10 |
| Hungary | 63 | 70 | 72 | 73 | 74 | 11 |
| Poland | 62 | 70 | 73 | 75 | 75 | 13 |

Sources: UN, World Health, OECD health statistics (annual); *UN Demographic Yearbook, 1979*, special historical supplement; UNICEF International Child Development Centre, *Children at Risk in Central and Eastern Europe*, 1997, p. 123.

Germany. The result is that by 1989 women in West Germany and Austria could expect to live three years longer than women in East Germany and five years longer than Hungarian women.

## II  Driving forward slowly

In command economies national income accounts were based on Marxist assumptions about value rather than on prices paid for products in the marketplace. Communist-bloc accounts of Net Material Product excluded services that were deemed not to be of productive value. Excluded services included not only capitalist activities such as banking but also such social services as education and health.

For what they are worth, official statistics of Net Material Product showed striking rates of growth of more than 7 per cent a year between 1951 and 1970. However, there were declines in growth rates thereafter. Estimates from Western sources, such as the CIA's research department, produced lower figures than did COMECON countries, and rates retrospectively estimated by Soviet experts in 1990 were lower still. For example, official statistics showed an average rate of growth in the economy of 3.6 per cent in the five years before Mikhail Gorbachev took office, while CIA estimates gave a growth rate of 2 per cent and revisions by Soviet experts estimated growth at 0.6 per cent a year (Lavigne, 1995: Table 4.1). Ordinary workers were not fooled by the ability of the commanders of the command economy to produce glowing macro-economic statistics. The bottom-up view of workers was expressed in the bitter epigram, 'They pretend to pay us and we pretend to work'.

In the succinct terminology of Janos Kornai (1992), the political economy of Communism was a shortage economy. In Poland, for example, basic foods were rationed in the 1980s. The shortages created by the non-market economy meant that citizens had to wait years to buy products readily available in West German and Austrian shops, and of much better quality too. The ability to obtain shortage goods was often influenced by who you were or who you knew. There were special shops for party functionaries and an under-the-counter supply of goods through informal networks.

Car ownership offers a simple material indicator of mass living standards, for throughout Europe in the postwar era car ownership rose as household discretionary income rose. Car ownership is not only a sign that a household has sufficient income to make a purchase equivalent to many months of wages, but also that it has sufficient income to keep the car supplied with petrol, a commodity that must be bought for cash and cannot be grown at one's dacha.

Immediately after the Second World War, car ownership was a luxury throughout Central Europe. For example, in the Federal Republic of Germany in 1950 there were only 13 cars per 1,000 people and in Austria only seven, compared to 266 in the United States. In 1960, the earliest year with comparative data, car ownership in Hungary and Poland was less than in Austria and West Germany a decade earlier. Moreover, in all three command economies of Central Europe car ownership was much less than in the market economies of West Germany and Austria (Figure 3.1).

A consumer boom of sorts began in the 1960s in command economies. Within a decade national levels of car ownership had increased by almost six times in Hungary, and in absolute terms had risen even more in East Germany and Czechoslovakia. However, because of their low starting point, all the command economies fell further behind Austria and West Germany. The subsequent rise in car ownership highlighted

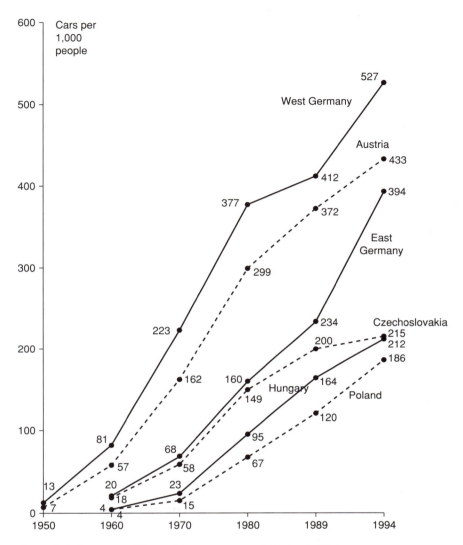

*Figure 3.1* Car ownership: making progress and falling behind.
Source: United Nations, *Demographic Yearbook*, various years. Final year for East and West Germany is 1993, and for Czechoslovakia, 1991.

differences in the progress of Communist-bloc countries. For example, in 1989 car ownership in Hungary had risen to 164 per 1,000, a third higher than Poland. However, it was one-fifth to two-fifths behind Czechoslovakia and East Germany.

When the Berlin Wall fell in 1989, all Central Europeans were more prosperous than when the Iron Curtain fell four decades previously. But the hard evidence of car ownership illustrates that people in a command economy were far less well off than their neighbours living in a market economy. The extent to which the lack of material goods reflected shortages and low income levels rather than consumer tastes is illustrated by East Germany. Before the Berlin Wall, car ownership there was similar to that of neighbouring Czechoslovakia. However, once German re-unification gave an enormous boost to the income levels of East Germans, car ownership among East Germans shot up so much that in four years it was almost double that of its Communist-bloc neighbours and rapidly catching up with West Germany.

Comparing material goods produced in market and non-market economies is not comparing like with like, because of great differences in the quality of the products. Automobiles illustrate this point: the East German Trabant or Wartburg was far inferior in every respect, including being more polluting, to cars produced in the Western economies of Central Europe, such as the Volkswagen or Vauxhall. Inferior cars were driven in Communist-bloc countries because the regimes forbade the import of products from market economies. The fall of the Berlin Wall gave consumers freedom to choose. The result quickly became visible on the streets and highways of Central Europe. Hungarians, Poles and Czechs and Slovaks abandoned the cars that they had been forced to buy in a non-market economy in favour of buying second-hand or new cars produced for a modern market economy.

### III  Promoting the welfare of the party-state

In late-nineteenth-century Central Europe, the German Chancellor, Prince Bismarck, pioneered the state provision of welfare services in Central Europe with the aim of maintaining support for an undemocratic regime from workers who benefited from these services and from the trade unions, churches and civil-society institutions that delivered these services. In Britain and Scandinavia, the introduction of democratic elections not only increased popular demand for maintaining and raising welfare benefits; it also made those responsible for promoting welfare accountable to the citizens they were meant to benefit. In reaction against Nazi totalitarianism, the postwar regimes of West Germany and Austria adopted this philosophy too.

On the other side of the Iron Curtain, the promotion of welfare had a different purpose: to build a Communist society. The goal of the party-state was not to promote individual welfare but to build Communism. In the first decades of the Soviet Union this meant creating the physical infrastructure of a modern society, for example, electricity stations, railways and factories that could produce military materials for use in the anticipated coming war with capitalism. The party-state did not have to worry about popular dissatisfaction with welfare services, because it was not subject to competitive elections. Nor did it have to worry about a taxpayer's revolt, for instead of taxing individuals heavily its total control of the economy enabled it to allocate resources for guns, butter or health care as it chose.

Under Stalin the Soviet Union did not offer welfare services as incentives to secure popular support. Instead, it offered ideological exhortations for people to make sacrifices in order to achieve the long-term goal of building Communism. Insofar as this was not sufficient, the party-state resorted to coercion. The achievements of the first five-year plans not only included showpiece electricity stations and buildings but also the graves of millions of people who lost their lives or had them foreshortened by Stalinist terror. The expansion of the Communist bloc after the end of the Second World War took in societies where the foundations of welfare systems had been created under Prussian and Habsburg regimes. Communist regimes replaced civil-society institutions delivering welfare with those that were under the control of the party-state.

*Providing and corrupting welfare.* Decades of peace and economic growth made it possible for Communist regimes to expand the provision of social welfare. Free secondary education was made available nationwide and new technical institutes and universities created. Doctors were trained, hospitals built and clinics made health care nominally free to all. The command economy's method of allocating labour produced full employment, albeit it also reduced the freedom of employees to move from one job to another and unions were organized to repress rather than promote demands for higher wages. Pensions were introduced while housing shortages meant that pensioners were often living with adult children and grandchildren. However, the anti-modern methods employed corrupted the ideals and practice of the modern welfare state. A leftwing Western critic described the provision of welfare as 'part and parcel of the totalitarian state project of forcing work out of reluctant citizens for purposes which seemed to benefit only the privileged party state apparatus' (Deacon, 1993: 182).

In modern societies the rule of law determines the benefits that individuals are entitled to claim from the state and the rules determining entitlement are administered fairly by bureaucrats. In anti-modern regimes, the laws may appear to be the same but the administration is not. Public officials sometimes demand money (including hard currencies) to admit children to a good school, for medical treatment or housing. A New Europe Barometer study at the start of transformation found two-thirds of Czechs and Slovaks used connections or cash payments to bend or break the rules governing entitlements to welfare benefits – and this was especially true in the pursuit of 'free' health care (Rose, 1993: 234ff; see also Tables 7.1, 7.2).

Education was free in economic but not political terms. Teachers were required to read out what sceptical pupils in Catholic countries referred to as 'the bishop's letter', that is, bulletins giving the party line on matters of political belief and action. Not only were classes in Marxism-Leninism compulsory but also refusal to parrot the party line in an examination could lead to a fail mark in a subject required for university entrance. In countries where it was not the home language, Russian was compulsory and the party-state carefully monitored the number of people allowed to learn English, for it was a language used in books that the Party did not want to be widely read. In Leipzig, young staff members in a Marxist-Leninist Department of Political Science were even discouraged from forming a reading group to discuss Marx's *Das Kapital*. They were told that if they wanted to know what Marx meant, they should not debate this among themselves but ask the Party what Marx really meant.

State-owned enterprises guaranteed employment for all. The command economy's use of monthly production targets created a work cycle in which there were brief periods of storming in order to produce, by hook or crook, statistics that appeared to meet the targets of the plan. Instead of replacing the instinct of profit with an emphasis on workmanship, the storming system rewarded the mass production of shoddy goods, and the shortages created by the plan made sure that there was a demand for these goods.

Linking welfare services to a person's place of employment meant that instead of services being universal benefits equally available to all according to need, access to more desirable welfare benefits often depended on the industry in which a person worked and the priorities of the party-state. This divided the labour force into insiders and outsiders in welfare terms. The fourth New Russia Barometer survey found that no one welfare benefit was taken up by as many as half of employees. However, the variety of benefits were such that 72 per cent of workers were receiving at least one welfare benefit in kind from their employer and this had hardly changed since transformation began. The median worker was in receipt of two employment-related welfare benefits. In order of importance, the chief benefits were medical care, child-care, holidays, food, housing and shortage goods.

The logic of the welfare state is that services should be allocated to those in greatest need. In a modern society, need is defined by characteristics of individuals, for example, mothers need maternity care, young people need education, and retired people need income from a pension. However, in a Communist regime need was defined by the priorities of the party-state. The provision of a low standard of basic services was sup-plemented by providing additional benefits for employees in industries of higher pri-ority to the state. The NRB surveys found that extra welfare benefits were most likely to be give to those in the military, the police and heavy industry, all of which are sec-tors of the economy dominated by the employment of males with no need for mater-nity leave and limited demand for child-care. By contrast, sectors where women were more likely to be employed, such as education and retailing, were least likely to pro-vide employment-related benefits. The skewed distribution of benefits is underscored by the fact that in places of work employing more than 1,000 people five-sixths received extra benefits, while fewer did so in small and medium-size enterprises.

The value of benefits appeared greater in Soviet publications aimed at Westerners than in the eyes of recipients. Half receiving benefits at work said they were of no value; the other half were prepared to put a positive rouble value on what they were given. However, only 3 per cent thought their work-related benefits were enough to be one of the most important resources in the portfolio of resources that they relied on to cope with the challenges of transformation (see Chapter 8). Nor did the provision of a welfare service at work give people an advantage in coping with transformation. Those who did not have any welfare benefits at work were just as likely as those who did to avoid destitution and get by without having to borrow money or exhaust their savings (Rose, 1996a: 54).

There was a great contrast between the ideals nominally espoused by the workers' party and the conditions of 'real existing socialism' in which subjects lived. Privately, people could express their disbelief of top-down pronouncements of the party-state by comparing it with their everyday lives. As the Communist era riddle put it: 'What is the difference between capitalism and socialism? Under capitalism man exploits man; under socialism it is the other way around'. The fact that this joke could be told to me by a Russian interpreter in Leningrad in 1976 shows that people could privately express what they thought. But the fact that people had to say the opposite in public showed that the party-state could compel people to maintain official illusions.

Demoralization was the result of living in an anti-modern system in which welfare was provided on terms that suited the state. A Hungarian social scientist has des-cribed the terms thus:

> The Soviet Union is here and it is here to stay. It will not let Hungary go its own way. Independence or a change of the system are out of the question. So forget about ideals and accept us as the lesser evil. Leave us alone to take care of pol-itics. In exchange, we will leave you alone to take care of your private life. Interference will be minimal and as predictable as possible. You will not have rights, civil or political, but you will enjoy a decent level of material welfare. . . . And honestly, you would not trade off welfare for liberty, would you? So you must

recognise that this world is not that bad after all. It is the best of all possible worlds, at least, under the hegemony of the Soviet Union.

(Kis, 1998: 337)

While the societies of Central and Eastern Europe and the Soviet Union were experiencing a higher standard of welfare at the end of the 1980s than at the end of the Second World War, they were not the only societies making progress. The fall of the Iron Curtain meant the revival of Central Europe as a social space. Czechs, Poles, Slovaks and Hungarians no longer had to rely on Marxist histories or socialist realist writings from earlier eras for knowledge about how their neighbours were living. People could see for themselves how the welfare of West Germans and Austrians had been increased by living in a modern society while they were conscripted into building what was meant to become, later rather than sooner, a workers' paradise.

Given the existential gaps in welfare between Eastern and Western Europe, the goal of transformation has been to catch up. This requires making up for decades of lost time in which socialist health care led people to die sooner than their neighbours, to waste time learning from books dictated by Party commissars rather than by knowledgeable professors, and to wait for years to buy an out-of-date and polluting automobile instead of a modern car.

# 4    The need for patience

What we thought would be easy turned out to be painful. I ask you to forgive me for not fulfilling some hopes of people who believed that we would be able to jump from the grey, stagnating totalitarian past into a bright, rich and civilized future in one go. I myself believed in this. But it could not be done all at once.

(Boris Yeltsin, Farewell address to the Russian people, 31 December 1999)

Autocratic regimes are good at teaching people to wait. Like it or not, their subjects must accept their dominance for the indefinite future. Communist rulers emphasized the need for subjects to be patient while waiting for the achievement of pure Communism. Like preachers of a millenarian religion, they preached the doctrine of *chairos*, the unknown moment in time when the patience of believers will be rewarded and God's (that is, the Party's) will is realized. Subjects of such regimes needed patience, whether they were waiting for the regime's promises to be fulfilled or for it to collapse.

Political regimes are sticky institutions that cannot be changed easily or often; Max Weber (1948: 128) has described politics as the 'strong and slow boring of hard boards'. However, Weber's focus on patience has had far less attention than his accompanying discussion about the revolutionary consequences of charismatic leaders. Yet revolutionaries require patience too. For more than a quarter century, Lenin and his colleagues suffered imprisonment, exile and the risk of execution in the hope that some day their time would come. A civil rights worker of the founder generation, Rosa Parks, patiently endured the indignities of being a black woman in the Deep South for 41 years of her life before refusing to move to the back of a Jim Crow bus in Montgomery, Alabama in 1955.

Patience is a necessary condition in evolutionary theories that postulate democratization is, according to Robert Dahl (1971: 47) 'a slow process, measured in generations'. The classic example is England, which took three centuries to evolve into a democracy. However, many theories of the democratic electorate emphasize impatience. The political business cycle has a time horizon limited by the four-year period between one election and the next. The government delivers an annual budget and programme of legislation. The media, now providing around-the-clock news coverage, demands a different story in the headlines every day and if a major problem erupts, it demands that the government announce a solution almost instantly. As British Prime Minister Harold Wilson was fond of remarking, 'A week in politics is a long time'.

New leaders of post-Communist regimes could not know how long it would take to overcome the costs of transformation and how long to achieve its full benefits. As Boris Yeltsin confessed, leaders could have unrealistic expectations of jumping from the past to the future while ignoring present difficulties. The political goals of *de*construction could be realized quickly. For example, the Berlin Wall was literally breached overnight, and in less than 12 months free elections across Central and Eastern Europe had turned the Iron Curtain into scrap metal. However, constructing new institutions of polity, economy and society was certain to take longer. Whether people regarded the costs of transformation as justified by subsequent benefits depended upon the patience of the electorate.

## I Patience in authoritarian regimes

The word *patience* is derived from the Greek root for suffering. Life in Communist-dominated Central or Eastern Europe required patience, for people not only had to wait without knowing when or whether their political dissatisfactions would ever be removed, but also to suffer the indignities of life in an anti-modern society. Patient subjects are likely to comply with the demands of an authoritarian regime, but their motives are different from those who positively accept it. Given uncertainty about how long the current regime can continue to impose its commands, patience is not justified by rational expectations but by hope or even, hope against hope, that change will occur some day. Patient people can with fortitude endure discouragement and difficulties waiting uncertainly for a transformation of their circumstances. After the Second World War Estonians, Latvians and Lithuanians, whether at home or in exile, refused to accept the integration of their territories in the Soviet Union. They patiently maintained that the three Baltic countries ought to be independent, a goal that came about after a half century of waiting.

Whereas patience leads to silent reservations about coercive authority, *impatience* can lead to protest. Protesters differ from patient subjects in their time horizon; they want to do something about a repressive regime and do it now. In response to events in the 1960s, Ted Gurr (1970) theorized that the greater the gap between what a regime did and what its citizens wanted, the greater the likelihood of popular frustration and then more or less spontaneous protests. If the regime suppressed the protests brutally, this would create an escalating round of disorder. Impatient protesters differ from patient revolutionaries, for the latter have long-term strategies. Their protests occur when the time is deemed right for advancing their goals. Students in the Communist bloc kept quiet when student protesters challenged authorities in Western Europe in the late 1960s. Communist-bloc students patiently suffered lectures on the pseudo-science of Marxism-Leninism because they knew what would happen to their careers if they impatiently protested against the regime.

In an established democracy the demands of protesters can be met without changing the regime. If people are dissatisfied with the government of the day, they can vote for a change of government while democratic institutions remain secure. If they are dissatisfied with all established parties, they can vote for new protest parties and their votes will encourage established parties to adapt to their expression of dissatisfaction. Insofar as politicians anticipate the reaction of voters at the next election, the waiting time for removing grievances is foreshortened.

In an autocratic regime time horizons are long, for there is no prospect of changing the government at the next election. An autocratic government does not limit its duration. Subjects do not know whether they or the regime will die first. The classic problem-solving method of dealing with dissatisfaction, searching for something different, cannot operate because people are not free to search for an alternative regime. However, in the privacy of their minds, individuals remain free to hope that some day a hated regime will be gone.

As the revolutionary commitment to totalitarian transformation waned, the immediate concern of Communist regimes was with compliance here and now. As long as people behaved as the government demanded and avoided the public expression of dissatisfaction, the regime could persist. The outward compliance of subjects gave some of the attributes of legitimacy; the chief defect was that compliance was not voluntary (Rose, 1969). Nonetheless, compliance meant that Communist regimes were accepted as being likely to outlive both their subjects and their opponents.

*Adapting to an unwanted regime.* In free societies people have three main strategies for responding to unsatisfactory situations: exit, voice and loyalty (Hirschman, 1970). In Communist systems two of these alternatives were prohibited. Exit was not allowed or was only possible in exceptional political circumstances, for example, the regime wanted to get rid of a potentially awkward dissident. Voice was silenced by censors and stifled by the political discussion being dominated by the verbal fog that was produced by the rhetoric of Communist party-states.

Communist regimes sought to achieve a show of loyalty, whether voluntary or dissembled, by a mixture of ideological rhetoric, coercion, inducements, and by the turnover of generations. Mundane incentives to go along with the regime encouraged ambitious subjects to lick rather than bite the hand that could reward them. Joining the Communist Party opened up opportunities for promotion at work, a decent flat or educational benefits for children. In the Soviet Union the death of generations old enough to have experienced Stalin's murderous collectivization of agriculture and purges of the 1930s removed from the population cohorts with grounds to refuse commitment. In Central and Eastern Europe the turnover of generations removed those who had experienced the behaviour of Soviet troops when they occupied parts of Poland and the Baltic states after the Nazi–Soviet Pact of August 1939, and in their 'liberation' half a dozen years later. It also marked the passing of those who opted for Communism when offered a stark choice between siding between a Stalinist and a Nazi regime.

Fatalistic resignation is a second-best alternative to loyalty. Subjects complied with what the regime wanted without regarding it as legitimate or desirable. In the words of the Hungarian Prime Minister Janos Kadar, 'He who is not against us is with us'. Fatalism encourages the belief that the regime is willed by forces beyond the control of individuals and will not go away because of anything its subjects can do. Fatalism can be a rational response to the powers of the state: 'If I can't change the system, I had better learn to live with it'. Fatalism contributes to a low-level political equilibrium in which a regime can exercise authority without legitimacy in the minds of its subjects.

In an earlier era resigned acceptance of the powers that be was normal because these powers were remote from their subjects. However, in a regime with a totalitarian vocation, it was difficult for an individual to maintain isolation from the state. The intrusive Communist efforts to mobilize a public show of support created a dual political personality, 'two persons in one body', with 'two sides, the hidden one and the visible one' (Dudintsev, quoted in White, 1979: 111). The visible person said and did what the state commanded while the hidden person thought what he or she wanted while patiently suffering the stresses of a political split personality. The institutionalization of such hypocrisy explains two phenomena – outward compliance with Communist regimes for four decades and their abrupt collapse once the capacity to coerce compliance was lost. In the words of a Soviet musician, 'Everything was forever until it was no more' (Yurchak, 2006).

## II  The legacy of patience

People who had waited patiently in hopes of being rid of a Communist regime had that hope realized. However, regime change did not bring about an end to problems of governance. The transformation of the economy was accompanied by treble-digit inflation and unprecedented levels of unemployment. The mistakes of governors gave ammunition to critics and electoral competition gave opposition parties incentives to attack it. Transformation made it possible to find out how patient people were prepared to be when confronted with these problems. Hence, the New Europe Barometer asked citizens of Bulgaria, the Czech Republic, Slovakia, Hungary, Romania and Slovenia about patience in its third-round survey, which went into the field in November 1993, by which time it was clear that the problems left by Communism could not be disposed of quickly. At this time popularly elected governments had become unpopular. Most parties in government at the time of the 1993–1994 NEB survey were voted out of office soon after.

People were not asked how long they thought it would take the new regime to deal with problems inherited from the past, because an essential characteristic of patience is that one does not know how long suffering may continue. Patience is the willingness to persevere indefinitely in the face of suffering and hardship. To measure political patience, people were asked whether they thought another system of government should be tried if the new regime could not produce results soon or whether they thought it would take years to deal with problems inherited from the Communists.

In an open society, patience is not a sign of coerced resignation but a recognition of the difficulties inherent in extricating a country from the legacy of Communism. Most Central and East Europeans did show patience in the face of problems of transformation. In all, 66 per cent were willing to give the government years to deal with problems inherited from the Communist regime (Figure 4.1). Moreover, those describing themselves as very patient outnumbered those who were very impatient by a margin of more than two to one. Everywhere in the region patient citizens outnumbered those who were not. The extent of patience varied among the six countries: it was highest in the Czech Republic, 81 per cent, and least high in Hungary, 51 per cent.

However, in Russia the level of impatience was higher because the collapse of Communism imposed greater psychological and material stresses than in Central and Eastern Europe. In the third New Russia Barometer survey in 1994, 54 per cent of Russians were impatient with their new regime, a group more than half again larger than in Central and Eastern Europe. In the Baltic states, the population was divided: two-thirds of Estonians and Latvians and four in seven Lithuanians, having waited so long to regain their independence, were prepared to be patient, while a majority of Russians were impatient.

*Q. Do you think it will take years for government to deal with the problems inherited from the Communists [patient] or, if our system can't produce results soon, that's a good reason to try some other system of government [impatient]?*

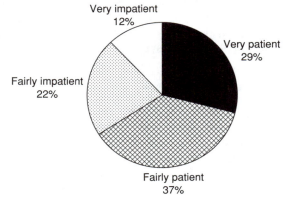

*Figure 4.1* The extent of patience.
Source: Centre for the Study of Public Policy, New Europe Barometer, 1994: Bulgaria, Czech Republic, Hungary, Romania, Slovakia, Slovenia.

*Who is patient?* There are many political, economic and social theories to explain why some citizens are patient while others are not. Hence, multivariate regression analysis is appropriate to test the relative importance of many potential influences. Since explanations postulate causes common to individuals in all transformation societies – for example, the importance of economic wellbeing, political values or education – respondents from all six NEB countries are here pooled in a single analysis. Table 4.1 reports those influences that are statistically significant. Collectively, they account for 12.7 per cent of the variance in political patience.

New regimes gained time from those who disliked the old regime. The more negative an individual was about the old regime, the more he or she was willing to be patient with the way new governors coped with their inheritance. In a complementary manner, citizens who were ready to reject their national traditions in favour of West European ways were also more likely to be politically patient. Patience was also boosted by the positive performance of new regimes in comparison with the past. Instead of having to accept heavy restrictions on their freedom, immediately after transformation citizens could say and do what they liked (see Chapter 10). The freer people felt, the greater their political patience. Because new regimes had more demands than resources, it was politically important how the new regime distributed scarce resources, either favouring party supporters and friends, as in the past, or fairly. Delivering services fairly encouraged patience, since people could believe that, if they waited their turn, whenever resources became available government would deliver what they were entitled to.

If people are only concerned with their current economic gratification, then those made worse off by transformation should be impatient, while those who take a long-term view will calculate that it pays to be patient in anticipation of the introduction of the market leading to material benefits in future. The familiar maxim – no gain without pain – was especially true of economic transformation. The analysis shows

*Table 4.1* Influences on political patience

| | *Variance explained by OLS regression: $R^2$ 12.7%* | | |
|---|---|---|---|
| | *b* | *se* | *Beta* |
| POLITICS | | | |
| Negative Communist political system | .02 | .00 | .11 |
| Prefers West European to national traditions | .10 | .01 | .11 |
| Government fairer now | .07 | .01 | .07 |
| Greater freedom now | .05 | .01 | .06 |
| ECONOMY | | | |
| Positive future economic system | .02 | .00 | .10 |
| Positive current economic system | .01 | .00 | .05 |
| Negative Communist economic system | .01 | .00 | .04 |
| Past household finances better | −.05 | .01 | −.05 |
| Fight inflation before unemployment | .07 | .01 | .08 |
| SOCIAL STRUCTURE | | | |
| Education | .04 | .01 | .04 |
| (All variables significant at .01 or better.) | | | |

Source: Centre for the Study of Public Policy, New Europe Barometer, 1993: Bulgaria, Czech Republic, Hungary, Romania, Slovakia, Slovenia.

that the more positive the expectation of the national economy in five years' time, the more willing people are to be patient with the current difficulties of government. If people were also positive about the current state of the national economy, this further re-inforces their patience. In a complementary manner, people who thought the old economic system better tended to be impatient with a system that put goods in shop windows but not enough money in their pockets to buy them. The same was true of people who felt their household finances had been better under the old regime.

Transformation gave citizens good reasons to be immediately anxious about inflation and unemployment, for both rapidly rose to unprecedented levels and both were the responsibility of the new regime. Inflation reached every household in society, while unemployment affected far fewer people, since about half the adult population were pensioners or otherwise outside the labour force. Two-thirds of NEB respondents gave fighting inflation a higher priority than dealing with unemployment. Even though inflation can result in prices visibly rising faster than earnings, this did not make citizens impatient with their new regime. Instead, it had the opposite effect, encouraging people to be more patient with a government burdened with responsibility for replacing a command economy with low prices and shortages with a market economy with higher prices and goods to buy.

Insofar as patience reflects fatalistic resignation, then more traditionally inclined people would be expected to be more patient, for example, those who are older or church attenders may await the promise of an after life and secularism could make people less patient with being denied satisfaction in the here and now. In fact, neither significantly affected patience. Nor were the impatient made up of young hotheads. Younger citizens were just as likely to be patient as older people. Whether people expected their household's future economic situation to be better or their current circumstances satisfactory had no significant effect on patience. Education was the only social difference that had a significant effect. It encouraged individuals to have a better understanding of problems of society, including the Communist legacy, and thus to be more patient with a government grappling with these problems.

## III Consequences of patience and impatience

Insofar as people are patient, they should be more ready to support their new regime as it deals with the problems it has inherited from its predecessor. But in a complementary manner, insofar as people are impatient, then not only should they be less inclined to support the new regime but also more ready to favour some form of undemocratic governance.

*Patience increases support for the regime.* At the time of the New Europe Barometer survey on patience, an average of 59 per cent of citizens were positive about the new regime, and this included an absolute majority in each of the six countries analyzed here. Endorsement was highest in the Czech Republic, where 78 per cent were positive, and lowest in Slovakia, where 52 per cent were positive.

The higher the level of political patience, the more likely people are to view the current regime positively. Among those who think the new government needs years to clear up the legacy of the Communists, 68 per cent are positive about the regime. Among those who are fairly impatient, support drops to 50 per cent and among the small proportion who are very impatient those negative about the current political system outnumber those positive. The correlation between patience and political support is confirmed by a multiple regression analysis. After controlling for the effect of many other influences, patience has a substantial and statistically significant influence on support for the new regime. Adding patience to the independent variables in Table 4.1 and making support for the regime the dependent variable can account for 28.5 per cent of the variance and patience has a significant beta of .08 and a b coefficient of .42.

If people are dissatisfied with their current regime, they need to identify an alternative to replace it. Otherwise, their impatience can generate frustration due to the lack of an alternative. Since Central and East European peoples have had first-hand experience of a variety of alternative regimes, including local dictators as well as Communist rule (see Chapter 17), impatient citizens ought to show substantial support for undemocratic alternatives. However, given the conflicts that have disrupted regimes in the region, there may be disagreement about what kind of regime could immediately do something about the problems of transformation.

Insofar as impatience with the new regime arises because its problems did not occur previously, then returning to a Communist regime would appear a logical alternative. However, in Central and Eastern Europe the dislike of the old regime was such that the third New Europe Barometer found only 15 per cent endorsed doing so. As expected, those most impatient with the new regime (31 per cent) were substantially more likely to endorse a return to the past than those who were fairly impatient (21 per cent) or those prepared to wait and see what the new regime could do (10 per cent). The importance of impatience is confirmed by a multiple regression analysis: it is third most influential among a dozen and a half potential influences on a desire to return to Communist rule.

Getting rid of parliament and elections and having a strong leader decide what to do about the problems of transformation attracted more support. In the 1993 NEB round, this was endorsed by 29 per cent of Central and East Europeans. As expected, the more impatient people are, the more likely they are to favour government by a dictator. There is a big gap in evaluating a move to dictatorship between the very impatient, 46 per cent, and the very patient, 23 per cent. A multiple regression analysis confirms that impatience is one of the four most important influences on the endorsement of dictatorship.

The patience developed during a lifetime of Communist rule among Central and East Europeans was extended to the regimes that faced the challenge of transformation. Patient citizens were not passive: they showed their dislike of particular governments and politicians by using their new democratic right of voting them out of office in a trial-and-error search for a government that could deal with the problems of transformation. A decade and a half after the fall of the Berlin Wall that patience was rewarded when governments shed their Communist legacy and claimed places as members of the European Union.

# Part II

# Coping with economic transformation

# 5   The need for a civil economy

I do not claim to be able to discuss the philosophy behind economic reform.

(Boris Yeltsin, 1994)

The abrupt collapse of the Communist system confronted policymakers with a challenge: How to transform an anti-modern economy into a modern market economy? However, the creation of a new economic system cannot be accomplished overnight. It took England upwards of a century to achieve the first industrial revolution, and countries that followed have required a half century to do so. For more than a generation, 100 third-world countries have been trying to develop into modern market economies, but their progress has been unsteady.

At the start of transformation, post-Communist governors could not ignore the legacy of the past, for it was all that was there. However, it was not conducive to the rapid creation of a market economy. The legacy of a command economy was different from the foundations on which market economies have been built. Early industrialization began in countries that already had a legal structure covering property rights and commerce, banking and financial institutions and markets where prices were related to supply and demand. In third-world countries these institutions have been less fully developed, but most have been free of the anti-modern legacy institutionalized throughout the Communist bloc.

In a modern market economy the state provides a legal framework within which institutions of the market can function. By contrast, Communist regimes rejected the idea of private property rights and the enforcement of contracts in favour of the party-state expropriating the property of the bourgeoisie and deciding when and how obligations were to be enforced. In place of a transparent system of market prices, the party-state substituted an opaque system allocating resources through its own plans and assessing output in terms of physical quantities rather than money values. In addition to the problem of creating new market institutions, policymakers also faced the problem of getting rid of the legacy of an anti-modern command economy designed with totalitarian aspirations.

The command economy was not, as in social democratic societies, a mixed economy with a state sector and a private sector. There was no place in the planned economy for private sector institutions to produce goods and services, just as in politics there was no scope for civil society institutions to operate independently of the party-state. Policymakers had to create a civil economy as well as a civil society.

The economic development of Germany illustrates the difference between modern and anti-modern economies. In nineteenth-century Germany there was the legal framework of a Rechtsstaat, a functioning economy of peasants, artisans and traders, and a civil society. Industrialization transformed both eastern and western parts of Germany to create a modern civil economy. In 1945 many of the major physical resources of the German economy were literally bomb sites and cigarettes and chocolates obtained from bartering with occupation armies were valued more than paper currency. In West Germany the devastation was met by the *Wiederaufbau*, the rebuilding of an economy that had once been the strongest economy in Europe. Reconstruction was possible because the institutional framework of a civil economy was still intact. Within two decades the rebuilt West German economy was booming.

By contrast, in East Germany the goal was not to rebuild the factories, commerce and financial institutions of Berlin, Dresden and Leipzig and other major centres created during industrialization. It was to replace capitalism with something different. The consequences of doing so led millions of East Germans to head west in search of prosperity before the Berlin Wall went up in 1961.

When the Berlin Wall came down, the governors of a re-united Germany faced a much more difficult task than that of their predecessors in the late 1940s. Instead of rebuilding economic institutions, market institutions needed to be created after an absence of more than two generations. Up to a point, this was feasible because there was a wholesale extension of West German laws and institutions to what had been the East German Republic (see Chapter 12). However, the consequence was not the transformation of East German lands into active participants in a modern market economy on the same terms as their West German cousins. Instead, it has been the provision of hundreds of billions of euros in subsidies in prolonged efforts to re-introduce a social market economy that made East German cities among the most prosperous cities in Central Europe before 1914.

## I  Civil and command economies

A market is a place where buyers and sellers produce and exchange goods and services. A marketplace requires accurate weights and measures, laws regulating the ownership and exchange of goods, money as a medium of exchange, and courts to enforce laws and contracts. It is the state, not the market, that enacts and maintains the laws that protect property. It is the state, not the market, that sees that contracts are enforced. It is the state, not the market, that maintains public order, without which enterprises cannot invest with security. To argue that a modern market economy can operate without the infrastructure provided by the state is to be an idiot in the original Greek sense of a person indifferent to civic responsibilities.

If the laws on which the market depends are made by a Rechtsstaat, and this was the case in the Prussian and Habsburg regimes, then a market economy is a *civil economy*. The point is illustrated by the fact that in universities of Central Europe the study of economics, like the study of political science, was originally part of an education in law. The German expression *Nationalwirtschaft* (national economy) reflects this outlook, as do the books of great scholars of economic development such as Max Weber, Joseph Schumpeter and Friedrich von Hayek. A civil economy can operate in accord with a variety of political values: it can be a social democratic economy, a free-market economy or a social economy. However, the institutions of a civil economy were absent at the start of post-Communist transformation, and most of those experienced in how they had operated were either dead or gone.

Because a Communist economy was a command economy, it was driven by politics. That is why the first seven chapters of Janos Kornai's (1992) magisterial exposition of the political economy of Communism are about power and political institutions. The party-state did not manage the economy; it *was* the economy. The justification for this was ideological. Marxism, especially the gloss given it by Lenin and Stalin, was a political as well as an economic theory. It rejected the central institutions of the market – private property, profit and capital – as causes of the exploitation and impoverishment of the masses. It rejected the institutions of the bourgeois state as a means of suppressing the masses in the interests of capitalism. It predicted that the longer the capitalist system developed, the closer it was to collapse. It claimed that Communism provided a more effective means of promoting economic growth and was also morally superior. Although the ideology was subject to continnal reinterpretation, one feature was constant: market institutions were proscribed. In the circumstances of the Soviet Union in the 1920s and of Central and Eastern Europe after the Second World War, Communism could only be achieved in the distant future. Meanwhile, subjects of the regime were expected to make sacrifices to advance toward that goal.

The power to give direction to the economy rested with the Party rather than the price system. The Party claimed to be acting as the vanguard of the proletariat, making decisions in the interests of workers by applying the principles of Marxist-Leninist science. If critics pointed out failings in a policy, this was treated as an indication that critics were 'spokesmen of the internal and external class enemy' (Kornai, 1992: 55). The Party's leading role was institutionalized through an elaborate apparatus integrating it with the state. The Party appointed the leading personnel in government, formulated policies in advance of commitments by public agencies and maintained Party cells within government ministries to monitor actions there. As a mass organization, the Party was active in the workplace and controlled trade unions. It encouraged workers as well as managers to meet monthly production norms by using both material and ideological carrots and sticks. The production of culture was treated similarly. In universities, broadcasting institutions, theatres and unions of writers or of composers, party apparatchiks monitored what was said and done. Works that were deemed to embody socialist realist culture were promoted and symphonies, paintings and books showing signs of ideological deviance were banned.

The five-year plan was the means by which the Party sought to impose its will on every form of economic activity. Planning under Communism was fundamentally different from the indicative planning and forecasts that Western governments make as part of their involvement in a civil economy. In a non-market economy the focus was not on money but on production quotas expressed in terms of goods, such as locomotives or aeroplane parts. Industries and factories were assigned targets, and achievement was monitored on a monthly basis. Managers in command economies became expert in exploiting connections to secure the goods and services needed to meet these targets. Workers became expert in the speedy production of goods without regard to quality. Because failure to meet plan targets could be labelled a political crime as well as an economic failing, managers doctored their accounts; the bottom line was the production of paperwork showing that the plan targets had been met.

Such were the pathologies of a command economy that in order to function effectively it required a shadow second economy to correct its deficiencies. In place of the institutions of finance capitalism that Marxists denounced as parasitical, there were wheeler-dealers who were experts in diverting goods and services from the paths laid down in official plans to those that could offer them something in return, whether it was access to luxury goods or dollars. Hence, the riddle: Why is Moscow like New York? Answer: In New York you can buy anything with dollars and nothing with roubles. It's the same here. The shadow economy offered functional means to overcome dysfunctional characteristics of the command economy by hook or by crook.

## II  The default position: an uncivil economy

Command economies could run without signals of supply and demand given by market prices, but they could not run without the political power needed to put the commands of bureaucrats into effect. Hence, the collapse of the party-state meant the collapse of the command economy and the creation of an economic void.

At the start of transformation there was an ideological debate about creating a third-way economy that combined the economic dynamism of a market economy with state controls 'socializing' the benefits of growth. In practice, the real choices facing policymakers were between two different kinds of market economies – a civil or an uncivil economy. A market could be immediately created by the non-enforcement of laws of a command economy. However, in the absence of laws and institutions to govern the market, it would not be a civil economy.

An *uncivil* economy combining legal and illegal activities was the default position for economies in transformation. In an uncivil economy individuals and entrepreneurs can buy and sell on terms accepted by both parties. Football fields were turned into bazaars in which people could sell everything from made-in-China designer clothes with Italian labels to plumbing wrenched from the toilets of decaying state enterprises. In the classic pedlar's mode, street traders bought cheap and sold dear wherever this was possible. Uncivil transactions can also involve the marketing of illegal goods and services such as sex or drugs, or buying favours from public officials such as guards. Doctors and teachers can extort 'tips' (that is, cash bribes) to provide services that by law are meant to be free of charge.

The collapse of the command economy left foundering state enterprises employing people to subtract rather than add value to what they produced. Enterprises with little hope of surviving in a market economy turned to tactics reminiscent of Gogol's novel *Dead Souls*. They created a virtual economy in which suppliers were paid with promissory notes and notes from customers were treated as if they were cash receipts. Barter, a common practice in the command economy, was also used as a substitute for cash transactions. Workers could be paid in kind or not at all; this was often accepted when the alternative was to be made unemployed.

Entrepreneurs showed their understanding of practices of the modern economy by manipulating its institutions in anti-modern ways. Corruption flourished. Whereas in a civil economy the state collects taxes from private enterprises, in an uncivil economy businesses sought to extract big benefits from the state. In Russia the tax exemptions and import licences given to bodies with names such as the Afghan War Veterans Union and the Humanitarian Aid Commission were worth hundreds of millions to those who controlled and used them for such things as selling cigarettes tax free. Peter Aven, a former Russian minister turned banker, described the system thus:

> To become a millionaire in our country it is not at all necessary to have a good head or specialized knowledge. Often, it is enough to have active support in the government, the parliament, local power structures and law-enforcement agencies. One fine day your insignificant bank is authorized to, for instance, conduct operations with state budgetary funds. Or quotas are generously allotted for the export of oil, timber and gas. In other words, you are *appointed* a millionaire.
>
> (quoted in Reddaway and Glinski, 2001: 603: italics added)

The disposal of state-owned enterprises was a high priority of anti-Communist policymakers wanting to be rid of major industries that were controlled by holdovers from the command economy. But the result was not privatization as the term is understood by economists and bankers in the Anglo-American world. It was privatization without a private sector or the rule of law. Moreover, the sale of state-owned enterprises presupposed that enterprises were legal entities separate from government departments and their accounts and balance sheets represented their actual financial circumstances rather than what the commanders of the command economy chose to write down. The result was a process variously described as Kremlin capitalism (Blasi, Kroumova and Kruse *et al.*, 1997), collision and collusion (Wedel, 1998), the looting of Russia (by murdered author Paul Klebnikov, 2000) or simply as 'kleptocracy', that is, rule by thieves.

Although ordinary people could not make significant sums of money from privatization, they could see the fruits of uncivil entrepreneurship and draw their own conclusions. When the first New Russia Barometer asked in 1992 for a description of those making money in an economy in transformation, substantial majorities saw the new rich as being hard-working, dishonest, intelligent, taking advantage of people and using domestic and foreign political connections (Figure 5.1). At a time of severe shortages of goods in shops, almost everyone thought the money of the new rich was helping the economy grow. However, a year later only one in three Russians thought moneymakers helped make the economy grow. Instead, 'biznessmen' were seen as get-rich-quick predators rather than investors for the long term.

The fall of the Berlin Wall did not mark the end of history. While people who had been subjects of a state with a totalitarian aspiration happily embraced a fundamental value of nineteenth-century liberalism – freedom from the state (see Chapter 10) – state action was still needed to provide the framework of law and institutions necessary to turn an uncivil into a civil economy. Moreover, the state's responsibilities today go far beyond those of the minimalist nineteenth-century nightwatchman state. Like their West European counterparts, post-Communist governments had major spending commitments on education, health care and pensions. Attempts to solve the shortfall of revenue by printing money were tried as a temporary solution for inadequate public revenue. But this only created a worse problem: treble-digit inflation and the further de-monetization of economic activity. In the short term, an uncivil economy makes government an ineffectual broken-backed democracy.

The ability to collect taxes is a defining characteristic of the modern state. The collapse of the command economy meant the new regime could no longer take what revenue it wanted from the cash flow of state enterprises. Nor was it possible to tax the uncivil economy. In the uncivil economy of Russia in the 1990s it was estimated

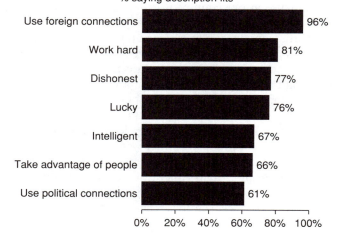

*Q. With the introduction of the market, some people have been able to make more money. Which of these words do you think applies to people who are now making money?*

*Figure 5.1* Attitude to people making money, 1992.
Source: Centre for the Study of Public Policy, New Russia Barometer, 1992.

that half of taxes were not paid, and tax collection could be based on negotiations and bluff rather than bureaucratic procedures. The great majority of Russians see taxation as an uncivil extraction that can be avoided by themselves as well as their employers. More than half say that there is no need to pay taxes if you don't want to do so, for the government will never find out, and three-quarters believe that paying a cash bribe to a tax official would evade payment of any taxes claimed. Russian opinions differ only on whether taxes can be completely ignored or whether a 'tip' to a tax official is needed to avoid legal obligations.

The attainment of sustained economic growth requires a civil economy. Uncivil activities, such as running an illegal taxi service or doing household repairs for cash-in-hand, are labour-intensive services that cannot generate employment and economic growth in the way that large-scale enterprises can. However, capitalists will not risk investing large sums in activities that depend upon illegality for profit. Because they have no legal title to their resources, uncivil entrepreneurs are discouraged from investing in enterprises that create thousands of jobs and promote long-term economic growth.

The existential challenge facing ordinary people at the start of transformation was much simpler than creating a civil economy. It was how to get enough to eat each day and cope with the radical changes in prices and wages. The need to get food was not new, for food shortages were a recurring problem of the agricultural policies of the command economy. The resources that people used to cope with transformation were also a legacy of the old system. Coping strategies did not enable people to become rich like 'biznessmen', but they did enable people to avoid destitution while waiting for their governors to create a more or less civil economy.

# 6    Getting enough to eat

In a country where the sole employer is the state, opposition means death by slow starvation. The old principle – who does not work shall not eat – has been replaced by a
new one – who does not obey shall not eat.

(Attributed to Leon Trotsky)

Food is a daily need of everyone. For that reason, societies need institutions that can
provide enough food to meet this basic need. In a command economy, the Party
was in charge of the production and allocation of food and, as Trotsky emphasized,
food was a political weapon that could be used make people keep to the party line.
However, since the agricultural policies of a command economy often made the supply of food problematic, this weapon could be a boomerang. If the command economy could not produce sufficient food for everyone, then it risked rationing and even
food riots, or the need to import food from capitalist countries.

In a modern market economy, making money is the object of agricultural production. The word farmer is derived from an old English term describing a person contracting for the use of land in order to produce crops that can be sold for enough to
meet the costs of production and leave a little profit. In such an economy the supply
of food is taken for granted. Farmers have invested money in fertilizers and equipment in order to produce more food with fewer farm workers. Until global demand
from Asia became great, increased efficiency has made food surpluses the characteristic problem of European and American agriculture.

By contrast, the collectivization of agriculture in command economies reduced
efficiency and made the supply of food to cities unpredictable. Peasant holdings and
the estates of large landowners were confiscated. Land was combined into large collective or state farms that were expected to provide an assembly-line output of food
for urban workers. Collectivization in the Soviet Union was exceptionally brutal: peasants who opposed it were shot or deported or left to die of starvation after they had
slaughtered their animals and eaten their seed corn. Collectivization was forcibly imposed
across Central and Eastern Europe except Poland. As an analysis of the experience
concluded: 'The forced collectivization of agriculture has been a searing historical
experience in Marxist regimes, during which tens of millions died from starvation and
mistreatment, while countless others suffered greatly' (Pryor, 1992: 3).

Collectivization demoralized agricultural labour. Workers on collective farms grew
what they needed for themselves or for sale or barter in the unofficial economy while
producing the minimum quantity and quality of food for the state plan. In response

to the shortcomings of collectivization, in 1954 Nikita Khrushchev launched a programme to cultivate an additional 41 million hectares of land. The programme was a spectacular failure. To feed Soviet citizens, Brezhnev began regular imports of food from the United States. By the 1980s the cost of importing food from hard-currency countries was a major problem for Mikhail Gorbachev.

For the ordinary urban household in Communist times, buying food was a problem. Even though subsidies meant food was cheap, there were chronic shortages in shops. For instance, until the fall of the Berlin Wall some East Germans regarded oranges as a Christmas treat rather than as a commodity to be found on the breakfast table every morning. In a shortage economy the answer to the question – Who grows food? – could be: Almost everyone who wants to eat. This meant that the disruption of transformation did not lead to widespread malnutrition or famine, because households had in place strategies used to get enough to eat in a non-market command economy.

## I Alternative systems for producing food

Societies differ first of all in the degree to which food producers are differentiated from other types of workers. In a primitive society almost every household will produce some or most of its own food, but in a modern society the great majority of people do not grow food. Instead, most workers produce goods and services while agriculture is a specialized activity of farmers. Societies vary in the complexity of food production and distribution. In a primitive society a household produces food for its own consumption or exchange within a village. In a modern society, the production and distribution of food is part of a complex system of international trade. Together, these two distinctions can be used to identify four ideal-type societies.

In a pre-modern society in which the great bulk of the population is rural, most households are more or less self-sufficient. There is little differentiation between those who grow food and those who do not. Where very little economic activity is monetized and exchanges are localized, they are also simple. Where transportation is limited, as in medieval Europe, this greatly restricts the shipment of goods between farm and market. Most growers of food are peasants, defined by Shanin (1990: 9) as households producing 'mainly for their own consumption and for the fulfilment of commitments to the holders of political and economic power'.

Differentiation between food producers and non-producers was the start of the transition from a self-sufficient to a modern market system of food production: 'Peasantry as a specific social class and a way of life develops into farming as an occupation' (Galeski, 1987). Within a transitional village, households could be differentiated between food producer, weaver, shoemaker, tavern keeper, priest, etc. Exchange could involve reciprocal services between people well known to each other, cash payments, or a mixture of the two. Finally, as monetization and transportation and modern monetization extend the reach of markets, village production becomes linked with urban centres in more complex networks that eventually extend into international trade. Polanyi (1957) called this shift the start of 'the great transformation' from a subsistence to a modern economy.

A modern economy is one in which the labour force is differentiated into a large proportion of people producing manufactured goods and services and a small proportion of farmers in rural areas. The percentage of the labour force in farming is below

3 per cent in Britain and the United States and in France, historically a peasant society, it is now only 5 per cent. Farmers specialize in the full-time production of
particular commodities for sale in a complex system of national and international markets. Specialization results in a wheat farmer buying meat at a store and often bread
as well. Food producers export their commodities to feed a large number of urban
dwellers, who in turn produce goods bought in the countryside. The growth of capital-
intensive farming means that farming is more and more about deploying capital effectively rather than about employing family members or hired hands. Even in nominally
rural areas a majority of the labour force no longer farms.

Karl Marx had railed against the 'idiocy of rural life' and the planners of the command economy sought to eliminate differences between urban and rural life by bringing technical education to rural areas and applying factory methods of production
to collective farms. Diagnoses of what was wrong with East European agriculture
assumed that 'the food chain being unable to meet the food requirements' (Ash, 1992:
2) was a problem that could be put right by altering faults in the existing system. In
the extreme case, reviews of transformation ignored agriculture, as if food for hundreds of millions of people would be produced as long as macro-economic policies
were effective.

The fourth alternative – a stressful system – describes non-market food production
at the time of transformation. All households faced the immediate problem: How do
we feed ourselves? People could not go to grocery stores to buy what they needed because
shortages remained a chronic problem. For example, in November 1991 one of my
collaborators in the New Russia Barometer queued for three hours in his suburban
food shop in order to buy six eggs. Factory and office workers did not produce food
because of some romantic rural notion but because they lived in a stressful economy
in which the alternative was to risk doing without food. Paradoxically, the attempt to
introduce specialization without markets led to the 'de-differentiation' of the labour
force.

The immediate consequence of the collapse of the command economy was to increase
stress. The collapse disrupted the 'pseudo-modern' economy of the Communist era and
introduced many uncertainties about the value of money, the market price of food
and the incentives for rural areas to send food to cities. In such circumstances, a household's capacity to go outside officially recognised channels was of critical importance
in getting enough to eat. Urban residents could cope insofar as they had already
're-peasantized' themselves, producing food for household consumption.

## II If you can, grow your own food

To get enough to eat amidst the uncertainties of transformation, households could avoid
a forced choice between being a farmer or a factory worker: they could try to be both,
working in a factory or office for money and growing food to make sure they got enough
to eat. Hence, in the early years of transformation the New Europe Barometer gave
detailed attention to how people got their food because this was a time when the
market was just starting to provide lots of food to buy – if you had enough money.

*Most who grow food are not farmers.* In a modern market economy being employed
in agriculture is the conventional definition of being a producer of food. Official employment statistics recorded that employment in agriculture was as low as 12 per cent in

Czechoslovakia and 13 per cent in Russia and slightly higher in Bulgaria. Poland was exceptional because the Communist regime did not abolish peasant farmers; 28 per cent of the Polish labour force was therefore classified as in agriculture.

Taking official statistics as conclusive evidence of who grows food is very misleading. First, labour-force statistics exclude people who are retired, students or others outside the labour force. Second, it is assumed that people who are not employed as farmers do not grow food and that urban dwellers lack access to plots of ground. However, late-nineteenth-century industrialization led to a movement throughout Europe for urban workers to have small allotments of land on the edge of the city where they could grow food or simply relax. Allotments with garden sheds or summer houses are familiar sights to anyone travelling in and out of European cities by rail.

To find out the extent to which households were producing food, whatever their place of residence or official occupation, respondents were asked: Does anyone in your household grow food on their own plot of land? If not, does anyone in your household help friends or relatives to grow food? The replies showed that from half to four-fifths of households were growing food, usually on their own plot of land rather than helping others (Figure 6.1). The highest percentage growing food was in Russia. Not only were rural dwellers almost invariably producing some of their own food but also almost three-quarters of households in Russian cities.

Instead of collectivized agriculture leading to the socialized production of food on state farms, the great majority of households growing food were not farmers. In Russia the proportion growing food who were not employed in agriculture outnumbered nominal agricultural workers by a margin of five to one, in Czechoslovakia by a

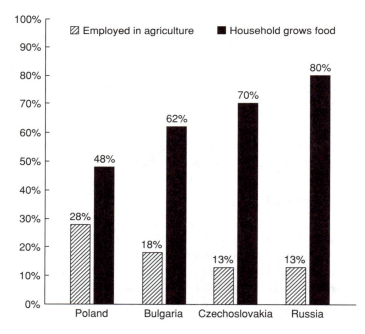

*Figure 6.1* Producers of food.
Sources: Centre for the Study of Public Policy, nationwide surveys in Bulgaria, Czechoslovakia, and Poland, 1991; New Russia Barometer, 1993.

margin of four to one, and in Bulgaria by a margin of three to one. Only in Poland were those employed in agriculture more than half of those growing food.

In a modern economy, people either grow food as a full-time job or they do not grow food at all. However, in a stressful society we would expect most people growing food to do so as one among a number of economic activities on which their household relies, and this is in fact the case. Small plots of ground do not require daily cultivation nor do potatoes, cucumbers and vegetables. Across the region, two-thirds of households grow food on a part-time basis and the median household works their plot several times a week during the growing season.

If a person spending at least several hours growing food is considered an agricultural worker, then at the start of transformation there were more agricultural workers in Russian cities than in the countryside and the same was true in Czechoslovakia. In Bulgaria the number of urban households engaged in daily agricultural tasks were equal to those nominally employed in agriculture. Growing food is not undertaken lightly by urban dwellers, because a plot of ground is not usually found just outside the door. In a large city it is likely to be an allotment some distance away from high-rise blocks of flats or at a *dacha* which is accessible every weekend. The commitment to growing food is shown by the willingness of the median Russian urbanite to spend between one and two hours making a return journey to his or her plot of ground and in Bulgaria, where cities are smaller, the median journey to and from a plot of ground has been upwards of one hour. Only a small percentage of part-time food producers have a plot of ground that is several hours away, for example, in the village where their family originated.

*Who grows food?* Although every household needs to eat, not all transformation households produced food. What can account for the difference? On a priori grounds, low earnings are one reason; people who have difficulty in making ends meet may rely upon their own resources because they cannot afford to buy all their food. Having the time to cultivate food is another potential influence; retired persons and those not in regular employment have more time to till the soil.

Only one condition is necessary to grow food: access to land. In a multiple regression analysis for each country, access to land is shown to account for nearly all of the variance in growing food and no other influence is of substantial importance (Rose and Tikhomirov, 1993: Table 3). While this may seem obvious, in the absence of economic necessity people could use their plot to grow ornamental flowers or for other leisure pursuits, as is often the case with gardening in modern societies.

Equally striking, a household's economic circumstances have no effect on the decision to grow food. Neither the number of employed persons in a household nor education has a statistically significant influence on growing food. Furthermore, the adequacy or inadequacy of income from the official economy is without any substantive impact. The greater availability of time during the week for growing food is also without effect: retired persons are no more likely to grow food than those in employment.

*Importance in a portfolio of resources.* Households that produce food on a part-time basis cannot generate enough to fulfil their needs. Nor is this necessary in a society in which nearly every household combines resources from a variety of economic activities, including a cash income in the official economy (see Chapter 8). The command economy's practice of selling basic foodstuffs at low prices made buying food economical – as and when it was available in shops. However, when the surveys analyzed here were undertaken, the stresses of transforming a command economy into a market economy meant that it was still common to queue to buy goods such as food. For example, in the autumn of 1991 nine-tenths of the shelves in a food shop of a middle-class Moscow housing estate were empty and a Bulgarian fortunate enough to travel to Amsterdam brought back food rather than toys for his children.

Since most households produce food for their own consumption, the relevant question is not – How much does the household production of food contribute to a country's Gross Domestic Product? but – How much does it contribute to a family's total food consumption? When asked about the extent to which they relied on home-grown food, the median household said that it accounted for some but not most of the food they consumed. In other words, the alternative to growing food was not starvation but going hungry or ill-fed with a disturbing frequency.

To determine the relative importance of household food production as compared to other resources, such as working in the shadow economy for cash in hand, the NEB asks people to choose from a list of nine options the two resources that are most important for their standard of living. In all four countries at least two-fifths of households considered growing food as one or the most important economic resources of their household, and in Russia the proportion rose to 50 per cent.

## III  Bringing the idiocy of rural life to the cities

The urbanization of the population of Central and Eastern Europe and the Soviet Union was a major achievement of the command economy, and it was cited by sociologists as an example of the modernization of Communist-bloc societies. By the time the system collapsed, three-quarters of the population of Russia and of Czechoslovakia were living in cities, as were two-thirds of Bulgarians and more than three-fifths of Poles.

The collectivization of agriculture was meant to end the idiocy of rural life by turning peasants into the equivalent of an urban proletariat. However, its effect was the opposite. The pathologies and inefficiencies of collectivized agriculture introduced the idiocy of rural life into cities. Confronted with the erratic supply of food in shops, urban residents cultivated potatoes, cucumbers and whatever else their plots would support. In terms of the logic of specialization in a modern economy, this was the reverse of the rational allocation of labour. But bringing the idiocy of rural life to the cities was rational for people who wanted to be sure of having enough to eat.

If agriculture had been organized along modern lines, households in big cities such as Moscow, Sofia, Warsaw or Prague could have relied upon markets to keep the stores well stocked with food and the percentage growing some of their own food would have been close to nil. In fact, this was not the case. Even though it is more difficult to grow food in cities, at the start of transformation an average of 51 per cent of households in big cities and 63 per cent in towns were growing some of their own food to compensate for the pathological character of collectivized agriculture. Since the population of urban areas is much greater than rural areas, the result was that the percentage of 'urban idiots' growing food was everywhere higher than that of rural idiots. In the extreme case of Russia, urban producers of food outnumbered rural producers by a margin of three to one and even in Poland, urban producers of food outnumbered those in the countryside.

*Reducing stress by retreating from the market*. The logic of pre-modern agriculture is subsistence: food is produced for consumption within the household rather than for sale. People who do so are cultivating the soil rather than a balance sheet. The production of food in Communist societies was far more complex than in societies where people depended on subsistence agriculture. Households could get enough to eat by combining food obtained by queuing in shops and home-grown produce. There were uncertainties due to the inefficiencies of the state system. There were also uncertainties about home-grown food production due to the vagaries of the weather. Transformation introduced another uncertainty: whether you would have enough money to buy the food that the shops offered. The result was a stress-inducing system of producing food.

Producing food for household consumption rather than for sale is a step away from the market – and this is the direction that people took to get enough to eat amidst the turbulence of transformation. In Czechoslovakia, 88 per cent said they only grew food for their own use and in Bulgaria 80 per cent consumed all the food they grew while four per cent often sold food. In Poland, where farming is more widespread, three-quarters never sold any of the food they produced and in Russia two-thirds grew food only for home consumption. For the rest, selling food was an occasional practice; less than 1 in 12 said that they often did so. The absence of commercial motivation is illustrated by the readiness of people to give food to friends and relatives. The percentage doing so is as high as that regularly producing food for sale. The retreat from the market is normal not only among urban residents but also in the countryside where more households were growing food for their own consumption than for sale. However, the success of households in getting enough to eat during transformation left unresolved the challenge of modernizing an anti-modern system of agriculture.

# 7   Social capital when government fails

Russia is not a modern society. Of course, there is industry in Russia. But there is no society.

(Abdurakhman Avtorkhanov)

Social capital networks are ubiquitous building blocks of society. However, these networks do not work the same in all societies. In pre-modern societies social capital typically involves informal face-to-face relations of family, friends and neighbours. What makes a modern society distinctive is that, in addition to informal networks, social capital includes large, impersonal bureaucratic organizations operating according to the rule of law such as social-security funds, departments of defence and tax-collection agencies.

But what is the role of social capital networks when there is government failure, that is, there are too many bureaucratic rules and too little adherence to bureaucratic norms? A surfeit of rules imposes delays, because many public officials must be consulted and individuals have to spend an unreasonable amount of time hectoring officials to compensate for organizational inefficiencies. The absence of the rule of law adds corruption to unpredictability. Do people retreat into informal networks to substitute for discredited formal organizations? Is this paralleled by social failure, that is, individuals displaying 'amoral familism' and refusing to cooperate with others outside their immediate household? Or do informal networks penetrate formal organizations, seeking to correct for their shortcomings through such anti-modern practices as favouritism and bribery?

The Communist system sought to organize every aspect of social life in order to control its subjects and secure compliance with its dictates. It made membership in Party-approved organizations from school-days onwards a necessary condition of qualifying for such benefits as the state offered. But it was simultaneously under-bureaucratized, because the rule of law did not apply. Thus, the system encouraged people to create informal networks for protection against the state or to subvert its commands. The result was more social capital than society.

## I  What social capital is and is not

In economics capital is an asset: money is the most familiar form of capital, but natural resources such as oil and human resources such as education are also capital assets. The accumulation of capital is instrumental: it is used to produce goods and services.

Money can be invested in stocks and shares or used to set up a business; natural resources can be mined and turned into energy; and education can provide skills that produce a well-paid job.

*The instrumental approach.* The political economy approach of James S. Coleman (1990: 302) is instrumental; social capital is defined by its function. It is used to get things done, that is, to produce goods and services whether or not money changes hands. Social capital is deployed in informal relationships between individuals; in contacts between individuals and formal organizations; and in relationships between organizations. Social capital networks can be formal or informal. The type depends on how things get done in a given situation. Informal networks may be used to organize a neighbourhood social event; informal networks and formal networks can be used to get a government grant for a community centre; and government contracts are meant to be awarded to firms through formal bidding processes.

Face-to-face relationships create informal networks between a limited number of individuals bound together by kinship, propinquity, friendship or mutual interests. Informal networks are institutions in the sociological sense of having patterned and recurring interactions. But they are not formal organizations, because they lack legal recognition, full-time officials and written rules. The characteristic output of informal networks is a small-scale, do-it-yourself service such as help in child-care or repairing a house. Reliance on informal networks was of primary importance in pre-industrial societies. For example, when Alexis de Tocqueville wrote *Democracy in America* in the 1830s, the United States was a rural society in which almost all relationships were face-to-face relationships, since more than 90 per cent of the population lived in communities of less than 2,500 people. To take it as a model of social networks today is to ignore a lot that has happened since that classic book was published.

The formal organizations that are pervasive in modern societies are legally chartered and bureaucratic; their revenue comes from the market, the state or voluntary contributions. A formal organization can have individual members, for example, a professional association of doctors, or its members can be organizations, such as an association of hospitals. In a study of corporatism, Schmitter (1995: 310) goes so far as to argue, 'Organizations are becoming citizens alongside, if not in the place of, individuals'. The links between individuals and organizations are often filtered by many intermediaries. This is true not only of government but also of joint stock companies, national trade unions and internationally organized churches. Formal organizations are a necessary part of a modern society, producing goods such as automobiles and services such as university education.

Informal and formal organizations can be complementary. Some involve horizontal ties, for example, a wedding in a church. Others involve vertical links, for example, trade-union members can have informal relations in their union branch and the work branch is affiliated to district and regional organizations and to national headquarters. However, a formal organization cannot behave like individuals interacting informally on the basis of friendship as interaction is based on formal rules and procedures. An informal network has fewer resources, but more flexibility and, in the literal sense, more sympathy with those it embraces. Informal cooperation is based on an 'inside morality' that Max Weber (1968) characterized as *Binnenmoral*; the complement is 'outsider morals' (*Aussenmoral*), which can justify the exploitation of formal organizations of the state.

The relationship between informal networks and formal organizations is contingent. Informal networks can have positive consequences within formal organizations, as in Edmund Burke's hypothesis that soldiers fight for their platoon rather than for a bureaucratic army. In an anti-modern Communist system, informal and formal networks often contradicted each other. Uncertainty about how a formal organization might behave encouraged the formation of informal horizontal networks that individuals used to insulate themselves from exploitative organizations. When individuals did have to deal with government institutions, they could try to 'de-bureaucratize' the relationship, using personal contacts, bartering or bribes to get what they wanted.

Membership of organizations is an inadequate measure of the use of social capital, for membership may be active, passive or a condition of employment, as in a closed-shop union or a students' union. The Communist practice of compulsory membership and the misrepresentation of members' views has left a legacy of distrust. Even though 53 per cent of Russian employees report being members of a trade union, less than half trust their local union leader to look after their interests, and only 11 per cent of union members trust national union officials to look after their interests. Consistently, the New Europe Barometer finds only a limited minority of people belong to any type of sports, arts, community or charitable organization. In the 10 new European Union member states, 16 per cent report belonging to such organizations and in Russia, only 5 per cent do so.

*Attitudes are not networks.* The social psychological approach treats social capital as a set of trusting attitudes that predictably lead to the creation of behavioural networks. Inglehart (1997: 188) defines social capital as 'a culture of trust and tolerance in which extensive networks of voluntary associations emerge'. Robert Putnam (1997: 31) postulates that the attitudes found in informal face-to-face groups spill over from one situation to another and also 'spill up', creating large-scale, civil-society organizations such as political parties that positively link individuals with national government. Fukuyama (1995: 26ff) qualifies this proposition by stating that the radius of social trust varies between societies, a view particularly relevant to the study of societies with a Communist legacy.

Empirically, the social psychological approach assumes that people will have a general disposition to trust both people they know and large formal organizations that are the constituent institutions of representative government. Putnam's assumption that trust spills up from informal to formal organizations is used to justify relying on trust in other people and membership in face-to-face groups such as bowling leagues as proxies for participation in social networks that get things done and that make democracy work nationally. However, a long chain of inferences is needed to link trusting attitudes with instrumental networks. In his definition of social capital, Putnam (1997: 3) conflates 'networks, norms and trust that facilitate cooperation and coordination for mutual benefit'. This makes it impossible to use the concept in cause-and-effect analysis. The test of the political consequences of social capital, restricted to Putnam's core concept of trust, finds that in Russia trusting attitudes have very little influence (Mishler and Rose, 2005).

Trust in people you know is relatively high: 72 per cent of Central and East Europeans do so and the same is true of 62 per cent of Russians (Figure 7.1). However, the radius of trust does not extend outwards very far, a critical condition for Putnam's theory that interpersonal trust leads to collective political action. Only two-fifths of new EU citizens trust most people in their country, and barely one-third of Russians.

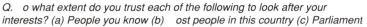

Q.  o what extent do you trust each of the following to look after your
interests? (a) People you know (b)   ost people in this country (c) Parliament

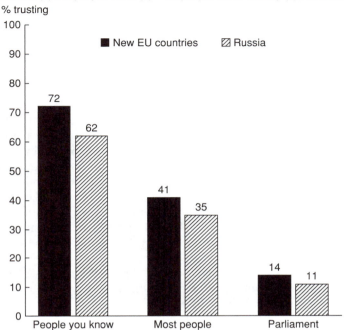

*Figure 7.1* The less you know people, the less you trust.
Sources: Centre for the Study of Public Policy, New Europe Barometer, 2004; New Russia
Barometer, 2005. Replies on a seven-point scale in which 5 to 7 is trusting; 4, neutral; and 1 to 3, does
not trust.

To make trust in people a proxy for social capital presupposes that this is tanta-
mount to trust in institutions. However, in post-Communist countries this is not the
case; instead of trust in other people being projected or spilling up into trust in national
political institutions the two are dissociated (Figure 7.1). Trust in Members of Parliament is consistently low; an average of 14 per cent in new EU member countries
and 11 per cent of Russians trust their nominal representatives.

There is a third way in which people can view social relations: they can be sceptical. Instead of confidently trusting or scornfully distrusting others a sceptic is uncertain (see Mishler and Rose, 1997). Such doubts can reflect a lack of experience or, in
the case of dealing with people you know, a mixture of good and bad experiences.
When a regime is transformed from a Communist system to a new democracy there
are good reasons for individuals to be doubtful or sceptical about trusting the capacity of new institutions to change human nature. In fact, the Barometer surveys find
that about as many new Europeans and Russians are sceptical of their fellow citizens
as are distrustful. As for Parliament, more are sceptical of it than positively trust it.
The existence of a sceptical bloc of citizens is significant, insofar as sceptics have an
open-minded approach to dealing with others and are willing to decide on the basis
of experience whether remote groups such as Members of Parliament are to be trusted
or distrusted.

## II Social capital in transformation societies

Every society has social capital networks, but their forms are contingent and can differ. Like a modern society, an anti-modern society has large formal organizations delivering education, health care and social services. However, such organizations are not predictable, for their outputs can be produced by opaque means, such as informal networks that break bureaucratic rules. In such circumstances individuals would be ill-advised to trust (that is, confidently expect) that they could get things done by relying on formal rules and procedures alone. On the other hand, the volume of services delivered by a Communist regime required it had to have some standard means of doing so. The repudiation of the Communist Party removed a major anti-modern influence on delivering public services, but the same public employees remained in place.

*Alternative networks for getting things done.* In the ideal-type modern society, people do not need a repertoire of networks to deal with formal organizations. Bureaucratic organizations predictably deliver goods and services to individuals as citizens and customers. In Weber's image, modern organizations operate like a vending machine: a person inserts a form to claim an entitlement and it is automatically delivered. In a modern society we do not think it unusual that electricity is supplied and billed without interruption; an airline ticket booked on the internet gives a seat on the scheduled flight; and wages due are routinely paid.

But what if modern organizations do not work in the ideal-type way? Given the centrality of money incomes in a modern society, the inability to pay wages or a pension is indicative of governmental failure. In the 1990s the effect of transformation meant that as many as half or more of workers and pensioners could be paid late or even not at all and in Russia the percentage was even higher.

Confronted with government failure, individuals have a choice of alternatives. Informal networks can be substituted for the failure of bureaucratic organizations or an attempt can be made to get what is wanted from government by personalizing relations with bureaucrats or using connections or bribery in an attempt to convince bureaucrats to violate rules. Fatalistically accepting that nothing can be done is a response of last resort.

The seventh New Russia Barometer was specially designed to probe the instrumental role of social capital (for details, see www.abdn.ac.uk/socialcapital). It was fielded in spring 1998, when Russians were still confronting the challenges of transformation. Since networks may be situation-specific, people were asked how they would go about getting what they wanted in a variety of familiar bureaucratic encounters, for example, obtaining subsidized housing, a place at a good school for a child, or admission to a hospital. Focusing on bureaucratic encounters avoids the anthropological fallacy of treating every relation as operating outside modern structures. It also avoids the formalist fallacy of assuming that government organizations actually do what citizens want them to do. Asking about activities familiar to most households assures replies with greater validity than questions about trusting national institutions known principally from television or the press. A multiplicity of alternative tactics were offered, including the possibility that the government organization worked as it ought to.

A majority of Russians did not expect government to provide services in a *modern* manner with vending-machine efficiency (Table 7.1). Only two-fifths were confident in the police protecting their home from burglars and barely a third believed a social-security office would pay a benefit if you filed a claim and did not push further. The

*Table 7.1* Alternative tactics for getting things done

|  | % endorsing |
|---|---|
| **MODERN ORGANIZATIONS WORK** | |
| *Public sector allocates by law* | |
| Police will help protect house from burglary | 43 |
| Social security office will pay entitlement if you claim | 35 |
| *Market allocates to paying customers* | |
| Buy a flat if it is needed | 30 |
| Can borrow a week's wage from bank | 16 |
| **INFORMAL ALTERNATIVES** | |
| *Non-monetized production* | |
| Growing food | 81 |
| Can borrow a week's wage from a friend | 66 |
| **PERSONALIZE** | |
| *Beg or cajole officials controlling allocation* | |
| Keep demanding action at social security office to get paid | 32 |
| Beg officials to admit person to hospital | 22 |
| **ANTI-MODERN** | |
| *Re-allocate in contravention of the rules* | |
| Use connections to get a subsidized flat | 24 |
| Pay cash to doctor on the side | 23 |
| **PASSIVE, SOCIALLY EXCLUDED** | |
| *Nothing I can do to* | |
| Get into hospital quickly | 16 |
| Get pension paid on time (pensioners only) | 24 |

Source: Centre for the Study of Public Policy, New Russia Barometer, 1998.

mega-network of the market offers those who can pay an alternative to government failure. However, less than 1 in 3 had enough money to consider buying a house and only 1 in 6 reckoned they could secure a bank loan. However, grocery stores sprang up with lots of goods on their shelves and this was the one modern institution that Russians expected to work as it should: 74 per cent said they sometimes went to shops that charged prices as marked on their products and did not cheat. While in a modern society this appears obvious, in Russia it was a novelty, since in the command economy food stores allocated goods by a combination of queuing, the black market and arbitrary fiat.

Individuals can avoid relying on undependable modern organizations by substituting *informal networks*. Four-fifths of Russian households, including a big majority of city dwellers, continue to grow some food for themselves. While only 1 in 4 has savings, informal social capital networks can supply cash when in need. Two-thirds reckoned they could borrow a week's wages or pension from a friend or relative. In a developing society such informal networks can be described as pre-modern. However, in the Russian context they are evidence of 'de-modernization', a means of avoiding the failure of bureaucratic welfare systems to provide social protection.

When a formal organization does not deliver and neither the market nor an informal network can be substituted, a person can try to *personalize* his or her claim, begging, cajoling or hectoring officials to provide what is wanted. The great majority of Russians do not expect to receive an unemployment benefit promptly after filing a claim. Hence, a common tactic is to pester officials until it is paid. This is not a retreat into a pre-modern informal network so much as it is a stressful attempt to compensate for major inefficiencies of bureaucratic organizations.

The behaviour of organizations in Soviet times encouraged *anti-modern* tactics, i.e. getting things done by bending or breaking rules (see Chapter 5). In Soviet times it was assumed that you had to know people in the Party or in a government office to get things done through a network of friends, friends of friends or even friends of friends. Connections remained important in transformation. For example, 24 per cent endorsed using connections to get a government-subsidized flat and 23 per cent reckoned a cash payment to a doctor was the best way to get medical treatment.

The assumption that everybody is doing it, whatever 'it' is, ignores the fact that access to networks is not universally available. To assess *social exclusion* the social-capital survey for each situation included as an alternative: Nothing can be done. Very few people felt that nothing could be done. Three-quarters to more than nine-tenths of Russians can draw on some form of social capital network to deal with the problems of everyday life. Only one-quarter have no idea of how to get a flat and as few as 5 per cent have no idea about how to get medical help. It would be misleading to label people as socially excluded on the basis of a single very general question, or to draw such inferences from indicators of low social status. Over all, less than 2 per cent of Russians felt they could do nothing in all or all but one of the dozen situations set out in Table 7.1. Reciprocally, only 7 per cent have networks that they can rely on in every situation or every situation but one.

Government failure is not a sign that nothing works but that formal organizations do not work as they do in a modern society. When a formal organization fails to operate routinely, most Russians have social-capital networks that they can turn to. The type of network is likely to vary with the situation. There is far more scope for informal networking in seeking a loan than in borrowing from a bank and more scope for bribery in seeking a flat than in obtaining food in a market economy. In most situations, only a minority relies on bureaucrats to deliver services to which it is entitled by going by the rules, but the majority does not.

## III  Redundancy in the face of uncertainty

Uncertainty is the bane of an anti-modern society. The presence of many public agencies in every town and most villages is evidence of what government can deliver – if only the right way can be found to achieve this. However, the experience of the intermittent failure of these organizations is a warning that they cannot be relied on to work all the time.

Instead of relying on a single network to get things done, people can rely on redundancy, that is, having several networks so that if one fails another can be tried until, by a process of trial and error, you get what you want. The pathologies of anti-modern organizations externalize onto individuals the costs of trying again and again until they get what they want. A person who can turn to a variety of networks multiplies his or her chances of getting what is wanted from an unpredictable organization. This method of getting things done may not be efficient, but in conditions of uncertainty it can be the most effective way to proceed in order to achieve satisfaction.

Job search is a classic example of redundancy in the use of networks; people can look for work by a multiplicity of means. Economic transformation makes most of those in employment worry about losing their job. Yet these anxieties are balanced by confidence in being able to find another job. In the depths of transformation almost two-thirds of Russians thought they could do so. Redundancy contributes to this confidence. Not only do four-fifths have some idea of what they would do to find a job but a majority can call on at least two different networks to search for work. Informal networks include asking friends (50 per cent) and family (11 per cent). Market networks include approaching employers directly (33 per cent); reading 'Help Wanted' advertisements (23 per cent); and moving to another city (3 per cent). Turning to a public employment bureau is mentioned by 19 per cent. Only 1 per cent suggest an anti-modern method, offering a payment to a personnel manager in return for a job.

Worry about thieves breaking into the house is another example of the usefulness of redundancy. Such worries are realistic, since at the time of the seventh NRB survey 30 per cent had had friends burgled in the past year and 7 per cent had had their own home burgled. When offered a list of six things that might be done to make a house safer, 83 per cent endorsed an informal social network, making sure someone is usually in the house. In addition, three-quarters endorsed the anti-modern alternative of keeping a fierce dog and half also favoured keeping a knife or gun handy. Complaining to the police was seen as useful by 43 per cent. A market response, moving somewhere safer to live, was a possibility open to 1 in 5. An overwhelming majority plays safe, endorsing more than one measure and only 2 per cent felt they could do nothing. The median Russian endorses four different methods of protecting their home against burglars.

Health care illustrates how satisficing works, since what is needed changes with the intensity of discomfort. In the year before the NRB survey, 42 per cent had no need to seek health care, since they had not felt ill. Of those who did feel ill at some point, a third did not think it necessary to visit a doctor, staying home and treating their aches and pains with a home remedy. If medical treatment was required, seven-eighths said they would rely on state services such as a clinic near their home or linked to their place of work. However, if the level of pain rises, very few accept the bureaucratic rule: Wait your turn. When asked what a person with a painful illness should do if a hospital says treatment will not be available for months, only 1 in 6 say nothing can be done. The most frequently cited tactic for queue-jumping is anti-modern; 44 per cent endorse using connections to get hospital treatment promptly and 23 per cent endorse offering money. The proportion ready to buy a 'free' service is greater than the fifth who would legally buy private treatment in the market. A begging appeal to officials can be tried at no expense; it was favoured by 22 per cent. These tactics are not mutually exclusive. A person in pain can proceed sequentially, first begging a hospital to speed up treatment, then turning to connections and, if that does not work, offering cash on the side to jump the hospital queue.

In a matter of weeks a household can combine anti-modern and modern market networks, buying some things in the market and buying public services by offering 'tips' to officials. The less money a household has, the more likely it is to turn to informal networks to produce what it needs. The use of connections to get things done need not require a cash expenditure. Access can often depend on idiosyncratic coincidences, for example, the occupations of relatives or friends or of schoolmates who have gone diverse ways.

The variety of ways in which people can get things done in a society in transformation means that lacking the resources to get what you want in a modern society is not that important. In an anti-modern society, vulnerability is greatest when a person's only network is their entitlement as a citizen to the services of public sector organizations that do not deliver them routinely. When government fails, the vulnerable are pushed into the ranks of the socially excluded. However, this is the exception among people who have learned under Communism how to cope with an anti-modern society.

A multiplicity of social-capital networks meant that instead of feeling helpless when government organizations fail and there is insufficient money to turn to the market, people confronted with the challenges of transformation could find ways of getting things done. When the seventh New Europe Barometer survey asked people how much control they had over their lives, the replies showed widespread confidence. In new EU member states, two-thirds felt they had a substantial measure of control over their lives, 15 per cent were unsure and only 2 per cent felt that they had absolutely no control over their lives. Among Russians, 46 per cent felt they had a substantial measure of control and only 5 per cent felt they had no control over what happened to them.

## IV  Comparing Russians across continents

Many argue that Russia is unique and this explains why social-capital networks there are different from what Putnam has postulated. However, in principle the basic propositions – social-capital networks are instrumentally productive and they differ from situation to situation within a country – are applicable across many countries. It is possible to test how generally applicable is the Russian evidence with survey data from Ukraine, the Czech Republic and the Republic of Korea, where Barometer surveys have asked comparable questions. Insofar as Russia is unique, responses in other countries should differ. Insofar as the pathologies of Soviet experience are distinctive, then Russians and Ukrainians should differ from Czechs as well as Koreans. Insofar as networks reflect the Communist experience, then Russians, Ukrainians and Czechs should be similar to yet differ from Koreans. Koreans can doubly claim to be different: not only do they have an Asian culture but also the political legacy of the old regime is that of an undemocratic but not totalitarian military dictatorship more akin to Latin America than to the Communist bloc.

People were asked in each of four countries the best way to get something from the government to which they were not entitled. Scenarios sketched situations where bureaucratic procedures were obstacles: refusal of admission to university to a youth with poor grades, eligibility rules for subsidized housing, a lengthy queue for admission to hospital or a delay in issuing a government permit. For each situation alternative networks were offered. Anti-modern alternatives were the use of connections, making up a story or offering a bribe. The pre-modern alternatives were to personalize demands by cajoling or hectoring officials. Turning to the market to buy a house or hire a tutor for a youth who needed better grades were other possibilities and passively accepting that nothing could be done was the final alternative. Overall, replies rejected theories postulating that everyone in a society behaves the same. In each country people were divided in their views of how to handle each situation, but they may not divide similarly.

The impact of Soviet life is shown by the consistency with which Russians and Ukrainians appear similar in their choice of social-capital networks. Four-fifths can think of a network to invoke in dealing with each situation; few are passive. The most frequently recommended tactic to get a flat, a government permit or prompt hospital

*Table 7.2* National differences in social capital

| | Anti-modern | Network Personal (% endorsing) | Market | Passive |
|---|---|---|---|---|
| *Getting into university without good enough grades* | | | | |
| Russia | 33 | 6 | 39 | 22 |
| Ukraine | 31 | 3 | 45 | 21 |
| Czech Republic | 7 | 2 | 72 | 18 |
| Korea | 3 | 2 | 37 | 57 |
| *Getting a better flat when not entitled to publicly subsidized housing* | | | | |
| Russia | 45 | n.a. | 30 | 25 |
| Ukraine | 34 | 10 | 28 | 27 |
| Czech Republic | 14 | 23 | 48 | 15 |
| Korea | 8 | 13 | 64 | 15 |
| *Action if an official delays issuing a government permit* | | | | |
| Russia | 62 | 18 | n.a. | 20 |
| Ukraine | 61 | 18 | n.a. | 21 |
| Czech Republic | 35 | 46 | n.a. | 19 |
| Korea | 21 | 45 | n.a. | 34 |
| *Getting treatment for a painful disease when hospital says one must wait for months* | | | | |
| Russia | 57 | 13 | 11 | 19 |
| Ukraine | 39 | 12 | 34 | 15 |
| Czech Republic | 24 | 31 | 31 | 14 |
| Korea | (Not applicable: no government health service) | | | |

Sources: Centre for the Study of Public Policy, New Europe Barometer, 1998; New Russia Barometer, 1998; Doh C. Shin and Richard Rose, *Koreans Evaluate Democracy: A New Korea Barometer Survey*, 1997, p. 26f. Due to rounding, here and elsewhere percentages may not add up to exactly 100.

Notes: Anti-modern: Offer bribe; use connections; make up a story. Personal: Beg, cajole or complain; hector officials to act. Market: Buy what you want legally. Passive: Nothing can be done.

treatment is anti-modern, such as paying a bribe or using connections; for university admission anti-modern tactics are second (Table 7.2). People socialized in the former Soviet regime rarely see pleading with bureaucrats as useful and only a limited minority see the market as offering an affordable solution to a problem.

The extent to which the Soviet legacy differs from that of Central and East Europeans is indicated by comparing Czechs with Russians and Ukrainians. Ex-Soviet citizens are four times more likely than Czechs to turn to anti-modern behaviour to get a youth into university and two to three times as likely to use corruption or connections to get a better flat. They are also almost twice as likely to break the law if having trouble getting a government permit and up to twice as likely to use anti-modern methods to get prompt hospital treatment. Furthermore, the distinctiveness of Czechs is not a consequence of passivity; Czechs tend to be less likely to think that nothing can be done. Differences arise because Czechs are more likely to rely on the market, a reflection of higher Czech incomes. They are also more likely to personalize and plead with bureaucrats, indicating a belief that the system will deliver what they are entitled to, even if bureaucrats need to be pushed to do so. It also suggests that Central and East European bureaucrats have been less committed to Communist norms and more likely to show sympathy to their fellow citizens in finding ways to get around an alien system.

Koreans are distinctive in the extent to which they passively accept that nothing can be done about the actions of government officials. While education is highly valued, Koreans tend to accept decisions of university admissions officials; 57 per cent think that nothing can be done to reverse a refusal of admission. Similarly, 34 per cent think that one must wait for a government permit to be issued and create a personal relationship rather than break the law in order to get government officials to act. Economic prosperity means that Koreans would prefer to buy a better flat rather than pay a bribe to get an upgrade in public housing. The absence of a universal health care system means Koreans are accustomed to getting hospital treatment by paying for health insurance rather than paying a bribe to a hospital admissions officer.

Comparison highlights the importance of the totalitarian legacy of the Soviet Union. In their social-capital networks, Koreans and Czechs have more in common with each other than either do with former Soviet citizens. For example, in the readiness to use anti-modern networks to get a flat, there is a difference of 31 percentage points between Czechs and Russians as against a 6-point difference between Czechs and Koreans. In their readiness to use anti-modern networks to get a university place there is a 26-percentage-point difference between Czechs and Russians and no significant difference between Czechs and Koreans. Similarly, there is a 27-point difference between Czechs and Russians in relying on anti-modern tactics to get a government permit and less than half that difference with Koreans.

The significance of a totalitarian legacy is underscored by further comparison with the People's Republic of China, which has a totalitarian legacy from its Marxist-Leninist Cultural Revolution yet is historically the pre-eminent reference point for Asian values. A survey in Beijing (by T. J. Shi, 1997: 53, 121ff, 268, 316n23) just before the Tiananmen Square massacre provides a 'bottom-up' picture of how Chinese people were getting things done when confronted by a government with a post-totalitarian as well as Asian character. Nine-tenths of Chinese did not passively accept the decisions of bureaucrats. Instead, people formed networks to allocate goods and services to themselves rather than to others with whom they were in competition. The networks were not used to change laws; individuals used networks or *guanxi* to influence the implementation of central directives by 'anti-modern' tactics familiar to students of the Soviet system.

There is no 'silver bullet' formula that can reduce or sum up all forms of social capital to a single number. To suggest that the Soviet legacy is unique invites the complementary suggestion that the social-capital legacy of Tocqueville's America is exceptional. Insofar as this conclusion is accepted, then the Soviet legacy is more important since it has affected upwards of half a billion people across the European continent and, if China is included, more than a billion and a half people across two very large continents.

# 8 Juggling multiple economies

The key to continuing good economic performance is a flexible institutional matrix that will adjust in the context of evolving technological and demographic changes as well as shocks to the system.

(Douglass C. North, Nobel laureate in Economics)

Dealing with an economy in transformation was a culture shock for Western economists trained to think in terms of money as the measuring rod of individual wellbeing and official statistics as an accurate reflection of what was happening to individuals in society. It was less of a shock to those who had been socialized in a command economy in which connections could get things that money couldn't buy and wellbeing could be measured in terms of freedom from the intrusive demands of a party-state.

There was a consensus among economic policymakers about the goal of creating a modern market economy. Moreover, NEB surveys have found that a big majority of ordinary people wanted economic experts rather than politicians to take economic decisions. However, there is no consensus among experts about what those decisions should be. Moreover, the advice of experts was often based on abstract models, in which theoretical clarity encouraged exogenizing (that is, leaving out) inconvenient facts that were intrusive, messy and insistent in societies in transformation.

While experts debated, ordinary households had to survive from day to day. Amidst the more or less creative destruction of the old system, there was no need for lectures on welfare economics. Nor was there need for training in entrepreneurship, for in Communist systems there was a veritable 'rainbow' of economies in which individuals could explore how to pursue their wellbeing. In the command economy, the aim was not so much to maximize income but to get by through juggling resources from multiple economies. A major aim of the New Europe Barometer when launched was to find out whether and how people were coping with the economic consequences of transformation.

## I Top-down and bottom-up economies

*Oikonomia*, the Greek root of the word 'economy', refers to the production of goods and services in the household rather than in large factories and office blocks. In premodern economies household production was a normal form of economic activity. That has been forgotten in modern market economies in which money is the medium for valuing goods and services, and what is not priced is neglected. This is especially true of top-down models of the economy that reduce production to a single aggregate figure of Gross National Product.

*Multiple dimensions of economic activity.* In transformation systems three economies – official, unofficial and household – existed side by side. All three types must be taken into account to understand why the view of the economy from the top differs from the view at the bottom (Rose, 1993a, 2000).

In *household* economic activity no money changes hands. For example, when a member of a household prepares a meal their unpaid labour is not counted in the official economy, while the food bought at the shop is. Similarly, do-it-yourself household repairs are not counted officially, while hiring a plumber is. In a transformation economy, a family can eat rather than sell the potatoes it grows and a plumber can do a repair for a relative without receiving any payment.

*Unofficial* economic activities involve money changing hands, for example, in street markets or among petty entrepreneurs who keep their accounts in their heads and their money in their pockets. When this happens there is no official record of money changing hands. In the party-state, receiving 'off-the-books' cash payments to a foreign bank account was confined to the privileged few. With transformation, any business firm with the contacts and the revenue could open a bank account in a foreign country such as North Cyprus or Switzerland and arrange for payments to be made there in order to secure big profits tax-free.

The *official* economy consists of all activities for which there are public records that government can use for managing the economy and for taxation. In a modern market economy, private as well as public employers are bureaucratic organizations that monitor and record economic activity. Private enterprises must keep full records of employees, purchases and sales in order to know whether they are making or losing money. The cash flow of firms is so large that bank accounts are needed for internal accounting purposes and to obtain finance. Income tax and social security contributions must be deducted from wages and paid periodically to government. The use of Value Added Tax (VAT) throughout Europe gives tax authorities the means to audit a business's purchases and sales. Up to a point, private sector firms may reduce their tax liabilities through ingenious and complex arrangements, but they must still meet their obligation to act as record-keepers for the official economy. Wage earners do not need to keep track of their earnings; employers routinely provide computerized pay slips to their employees and to the tax authorities and pensioners receive their primary income from a government agency. Since opportunities for cash-in-hand work in the shadow economy tend to be limited, official tax records provide a fair account of household resources.

The relevance of different types of economic activity varies with the context. The standard national accounts that constitute the official record of the economy assume that the great bulk of economic activity involves money changing hands. Such conditions have only recently been met. For most of history, a large part of economic activity was not monetized and economic historians confront many problems in creating a full account of economic activity in a pre-modern society. In other words, official records are not sufficient evidence of economic activity. Moreover, in an economy in transformation this is not the case. Households monitored their circumstances by putting their hands in their pockets or purse to see how much money they had from unofficial as well as official sources. Consumption was monitored by looking at what was on the dinner table.

*What you see depends on where you look*. When command economies imploded, this stimulated radical re-adjustments in economic activity. Individuals had an incentive to turn to household production as wages lost value with inflation. The rewards of unofficial cash-in-hand work grew enormously, but the demand was limited since not many people had cash to spend. Firms forced to shift from accounts involving plan targets to profit-and-loss statements could switch from falsifying records showing the achievement of plan targets to falsifying records to show that they were solvent. When this was not the case enterprise managers could appeal to politicians for subsidies.

Policies for the management of transformation were widely debated, ranging from the 'big bang' theory that unpopular major decisions should be taken early on, while the Communist legacy could still be blamed, to the 'soft landing' theory that change should be gradually introduced as and when feasible. However, competing proposals often shared two mistaken assumptions. First, the idea of managing change repeated the Communist error of assuming that fundamental changes occurring during transformation could be controlled by national governments or by intergovernmental agencies such as the International Monetary Fund in Washington, DC. The process was not manageable, in the sense of having a steering wheel that policymakers could get their hands on and thereby steer the economy. Second, it was assumed that whatever the uncertainties about the past and the future, there was satisfactory evidence of the current economic situation.

Policymakers depend on highly aggregated data about the national economy to guide decisions about economic growth, inflation, unemployment and collecting enough tax revenue to meet public-expenditure commitments. The statistics used, such as the Gross National Product or the rate of inflation, are not tangible facts that can be touched or photographed; they are intellectual abstractions constructed by the sophisticated aggregation of many official statistics. The rationale for each statistic is documented in footnotes, but rationales may alter as economic conditions change or for political reasons, for example, a desire to lower unemployment by reducing the number of people counted as unemployed. In a modern market economy such high-level abstractions as the rate of national inflation may be used to infer what is happening at the enterprise and household level. However, in a system in transformation such measures can only be used with confidence *after* a command economy has become a modern market economy.

At the highest level, policymakers often saw what they wanted to see, and treated the removal of a Communist regime as sufficient to justify confidence in new leaders. This was particularly the case in the treatment of Boris Yeltsin in his first presidential term. For example, the executive director of the International Monetary Fund, Michel Camdessus (1994), returned from a trip to Moscow expressing a very positive view of the Russian economy. As evidence, Camdessus cited personal assurances from Prime Minister Viktor Chernomyrdin; talks with senior ministers and selected members of the Duma; and meetings in which he was 'especially impressed with religious leaders', who assured him that 'Russia's traditional spiritual values would enable the Russian people not only to cope with the difficulties of the transition process but also to make it more human'. When questioned about allegations that the Russian government was cooking its books, Camdessus contemptuously dismissed this suggestion as 'something that for a Frenchman is rather indigestible, the idea of a bizarre cuisine with numbers'.

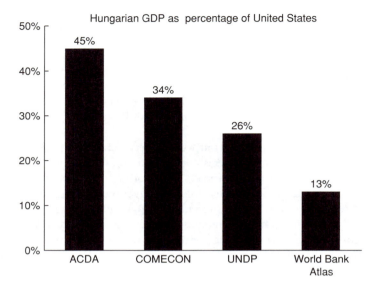

*Figure 8.1* Alternative measures of GDP, Hungary 1990.
Source: Paul Marer *et al.*, *Historically Planned Economies*, 1992, Table 1, p. 45. ACDA refers to United States Arms Control and Disarmament Agency; COMECON is the Communist bloc conducting trade in roubles.

Four years later the IMF invested US$6 billion dollars in a forlorn attempt to prevent rouble devaluation – to the benefit of Russian speculators if not the Russian economy (Lopez-Claros and Zadornov, 2002).

Confronted with circumstances far beyond their experience, Western economists responded by doing what their professional culture had trained them to do: producing economic statistics based on official records. The first challenge was to determine the state of the national economy in 1990, when transformation began in Central and Eastern Europe. The problem was not the absence of data but the diversity of statistics produced by national and international institutions on the basis of different assumptions and methods leading to very different results. Figure 8.1 uses data from Hungary, which has had the most sophisticated group of economists in the region, to illustrate this point.

Whatever the method of calculation, Hungarian GDP per capita appears as much less than that of the United States. However, there is a magnitude of difference between the most and the least favourable calculation. The highest is that of the American government's Arms Control and Disarmament Agency, which estimated the Hungarian standard of living at 45 per cent that of the United States. By contrast, the World Bank rated it at only 13 per cent of the American standard. The estimate of the United Nations Development programme is more than twice as favourable as that of the World Bank, but barely half that of the Arms Control Agency. Moreover, the US government agency rates the Hungarian economy as one-third larger than did the official Communist trade bloc agency, COMECON.

Official intergovernmental statistics reported that people had little money to live on. For example, at the start of transformation Russian GDP was estimated as being worth only $1,660 in US dollars, the equivalent of little more than $30 a week. Yet observation on the ground indicated that such numbers were 'too bad to be true'. People did not spend dollars but roubles, forints, zlotys or whatever their national currency was. The lack of realism in official exchange rates led intergovernmental authorities to produce an alternative calculation of Gross National Income, adjusted for purchasing power parity. This multiplied Russian income by almost five times to $8,010.

It was important for Western policymakers to have measures of the economy at the start of transformation in order to monitor progress henceforth. Intergovernmental agencies responded to this demand by arriving at a consensus about statistics of the Gross Domestic Product of more than two dozen post-Communist countries. These figures were calculated on the basis of available data, and the methods documented in copious footnotes and appendices. However, the numbers produced were not facts but counter-factual statements about the market value of economic activity in countries that had not yet institutionalized a market economy.

Since the state-owned economy initially accounted for nearly all of officially reported national income, success in reducing the state's control of the economy meant a massive contraction of officially recorded Gross Domestic Product. Policies to downsize the economy inherited from the old regime quickly produced results. Everywhere, the official economy contracted (Figure 8.2). The chief difference was the scale of the contraction. It shrank by as much as 43 per cent in the Russian Federation and 49 per cent in Latvia, while the reported contraction was only 7 per cent in Poland and 12 per cent in the Czech Republic. The duration of the contraction differed too. The bottom was not reached in Russia until 1998 and in Romania until 1999. By contrast, national economies were ready to turn around by the start of 1992 in Poland, and a year or two later in Slovenia and the Czech Republic.

The problems of official statistics were not only over the heads of ordinary people but also beyond their concern, since they omitted household and unofficial economic activities. Bottom-up indicators – for example, how much time people had to spend

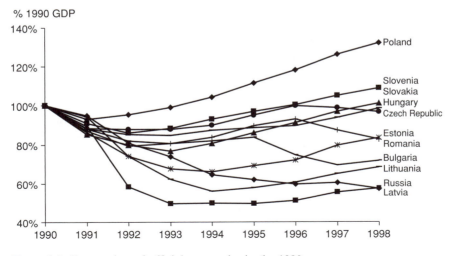

*Figure 8.2* Contraction of official economies in the 1990s.
Source: EBRD, *Transition Report 2001*, Table A.3.1, p. 59.

queuing in shops – produced more relevant empirical evidence. In the autumn 1991 NEB survey, the average Central or East European household devoted at least one hour a day to queuing. A year later, the second NEB survey found that those spending at least an hour a day queuing had fallen to 23 per cent of Central and East Europe. By the third NEB survey the transition to a market economy was nearly complete: the proportion spending an hour a day queuing was only 8 per cent. Shortages were worse in Russia: in January 1992 the median Russian household spent about two hours a day queuing. While an end to queuing showed that most people were living in a market economy, this was not an end to the problems of households. A shortage of goods was replaced by a shortage of money to buy the goods that shops now had on their shelves.

In the first years of transformation, the immediate threat to workers was not unemployment, which official statistics monitored, but going without a wage, which official statistics did not. Yet the stresses of transformation meant that employers were often unable to pay wages on time and, instead of making employees redundant, did not pay them. And because workers saw no immediate prospect of finding another job, employees often preferred to be non-waged workers or take unpaid time off to work in household or unofficial economies, rather than sever connections with their job in the formal economy.

In spring 1995, when NRB tracking of this phenomenon began, 52 per cent of Russian workers had been paid late or not at all in the previous year. In effect, employers were extracting forced loans from their labour force and, when monthly inflation was substantial, reducing their costs by paying back wages with devalued currency. The state was most likely to be delinquent in paying its employees. Hospitals and schools compensated for shortfalls in tax revenue by not paying teachers, nurses and doctors regularly. Similarly, state-owned factories delayed paying workers and the same was true in state enterprises. The new private sector, consisting of firms that did not exist before 1992, was most likely to pay employees regularly. As late as 2000 an absolute majority of Russians in employment were sometimes not being paid as they should be and only in 2003 were as many as three-quarters of employees being paid as they should. In every economy in transformation people were challenged to find ways of coping with their basic needs when they were working without being paid.

There was anxiety among Western policymakers about the political consequences of transformation. There were fears that if a social safety net was not introduced and financed by big grants from the World Bank, the European Union and other sources, then people under stress from the contraction of their official economy would revert to a Communist regime or to a populist dictator. Such fears ignored evidence of the poor performance of command economies (Chapter 3). More immediately, the fears assumed that ordinary people lived in a one-dimensional world in which the only economy that mattered was the official economy.

## II Two economies make a difference

The household is the basic unit of the micro-economy, for it enables individuals to ensure against risk by pooling resources. If one person is not paid a monthly wage due, the spouse may be paid. High levels of female employment in command economies have made two-income households the norm. Chronic housing shortages have made the doubling or trebling of generations common, thus adding a third income from a pensioner, a working youth or both. Within a household, individual members can give priority to different economies, for example, a grandmother can draw a cash pension; a husband can be a factory worker paid in money and goods in kind; and a housewife can produce goods at home and sell some in unofficial street markets. A single individual can also be involved in multiple economies, working in a government office in the morning and as a taxi driver in the evening.

In an economy in transformation, the first object is not to get rich but to survive. People face existential problems: how to get enough food each day, how to heat their house and how to keep clothes in good condition. In order to maintain total welfare in the family, the rational strategy is to combine goods and services from three economies. Total Welfare in the Family (TWF) equals:

$$TWF = OE + UE + HE$$

*OE* represents the official monetized economy, *UE* represents the monetized but uncivil economy and *HE* represents the household economy in which goods and services are produced and consumed without any money changing hands (Rose, 1986).

In an economy in transformation, the most risky strategy to maintain welfare is to rely solely on individual earnings in the official economy. When the New Europe Barometer asked people at the start of transformation – Do you earn enough from your regular job to buy the things you really need? – everywhere two-thirds or more said they did not. In 1992 the proportion able to earn enough from their regular job was as low as 11 per cent in Hungary, 22 per cent in Belarus and in 1993 less than 20 per cent in Latvia, Lithuania and Ukraine.

*Participation in nine economies.* In times of transformation, a multiplicity of economies provided a social safety net. To lose your job in the official economy did not mean that you became economically inactive. Instead, it was a stimulus to find activities outside the official economy and many different possibilities were at hand (Table 8.1).

*Table 8.1* Participation in nine economies

|  | *(Households)* |
| --- | --- |
| *OFFICIAL economies: legal monetized* | (97%) |
| Member of household has regular job | 72 |
| Receives pension, welfare benefits | 39 |
| *SOCIAL economies: non-monetized a-legal* | (90%) |
| Household production food, housing | 68 |
| Exchange help friends, neighbours | 64 |
| Queuing more than an hour a day | 23 |
| Gets, gives favours free | 15 |
| *UNCIVIL economies: monetized, illegal* | (34%) |
| Pays, receives bribe | 21 |
| Job in second, shadow economy | 19 |
| Uses foreign currency | 2 |

Source: Centre for the Study of Public Policy, New Europe Barometer, 1992: Mean: Bulgaria, Czech Republic, Hungary, Poland, Romania, Slovakia. Uses foreign currency: data from 1993.

Nearly every household is involved in the official economy with members as wage earners or recipients of a pension. In Czechoslovakia 65 per cent reported that at least two members of the household were employed in the official economy and in Bulgaria, 50 per cent. Since retirement age in Eastern Europe is below the norm in OECD countries and pensions are low, significant numbers of pensioners have also remained active in the official economy. In Czechoslovakia one-quarter of persons old enough to draw a pension but below age 70 continued working in the official economy.

When a regular job fails to provide enough, the commonest response is to retreat into a pre-modern economy without money. Far more people were active in household social economies involving production and exchange without money than in paid employment. While such activities are often undertaken in Western households, they are usually hobbies rather than imposed by economic necessity. Exchanging help with friends and relatives is equally important. Whereas in a modern society a car ride may be given for convenience to a friend who also has a car, in economies in transformation there can be an exchange of help between a household with a car and another with a plot for growing food. Shopping in a market economy can be done at leisure or quickly, because shops are full of goods. However, in a command economy, 'To queue is to work, and to do extra work. Standing and waiting takes time and is more unpleasant than most money-earning work or normal housework' (Wiles, 1983). In 1992 many households had non-waged workers in the retail distribution industry, because they daily spent an hour or more queuing.

Uncivil economies in which people were paid cash in hand continued during transformation. More than one-fifth received or paid bribes to get access to nominally free health and education services. Almost one-fifth were working occasionally in service-sector jobs and paid 'off the books' to avoid income and social-security taxes. Bribery was widespread as long as bureaucratic controls meant that many jobs gave people a marketable asset through employment in providing social benefits. By contrast, having household repairs undertaken by cash-in-hand labour could be achieved more cheaply by do-it-yourself work. One in eight households reported that in the midst of inflation they sometimes used foreign currencies. Those who did not were not showing a vote of confidence in the lev or the zloty but reflecting their lack of access to foreign money as they were not taxi drivers in capital cities or workers on trains going between Warsaw and Berlin.

*Assembling portfolios of resources.* Normally, households were involved in many economies. The median household was involved in five economies in the Czech Republic and in four economies in Bulgaria and Russia. Moreover, it was common to be active in all three types of economies – official, household and uncivil. This was the case in two-thirds of households in what was then Czechoslovakia, in just over half of households in Russia and 3 in 7 in Bulgaria. Households involved in only a single economy were deviant: in 1991 and early 1992 only 2 per cent in Czechoslovakia and 3 per cent in Russia were involved in just a single economy.

However, people do not invest their efforts equally in every type of economy. For those in employment, a job in the official economy usually claims the most hours in the week. A job in the cash-only second economy is invariably a part-time job; the average time spent working in a shadow job was nine or ten hours a week. The reported time spent helping friends and relatives was more limited. Since pensioners are not committed to going to a job every day, they have more time to engage in social economies, for example, queuing in shops, cultivating a vegetable plot or looking after grandchildren.

While the need to cope was universal, the way in which households responded differed more within countries than between them. The critical goal was to assemble a *portfolio* of resources in order to survive. The portfolios can be characterized by activities that NEB respondents identify as most and second most important in meeting their needs.

The commonest strategy, adopted by 55 per cent of households, was to rely on a pre-modern *defensive* portfolio. Instead of relying solely on their job or pension, to defend themselves against destitution people relied as well on social economies in which no money changed hands. The household economy can substitute domestically produced services for things that would be bought in the market in a modern market economy and spend its available cash on goods that cannot be produced at home, such as electricity or petrol. A defensive portfolio is pre-modern, because informal social ties are important as well as the cash nexus.

Going on the offensive by becoming *enterprising* was the strategy of one-fifth of households. Given the shortage of cash in post-centrally planned economies, earning money in uncivil economies was usually second in importance to an income in the official economy. From the perspective of an individual seeking to maximize material well-being, earning money from bribes, or dealing in foreign currencies is rational. But from a macro-economic perspective, it is not laying the foundation for a modern market economy. Scoffing at the law is an anti-modern activity.

The *vulnerable* depend for their wellbeing solely upon the official economy. They are vulnerable because the official economy was most influenced by the shift from the command to the market economy. The vulnerable were not necessarily poor; they could be civil servants in a ministry that was no longer needed, academics who had won favour by following the party line or skilled workers in factories making products for which there was no demand in the market. At the height of transformation less than one-sixth of households were vulnerable.

Paradoxically, *marginal* households were least at risk from transformation, because they had no direct stake in the official economy. They lived from day to day outside the official accounts of net material or Gross National Product. Their most important economy was social – looking after household needs or relying on help from friends and relatives.

## III  Coping without destitution

In a transformation economy every family faces a hard budget constraint: it cannot consume more than its portfolio of economies can provide. To avoid destitution households rely on a multiplicity of economies, thus avoiding the fate predicted in the blunt Bulgarian proverb, 'If you have to live from one job, you will starve to death.'

*Coping.* The New Europe Barometer measures the capacity of households to cope by asking: *In the past year has your household saved money, just made ends meet, spent savings, borrowed money from friends or relatives, or done both?* If a family does not borrow money or spend savings, then it can get by indefinitely, whether its standard of living is high or low. In 1992 a total of 67 per cent of Central and East Europeans were coping, that is, getting through the year without borrowing or spending savings. The proportion able to do so ranged from a high of 80 per cent in Slovenia to a low of 47 per cent in Bulgaria.

A critical difference between a modern and a transformation economy is that in the former most people can get by with what they earn in their normal job or receive as a pension. However, this was not the case in economies in transformation. Whereas in Austria 70 per cent reported they earned enough from their regular job to get by, less than half could do so in transformation societies. For most households, a portfolio of economies made all the difference between being able to cope without borrowing money or drawing on savings. Whereas in Austria a portfolio of unofficial and household resources increased the number of households able to cope by only 12 percentage points, in societies in transformation involvement in a multiplicity of economies trebled the proportion that coped.

Coping is not the same as living comfortably. People could cope by giving up what had previously been taken for granted, for example, a seaside holiday or going out for a meal every weekend. Throughout the 1990s many households in Central and Eastern Europe felt dissatisfied with their standard of living. In 1992 only 32 per cent were coping and satisfied. The largest category of households (35 per cent) were coping with their portfolio of resources but dissatisfied with their standard of living and 27 per cent were dissatisfied and not getting by. Doing without is not the same as destitution. A household without a car is not lacking in basic necessities nor would it be a sign of relative deprivation in post-Communist societies in which up to two-thirds of households did not own a car.

Destitution occurs when a household must often do without the necessities of daily life, such as food, heat and clothing. It is thus a matter of the frequency of deprivation; there is an enormous difference between going without meat or heating once in a while and going without often. Given a multiplicity of economies, destitution cannot be inferred from whether a person is employed or unemployed, since the wages of an employee may be devalued by inflation if paid late or they may not be paid at all. To measure the extent to which households were doing without necessities during transformation, the New Europe Barometer asked how often people had gone without food, heating and electricity, and clothes in the past year.

In the 1993 NEB survey, 68 per cent of Central and Eastern European households never had to go without food; 72 per cent never had to do without heating or electricity, and 50 per cent never went without clothes that they really needed. At the other extreme, 5 per cent said they often went without heating or electricity, 7 per cent often did without food and 12 per cent were often unable to buy the clothes that they really needed.

Since destitution arises when people often go short of food, heating and clothing, an index can be created by assigning a score for the frequency of doing without each necessity – 3 for often doing without; 2, sometimes; 1, rarely, and 0, never doing without a necessity. Combining the scores for food, heating and clothing gives an overall index of destitution ranging from 0 for never doing without necessities to a high of 9 for often lacking all three necessities. In Figure 8.3 those with an index score of 7 to 9 are described as often doing without necessities; 4 to 6 as sometimes doing without; 1 to 3 as rarely doing without and 0 as never doing without.

Notwithstanding the macro-economic difficulties of transformation, the great majority of households economized without destitution. Even when the official economy was contracting a great deal, more than two-fifths of Central and East Europeans never had to do without necessities. The median group, more than one-third of the total, only rarely did without necessities. Those who sometimes went without necessities constitute one-sixth of the population. Only 6 per cent often went without the necessary food, heating or clothing.

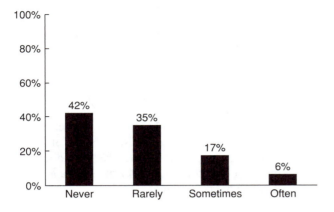

*Figure 8.3* Frequency of doing without food, clothing, heating or electricity.
Source: Centre for the Study of Public Policy, New Europe Barometer, 1993: Czech Republic, Hungary, Poland, Romania, Slovakia, Slovenia.

*Adaptation and resilience.* The upheavals of transformation meant that people could not live as before: in order to cope they were forced to adapt. But for some people this is easier said than done. The ability of people to get by without borrowing or spending savings and to avoid doing without necessities indicates the extent to which they have adapted. It also differentiates those who have problems in adapting but bounce back from these difficulties, and those threatened with long-term destitution (Rose, 1995b).

*Adaptable* people do not wait for national governments and foreign advisers to decide what to do about the official economy. Even if (or especially if) dissatisfied with their economic circumstances, people can make use of social or uncivil economic resources to supplement what they can get from the official economy. The proof of adaptation is that a household can get through the year without borrowing or spending savings and never or rarely doing without basic necessities. In 1993, when the NEB survey began collecting this data, 36 per cent of Central and East Europeans had completely adapted; they could get by without borrowing money or spending savings and never had to do without necessities. An additional 24 per cent had almost done so, living within their means and only rarely doing without necessities.

When the impact of transformation cannot be avoided, people need to be *resilient*, that is, able to get out of difficulties as well as getting into them. One strategy for bouncing back is belt-tightening, for example, only eating meat on Sundays and filling up on the cheapest foods during the week. Another strategy is stretching an existing stock of goods, such as household furnishings, to make them last longer. A third is mending and making do, patching clothes that become worn. Doing without, borrowing or spending savings is thus confined to temporary emergencies. Resilience in the face of difficulties is evidence that a household is adapting to the challenges of transformation, albeit not always successfully. One way or another, 34 per cent of households were resilient. In the early 1990s 10 per cent showed resilence by sometimes but not often doing without necessities and 24 per cent borrowed or spent savings in order to avoid destitution.

The evidence of *destitution* is not low income, for in societies in transformation the meaning of money is problematic. While the value of money is unclear, going without food, heating and clothing is evidence of deprivation and doing so often throughout the year shows that a household is unable to bounce back from difficulties but is threatened with being destitute. Of Central and East European households 6 per cent showed evidence of destitution in 1993, often having to do without basic necessities.

Thinking in terms of juggling a multiplicity of economies can reconcile official statistics implying that a quarter or a third of households were living in poverty during transformation with the absence of the malnutrition and starvation that characterized the region in the Second World War. The very negative statistics of the official economy were not the only resource of households. Having experienced the failures of the official economy in Communist times, people had a portfolio of unofficial resources that they turned to in order to get what they needed and often more than they needed (see Chapter 9).

Because transformation is only one stage in the dynamic process of moving from a command to a market economy, the question is not whether households are forced to do without some necessities at some point in time but whether people adapt or become permanently destitute. In the unprecedented circumstances of the early 1990s there could be no certainty of what the future would bring. But there were hopes that economies could adapt so that households could stop juggling resources in order to get by and begin to enjoy the benefits of a modern market economy.

# 9 Stresses and opportunities
## The impact on health

One of the most significant health problems in the late twentieth century: Why was life expectancy declining in the former socialist countries?
(William Cockerham, *Health and Social Change in Russia and Eastern Europe*)

The transformation of Communist into post-Communist societies has imposed stresses and created opportunities. Which of these can be seen to have the greater impact can be greatly influenced by *when* one looks. The immediate impact of the collapse of Communist regimes was often said to bring 'more shock than therapy' (Gerber and Hout, 1998). The consequences of shock were most dramatically illustrated by the decline of life expectancy in Russia and other post-Soviet states in the 1990s, as Cockerham (1999) and others have highlighted. However, the subsequent economic growth of post-transformation economies at rates double or treble that of established market economies has offered new opportunities for a healthier and longer life.

The impact of stresses and opportunities depends too on *where* one looks. Whereas Russian health statistics have been bad for many decades, in all seven EU member states that were never integrated in the Soviet Union male life expectancy has improved since the fall of the Berlin Wall. The tendency to focus on Russia rather than Central and Eastern European societies should not lead to the mistaken projection of Russian conditions onto countries no longer subject to its domination. In his annual address to the Russian Federal Assembly on 25 April 2005, Vladimir Putin defined the Russian attitude toward transformation in the following terms: 'The collapse of the Soviet Union was the greatest geopolitical catastrophe of the century'. However, in Central and Eastern European countries the same events are celebrated as regaining independence from Moscow.

Assessments of transformation also depend on whether societies are examined *in aggregate terms or by examining individuals* (Rose and Bobak, 2007). Changes in *national* health statistics rely on averages for a country's population. However, aggregate statistics cannot show how opportunities and stresses have been distributed between individuals within a society and how these consequences differ. Some people have benefited, others have paid heavy costs and in the course of two decades many people have experienced both stresses and benefits. Therefore, this chapter asks: How has the combination of stresses and opportunities resulted in some individuals being healthier than others?

## I Health in post-Communist countries

The anti-modern character of Communist societies subjected individuals to many stresses. There were stresses from restrictions on personal freedom and from pressures to conform in public to values that were rejected in private. While jobs were secure, the binge method of production led to periods of storming to meet plan targets followed by periods of slack and sloth. These stresses encouraged smoking, binge drinking and other forms of unhealthy behaviour.

Between the end of the Second World War and the fall of the Berlin Wall, health was improving in Communist-bloc countries but the rate of progress was so slow that the result was a widening gap with health in West European societies (cf. Chapter 3). Moreover, a fact often lost sight of, in the Soviet Union health was declining in absolute as well as relative terms. During Leonid Brezhnev's time in power the officially reported life expectancy of Russian men actually *fell* by 2.8 years and did not regain its 1965 level until 1989. Moreover, although Baltic peoples saw themselves as Europeans, their incorporation as Soviet republics resulted in worse levels of health there than elsewhere in Central and Eastern Europe.

Since the fall of the Berlin Wall, in Central and Eastern Europe health has been improving. Three countries – Slovenia, the Czech Republic and Slovakia – have been experiencing a steady rise in life expectancy since then. In four more countries the shock of transformation caused a limited short-term fall in the early 1990s but this was followed by a recovery; thus life expectancy was significantly higher in 2005 than it was in 1990. In the Baltic states, which had been part of the Soviet Union for more than four decades, life expectancy was as low or lower than in nearby Soviet republics. Moreover, life expectancy fell further than in their neighbours to the west. From this trough life expectancy has risen so that today it is higher than at the start of transformation in Estonia and Latvia, and has recovered from shock in Lithuania too. Over a decade and a half, the troughs in life expectancy created by the short-term stresses of transformation have been less than the peaks achieved through the longer-term consequences of the opportunities of living in a post-transformation Central or East European society.

However, in Soviet successor states the pattern has been in the opposite direction. Not only did life expectancy fall in the 1990s but it has failed to improve in this decade (Table 9.1). The effect has been worst in Russia, where life expectancy, already low at the end of the Soviet system, has fallen by 4.9 years between 1990 and 2005. Most of this decline is accounted for by official statistics recording an extraordinary fall in officially reported life expectancy of 3.1 years between 1992 and 1993. As in the Brezhnev years, there has been fluctuation; life expectancy was at its lowest in 1994, then 'peaked' in 1998. The subsequent boom in the economy and the greater predictability that President Putin has introduced into Russian society has not been matched by improved health: in 2005 male life expectancy was back to the same level as it was in 1993. A similarly fluctuating pattern is evident in Belarus and Ukraine. The result has been a growing divergence in health across the region. In 1990 there was a gap of 1.1 years in life expectancy between the average for Russia, Ukraine and Belarus and what were to become the new EU member states. By 2005 the gap in life expectancy had widened to 7.7 years.

*Individual health varies within as well as between countries.* Unfavourable national statistics encourage the description of Russia as an unhealthy society. However, just

*Table 9.1* Troughs and peaks in national life expectancy

| | 1990 | Male life expectancy in years | | 2005 |
| | | Fall (year) | Peak (year) | |
| --- | --- | --- | --- | --- |
| *New EU countries* | | | | |
| Slovenia | 69.4 | No fall | +3.8 (2003) | 73.2 |
| Czech Republic | 68.1 | No fall | +4.0 (2001) | 72.0 |
| Poland | 66.5 | −0.4 (1991) | +4.3 (2005) | 70.8 |
| Slovakia | 66.6 | No fall | +3.5 (2005) | 70.1 |
| Bulgaria | 68.1 | −1.0 (1995) | +0.9 (2005) | 69.0 |
| Hungary | 65.1 | −0.6 (1993) | +3.5 (2004) | 68.6 |
| Romania | 66.6 | −1.4 (1997) | +2.2 (2005) | 68.2 |
| Estonia | 64.6 | −3.5 (1995) | +2.7 (2005) | 67.3 |
| Latvia | 64.2 | −3.5 (1994) | +2.9 (2004) | 67.1 |
| Lithuania | 66.4 | −3.8 (1994) | +0.4 (2000) | 66.4 |
| *Post-Soviet countries* | | | | |
| Belarus | 66.3 | −4.1 (1999) | −2.9 (2000) | 62.9 |
| Ukraine | 66.0 | −5.0 (1996) | −3.0 (1998) | 62.2 |
| Russia | 63.8 | −6.2 (1994) | −2.5 (1998) | 58.9 |

Source: UNICEF, *Innocenti Social Monitor* (2007), Table 4.3.

Note: Latest figures for Latvia and Lithuania are from 2004.

as some people have above-average incomes in a poor society, so even in a society where average health is sub-standard, many people still have good health. Because the New Europe Barometer interviews people in many countries, it can be used to analyze differences in health between people living in the same country as well as differences in national means for health. Focusing on the health of individuals avoids drawing inferences about health from mortality statistics, which can be heavily influenced by pathological groups who can be unrepresentative or even deviant within their society, such as alcoholics or drug addicts.

In every post-transformation society there are substantial differences between individuals in their self-assessed health. Over all, 42 per cent say their health is good or excellent; 40 per cent describe it as average; and 18 per cent report bad or very bad health (Table 9.2). Those in good health outnumber those with bad health by a margin of more than two to one. If generalizations are to be made about national differences, then this evidence shows that the population of post-Soviet countries has a lower proportion of people with above-average health than do new EU member states and their minority in poor health is larger.

Differences in health between countries are much less than differences within countries. When excellent health is scored as 5 and very bad health as 1, the median country has a health score of 3.3. There is a difference of only 0.6 of a point between the country with the highest mean level of health, Slovenia, and the countries with the lowest mean health scores, Ukraine and Belarus. Although the self-assessed health of Russians is not so positive, the difference between its mean health rating and what is typical of new EU member states is much less than the contrast between the 31 per cent of Russians with good or excellent health and the 22 per cent with poor or very poor health.

*Table 9.2* Individual health after transformation

*Q. Over the past 12 months, would you say your physical health has been: very good, good, average, poor, very poor?*

| | Very good % | Good % | Average % | Poor % | Very poor % | Mean |
|---|---|---|---|---|---|---|
| *New EU countries* | | | | | | |
| Slovenia | 17 | 39 | 34 | 8 | 2 | 3.6 |
| Slovakia | 16 | 36 | 34 | 11 | 3 | 3.5 |
| Romania | 14 | 42 | 27 | 14 | 3 | 3.5 |
| Czech Republic | 12 | 35 | 39 | 12 | 2 | 3.4 |
| Poland | 16 | 33 | 31 | 15 | 6 | 3.4 |
| Latvia | 6 | 40 | 41 | 12 | 2 | 3.4 |
| Bulgaria | 10 | 37 | 33 | 16 | 5 | 3.3 |
| Estonia | 6 | 33 | 46 | 13 | 2 | 3.3 |
| Hungary | 9 | 32 | 36 | 18 | 5 | 3.2 |
| Lithuania | 5 | 29 | 49 | 15 | 3 | 3.2 |
| *Post-Soviet countries* | | | | | | |
| Russia | 3 | 28 | 47 | 18 | 4 | 3.1 |
| Belarus | 3 | 24 | 48 | 22 | 4 | 3.0 |
| Ukraine | 2 | 24 | 50 | 20 | 4 | 3.0 |

(Range: health very good 5; very poor 1)

Source: Centre for the Study of Public Policy, New Europe Barometer, 2004; New Russia Barometer, 2005. Due to rounding, here and elsewhere percentages may not add up to exactly 100.

## II  Individual differences influencing health

An individual's health develops as the consequence of an accumulation of influences over the life course. When the Berlin Wall fell and the Soviet Union moved toward dissolution, the average adult in the Communist bloc was already in his or her early forties. Thus, many experiences having a continuing influence on health were fixed long before the shock of transformation, for example, conditions of childhood in the 1950s, education, and occupation, as well as the effects of growing up in a society where health care was inferior to Western Europe. Some stresses were literally incomparable, such as living in the Communist bloc during Stalinism.

The disruptions of transformation affected individuals materially (income fell); psychologically (there was great uncertainty about what would happen from one week to the next); socially (the status hierarchy based on Communist values and patronage was no more); and as citizens (political regimes disappeared and sometimes states as well). However, all individuals did not respond identically; the stresses were experienced more sharply by some citizens than others. Thus, the first hypothesis about the consequences of transformation is: *The more an individual has felt the stresses of transformation, the worse their health.*

However, because it created opportunities transformation was also a crisis in the positive sense. Opportunities have been material, working for private sector enterprises that can offer higher wages than state enterprises of the command economy. They have also been social psychological, such as gains in freedom from the state. The shortage economy has been replaced by shops offering an abundance of consumer goods to those with the money to buy them. By the time of the 2004 NEB survey, the majority of citizens were enjoying a higher material living standard than before. In 90 per cent of households there was a colour television set; in 48 per cent a video cassette recorder or other electronic home entertainment device; and in 47 per cent a car. Thus, the second hypothesis is: *The more an individual has experienced opportunities of transformation, the better their health.*

Major stresses and opportunities augment rather than replace the effect on health of individual attributes. An individual's age inevitably influences health and other social resources, such as education and social class, can be important in themselves and by influencing how individuals react to stresses and opportunities. Hence, the third hypothesis is: *The more social resources an individual has, the better their health.*

Given so many potential influences, the first step is to identify the extent to which individual stresses, opportunities and resources influence health. Table 9.3 reports the combined effect of many different measures of stress, opportunity and social resources. Altogether, these varied influences account for 33.4 per cent of the variance in health. But they are not of equal importance – and the combination of positive and minus signs emphasizes that significant influences push in opposite directions.

The most important influence on self-assessed health is independent of transformation: it is age. In stable societies, the progress of a person from youth to middle age and then old age leads to a gradual decline in health and the same is true in post-transformation societies. The only difference is a tendency for post-Soviet citizens to feel older at a relatively younger age. Among respondents age 35 to 44 in the 1998 NRB survey, more than half felt too old to learn something different than their Soviet-era occupation. Age is linked to gender differences. Because women tend to live longer than men, average health of women tends to be less good than that of men.

*Table 9.3* Individual influences on health

| | | | |
|---|---|---|---|
| *Dependent variable: self-rated health* | | | |
| *Variance explained by OLS regression: $R^2$ 33.4%* | | | |
| | *b* | *SE* | *Beta* |
| *Stresses and opportunities* | | | |
| Can control life | .06 | .00 | .14*** |
| Don't earn enough to get by | −.08 | .01 | −.07*** |
| Number of consumer goods | .05 | .01 | .05*** |
| Public officials corrupt | −.06 | .01 | −.04*** |
| Income quartile | .04 | .01 | .04*** |
| Income better in past | −.03 | .01 | −.04*** |
| Victim of crime | −.09 | .02 | −.04*** |
| Never content with living standard | −.07 | .02 | −.03*** |
| Income better in future | .02 | .01 | .02* |
| Sees country as democratic | .00 | .00 | .00 |
| *Individual resources* | | | |
| Age | −.02 | .00 | −.38*** |
| Female | −.14 | .01 | −.07*** |
| Social status | .04 | .01 | .04*** |
| Education | .04 | .01 | .04*** |
| Can borrow money if needed | .03 | .01 | .03*** |
| Trust people you know | .01 | .00 | .01 |
| (***Significant at .001 level; **.01 level; *.05 level) | | | |

Source: Centre for the Study of Public Policy, New Europe Barometer, 2004.

The stresses of transformation challenged individuals to rise above events, actively coping with stresses, taking advantages of opportunities and in many cases doing both. A standard social medicine measure of the extent to which people are confident of controlling their lives is: *Where would you place yourself on a scale where 1 represents having no freedom or control over how your life turns out and 10 represents having a great deal of free choice and control?* (Syme, 1989). Across all NEB countries the mean for replies was 6.1, showing that most post-transformation citizens feel that they have some or a lot of control over the challenges that they have faced. However, the standard deviation of 2.1 around that mean emphasizes that within every NEB country individuals differ in their degree of confidence. After age, the psychological consequence of transformation is the single biggest influence on health. By the time of the 2004 New Europe Barometer survey, most people were confident of being able to control their lives and this had a substantial positive impact on health (Table 9.3). However, individuals who had themselves been victims of crime, or whose family members had been victims of crime, tended to be less healthy.

Economic transformation created material stresses and opportunities, and both have had a significant influence on health. A higher level of income, having more consumer goods and an expectation of a better income in future lead to above-average health. On the other hand, individuals who feel they don't earn enough from their regular jobs, that their income was better in the past and that they will never be economically content are likely to have average or below-average health. Although limited, the effect of feeling that income had fallen significantly depressed health, while the effect of anticipating a rising income had no significant effect.

Politics triggered the pervasive transformation of society but, after controlling for other influences, specific features of regime change were shown to have little effect on health. While those who saw government as more corrupt were inclined to feel a little less healthy, seeing the new regime as democratic had no significant influence on health.

The resources an individual can draw on to cope with and take advantage of transformation significantly influence health. In common with modern societies, people who have had a better education and a higher subjective social status are significantly more likely to have better health and those who are low in both resources tend to have average or below-average health. Access to social capital has little effect on health (cf. Rose, 2000a). There is no statistically significant relationship between trust in people you know and health, and belonging to an organization has only a slight influence. The one way in which social capital can be good for health is if people have a network of friends from whom they could borrow money if faced with an interruption of earnings or pension. Since most NEB respondents have not had to borrow money during the past year, this informal form of social security is first of all a psychological rather than a material asset.

## III  Multiple pressures in opposite directions

To say that the average man or woman in the Czech Republic or Slovenia has better health than his or her counterpart in Russia invites the question: Why? One explanation is that this is due to the collective attributes of a society. For example, citizens of Central and Eastern Europe now have more opportunities because their countries are members of the European Union while post-Soviet citizens remain subject to more stresses. Yet whatever a country's collective level of Gross Domestic Product or freedom, individuals' perceptions of national conditions are not identical. Individual characteristics, such as age or psychological control, will continue to affect their health.

*Adding in national context*. Epidemiology emphasizes that context can have an effect on health independent of the characteristics of individuals who constitute a nation's population. A medical sociologist who has intensively studied post-Communist countries concludes, 'People do have the capability to act independently of social structures in their lives, but the occasions on which they do so appear to be rare' (Cockerham, 2007: 56). Moreover, the epidemiological hypothesis – *The more positive the national context, the better the health of individual citizens* – is consistent with the national differences reported in Table 9.1.

Deciding which features of national context promote better or worse health is an open question. Whereas the legacy of Communism may account for health in post-Communist countries tending to be worse than in EU countries, poor health could also be blamed on the lower Gross Domestic Product per capita of post-Communist countries or on a spurious correlation between distance from Brussels and a decline in health. However, such explanations do not account for differences in health within Communist-bloc countries. To attribute it to distinctive national cultures is inadequate, since countries with different cultures, for example, Slovenia and Romania, have much the same average level of health.

National context can be characterized along a variety of different dimensions, for example, Gross Domestic Product per capita, the level of corruption, the extent of repression under Communism or the degree of freedom achieved since. Many measures of national context tend to correlate strongly with each other, for example, countries that have a high Gross Domestic Product per capita tend to be less corrupt and more democratic. Because national context operates at two levels – characteristics of a country as a whole and the way that individuals respond to their national context – it is necessary to use multi-level statistical modelling to determine the relative importance of each. The number of variables that can be included must be restricted to less than the number of countries included here. Therefore, individual characteristics showing little or no influence in Table 9.3 have been excluded. One contextual variable, Gross Domestic Product per capita, reflects the state of the national economy, while the other, whether a country has been accepted for membership in the European Union, summarizes a host of political achievements of a post-transformation government (see Chapter 19).

Combining individual and contextual influences confirms the importance of individual influences. Age remains of greatest importance (Table 9.4). The extent to which individuals have benefited from opportunities, for example, controlling their lives and prospering materially, continues to have a positive influence on health. So too does being subject to stresses from having inadequate earnings or a better income in the past.

The need to take individual differences into account is demonstrated by the fact that even though the economic circumstances of an individual significantly influence individual health, the national level of Gross Domestic Product has no significant influence (Table 9.4). Living in a relatively prosperous country cannot compensate for being in the lowest quartile of income while living in a relatively poor country can be compensated for by being in the top quartile of income within it. The one contextual characteristic that does affect health is living in a country that has succeeded in moving from being part of the command economy in a one-party state to being a democratic rule-of-law state with a market economy, an achievement recognized by

*Table 9.4* Multi-level model of influences on health

|  | *Dependent variable: self-rated health* | | | |
| :--- | :---: | :---: | :---: | :---: |
|  | \multicolumn{4}{c}{*Variance explained by multi-level model: pseudo R² 33.8%*} |
|  | RMLE | se | T ratio | P |
| *Stresses and opportunities* |  |  |  |  |
| Can control life | .06 | .00 | 13.62 | .000 |
| Don't earn enough to get by | −.11 | .02 | −6.95 | .000 |
| Number of consumer goods | .05 | .01 | 3.94 | .000 |
| Income quartile | .03 | .01 | 3.48 | .001 |
| Income better in past | −.02 | .01 | −4.31 | .000 |
| *Individual resources* |  |  |  |  |
| Age | −.02 | .00 | −17.00 | .000 |
| Social status | .05 | .01 | 4.07 | .000 |
| Female | −.13 | .02 | −6.02 | .000 |
| Can borrow money if needed | .04 | .01 | 4.59 | .000 |
| *Context* |  |  |  |  |
| EU member state | .30 | .07 | 4.24 | .00 |
| GDP per capita PPP$000 | −.01 | .01 | −.69 | n.s. |

Source: Centre for the Study of Public Policy, New Europe Barometer, 2004. Calculation of impact explained in text; n.s.: not significant.

admission to the European Union. The benefits for health are not caused by actions of the European Commission in Brussels, but by actions taken by national governments to reject past institutions and practices and make the country fit for a 'return' to Europe.

*The impact on balance.* The impact of different influences – that is, how much or how little they increase or decrease individual health – can be calculated from the multi-level model statistics. The Restricted Maximum Likelihood Estimators (RMLE) show just how much better or worse an individual's health will be if there is a 1 unit change in the value of an independent variable. Thus, if two people are alike in every respect except that one now lives in a country meeting EU standards while the other is in a post-Soviet society, the former's health will be 0.3 points better on the 5-point scale measuring health (see Table 9.4). If the influence has a range of values, for example, from having 3 to having 0 major consumer goods, then there is a 3-unit difference between the maximum and the minimum number of consumer goods. Multiplying this by the RMLE coefficient of .05 results in a difference of 0.15 points on the health scale for a person with all the consumer goods and none.

Social resources, especially those that are given, have the greatest impact on health. At the extremes of age, health is altered by almost one and one-quarter points from the average. Whereas a middle-aged person is likely to have average health, an 80-year-old will rate their health as poor while an 18-year-old will view their health as good. In addition, being female will further depress health while being male will improve it (Figure 9.1). But some people also have resources that can boost their health independent of age. The limited percentage of people who are higher in social status tend to have better health and the same is true of the larger proportion of people who could borrow money from friends if they needed to do so. However, the impact of these resources is gradually overtaken by the impact of ageing.

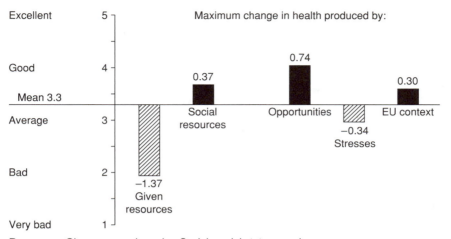

Resources: Given: age and gender; Social: social status, can borrow.
Opportunities: Controlling own life; buys major consumer goods; upper two income quartiles.
Stresses: Inadequate earnings; lower two income quartiles; income better in past. EU context:
country EU member not post-Soviet state.

*Figure 9.1* Impact of multiple influences on health.
Source: Centre for the Study of Public Policy, New Europe Barometer, 2004. Derived from multi-level model in Table 9.4.

The psychological effect of feeling in control of one's life has a big impact on health too. It is more than three times greater than the impact of having a lot of consumer goods and a sense of self-confidence is more widespread in society than lots of material goods. A family's absolute standard of living, as reflected in the number of its household consumer durables, has a bigger impact on health than does relative income, as indicated by being in the highest rather than the lowest quartile in a country's income distribution. Together, these three influences can raise an individual's health by more than three-quarters of a point on the health scale.

Stresses that have continued after transformation continue to depress health, but their impact is less than half that of the opportunities. Economic difficulty – not earning enough to get by without borrowing or saving – reduces health by more than one-fifth of a point and there is a lesser impact from having one's income drop substantially or being in the bottom quartile of a country's income distribution. The substantially greater importance of high or low consumption standards and earnings as against income quartile indicates that in countries in transformation it is absolute rather than relative differences in income that affect health more. This is consistent with the fact that when shocks hit less prosperous countries a household's first priority is to avoid destitution and achieve a sustainable position from a portfolio of resources. Catching up or narrowing the gap with those who are better off is a concern that can come after successfully adapting to transformation.

Because resources, opportunities and stresses vary between individuals within every country, the direct impact of national context is limited. After taking individual differences into account, the level of a country's Gross Domestic Product does not significantly influence health. Because GDP per capita is an average for the whole population, it cannot account for the wide variations in health within poorer countries, such as Ukraine and Bulgaria, as well as better-off countries, such as Slovenia and the Czech Republic (Table 9.2). The importance of looking at individual rather than aggregate measures of material wellbeing is underscored by the fact that, even though GDP has no significant impact, four measures of individual circumstances – earning enough, possessing more consumer goods, income quartile and comparison with past earnings – are significant in affecting health after controlling for the effects of social resources and national context.

Living in a country that is in the European Union rather than a post-Soviet state is the contextual measure that does have a positive impact on health. For two people alike in every individual characteristic, living on the western side of the border between Poland and Ukraine or Estonia and Russia will improve health by almost one-third of a point on the five-point scale. A country's membership of the European Union cannot alter the impact of age on its citizens' health. However, the transformation in Central and Eastern Europe since the fall of the Berlin Wall has enhanced the quality of life there much more than in successor states of the Soviet Union. Differences in quality of life are also likely to reflect differences in historical legacies: post-Soviet states lived in a ruthlessly anti-modern society much longer than did the Central and East European countries that are now members of the European Union. The quality of life is not a surrogate for national prosperity, since there are big variations in GDP per capita among the 10 new EU member states: in Slovenia and the Czech Republic it is twice that of Romania and Bulgaria, and Russia also has a higher GDP per capita than the two Balkan states. For CEE citizens, the collective benefit of being in a country that has 'returned' to Europe has almost as big a positive impact on health as the stresses induced by a big fall in income and lack of earnings.

Taken singly, all four hypotheses about the determinants of individual health have varying degrees of support. In statistical terms, the different types of impact displayed in Figure 9.1 can be added to each other to provide examples of those whose health has benefited most and least from the opportunities and stresses of transformation. Thus, a youthful male who is an EU citizen with a high sense of self-control, social status, access to consumer goods and income can be expected to have excellent health, while an elderly woman in a post-Soviet state with a sense of helplessness, low social status, no consumer goods and an inadequate income will have poor or very poor health. However, these ideal-typical examples are extreme; they describe very few individuals. Most people fall between these extremes, for example, being middle-aged rather than 18 or 80. To ignore this is to fall victim to the journalistic fallacy that what is out of the ordinary, and therefore newsworthy, is typical rather than atypical of post-transformation societies.

For most individuals health involves balancing pressures that have an impact in opposite directions: for example, having confidence that you can control what happens to you offsets the impact on health of being middle-aged and being an EU citizen more than offsets the impact of being of low social status. For a person who is average in terms of opportunities, stresses and social resources, the net impact of influences is, with two exceptions, virtually nil. The two exceptions are nationality and gender, which reflect differences in kind rather than degree. These two differences push in opposite directions: being a citizen of an EU country has more than twice the positive effect on health than the negative effect of being a woman. Moreover, the poorer health of Russian women is less due to their being women than to their being Russian.

Although individuals cannot stop themselves from ageing, the analysis shows that there are ways in which its negative impact on health can be offset. The chief coping mechanism is psychological, gaining a sense of control over your life. Whereas on material circumstances, may fall with ageing, other influences on health do not, such as having friends to whom one can turn for help if needed. Although government cannot prevent its citizens from ageing, it can reduce collective stress and increase individual opportunities that affect health. The preceding analysis indicates that the performance of 10 Central and East European governments have succeeded in doing so, while Russia, Belarus and Ukraine have not been effective in counteracting the baneful effects on health of the legacy of the Soviet Union.

# Part III

# Coping with political transformation

# 10 Freedom as a fundamental gain

> I am normally said to be free to the degree to which no human being interferes with
> my activity. Political liberty is simply the area within which a man can do what he wants.
>
> (Isaiah Berlin, *Two Concepts of Liberty*)

Freedom is a basic political right that is today valued not only by democratic
governments but also by international organizations such as the United Nations that
have unfree as well as free countries as members. But what is freedom? And how much
freedom is there around the world today? The persisting debate about the meaning
of freedom – or liberty, a word often used interchangeably – shows that freedom
is a valued symbol. But the multiple uses of the word among philosophers causes
confusion.

For people who lived in a Communist regime, freedom was important because it
was absent. Security services spied on them and people who questioned the party line
risked losing their jobs, harassment or worse. The party-state carried out an incessant
ideological campaign that sought to crowd out other ways of thinking and speaking.
These institutions gave ironic support to Lenin's claim in *State and Revolution*,
'Where the state exists, there can be no freedom'. Even though the party-state could
not control everything that people said and did, it could and did prevent people from
saying what they thought in public, reading what they wanted to read and travelling
where they wished.

Freedom from the state requires no more and no less than abandoning the apparatus
of oppression, such as a state security police whose informers reported on their
friends; border guards ready to shoot to kill people; and Party apparatchiks assessing
applicants for university places on the basis of Party loyalty. All these institutions have
now been consigned to the dustbin of history. The monuments to freedom are the empty
plinths on which formerly stood statues of Marx, Lenin and Stalin.

An immediate benefit of the weakness of new regimes was that people gained freedoms that they had previously lacked. But Dostoevsky claimed that in Slavic cultures
people could not stand 'too much' freedom; this doctrine was often invoked to explain
Russian compliance with the Soviet regime. Moreover, the turbulence that came with
freedom was often contrasted with the order achieved by the Communist suppression
of freedom. This chapter uses New Europe Barometer survey data to analyze the extent
to which people in post-Communist countries have experienced a gain in freedom as
the result of transformation.

## I Alternative ideas of freedom

*What freedom is.* In *Two Concepts of Liberty* Sir Isaiah Berlin (1958: 7, 22) has given classic expression to the idea of freedom as a negative condition, *freedom from* the state, whether the state is paternalistically seeking to 'propel people toward goals which the social reformer sees but others may not' or whether it is coercing subjects for the benefit of rulers. The emphasis on the absence of coercion by the state is a point especially relevant to people who had lived under Communism. The brevity of the definition is its strength; it avoids overloading the term with multiple meanings. Negative freedom is not treated as an absolute value. Berlin explicitly recognizes that in some circumstances there can be good reasons to limit the freedom of individuals to act in order to achieve some other end. But having been born in Riga and having left St Petersburg as it was exchanging one form of repression, anti-Semitic Tsardom, for another, Marxist-Leninist Communism, Berlin gave priority to freedom from a state that might not be beneficent.

Although Berlin's discussion of freedom takes the form of a lengthy essay, his definition is immediately relevant to empirical social science. Freedom from the state can be measured along two dimensions – the number of areas of everyday life in which individuals can act without governmental obstruction and the degree to which individuals can act free of interference. Freedom is thus a variable that can be more or less present within particular areas of society and a political system can be evaluated by the degree and scope to which its citizens are or are not free.

Freedom is about the activities of individuals and only indirectly about the government that permits or limits freedom. People can enjoy a degree of freedom in a pre-democratic Rechtsstaat that accepts legal limitations on its capacity to control the lives of individuals. Such a regime is a civil society in which institutions such as universities, business enterprises, trade unions and churches can act freely to an extent laid down in laws that constrain the state rather than its subjects.

The modern relevance of 'freedom from' is emphasized by Linz's (2000) distinction between totalitarian and authoritarian regimes. A totalitarian regime strives to maximize its power to interfere in areas of everyday life considered 'private' or 'non-political' in a civil society. It also seeks to repress the efforts of individuals to create social activities free from the state's control. By contrast, an authoritarian regime may allow individuals to do many things free from state interference while still maintaining restrictions upon some, for example, censoring books, plays and even operas. In the evolution of democracy in Europe, the achievement of legal and civil rights that gave individuals some freedom to organize to promote their interests occurred up to a century before the majority of adults gained the right to vote.

Writers in the Anglo-American tradition take freedom from oppression for granted. When governments of advanced industrial democracies run into economic difficulties political commentators assume that this threatens 'big' trouble in the political system, and if something is not done then democracy itself may be in danger from whatever social or economic condition is defined as troubling. Yet such threats have not materialized in the past two decades. The biggest changes have resulted from voters exercising their democratic right to turn the government of the day out of office – and democratic political systems have not become undemocratic.

*What freedom is not.* Defining freedom in terms of a single attribute makes it easy to identify what freedom is not. It is not concerned with individual limitations due to physical incapacity (for example, old age or blindness), lack of skills or knowledge (e.g. inability to play the piano) or being without material goods due to a lack of money. Many political values are omitted, including such political rights as the capacity to influence the state through democratic processes. Berlin (1958: 10) emphasizes that restricting the meaning of freedom is necessary to differentiate a variety of desirable and often competing political goals.

> To avoid glaring inequality or widespread misery I am ready to sacrifice some or all of my freedom. I may do so willingly and freely; but it is freedom that I am giving up for the sake of justice or equality or the love of my fellow men. I should be guilt-stricken and rightly so, if I were not, in some circumstances, ready to make this sacrifice. But a sacrifice is not an increase in what is being sacrificed, namely freedom, however great the moral need or the compensation for it. Everything is what it is: liberty is liberty, not equality or fairness or justice or culture or human happiness or a quiet conscience.

Positive conceptions of freedom endorse the ability of individuals to achieve their aspirations as well as to avoid constraints imposed by the state. A classic example is T. H. Marshall's (1950) dynamic conception of freedom. The achievement of civil rights, freedom from, was followed by the achievement of franchise rights (democracy, or freedom to influence government) and then social rights (e.g. education, health care, social security, freedom to realize individual welfare). Marshall was writing about the achievement of a welfare state in Britain, where the state respects negative freedoms as well as promoting positive welfare, and the model may also be applied to Scandinavia. Where freedom from a repressive state is assured, political debates focus on whether and how the state should or could help more people meet their needs and aspirations.

Freedom from the state is complementary to the civic virtue of individuals seeking to influence the state through political participation, for it is about limiting the scope of activities that should be subject to political action. It differs from collectivist philosophies that claim to know what activities individuals ought to pursue and assume that political institutions ought to encourage individuals to do what is in their true interest and forbid what is not. While Berlin (1958: 18) recognizes that some idealist prescriptions may reflect 'democratic optimism', he also notes, bearing in mind the tyrannies invoked in the name of Marxism, that they can be 'a specious disguise for brutal tyranny'.

There are examples of non-democratic regimes reducing freedom in many areas of private life and in return offering increased education, health care, social security and job security, The first steps toward the welfare state in Europe were taken more than a century ago in the Prussian Kaiser's Reich as an 'authoritarian defence' against democratization (Flora and Alber, 1981: 46ff). A trade-off between freedom from and claims to social welfare became increasingly important as the Soviet Union reduced its totalitarian pressure and offered welfare benefits to workers who accepted restrictions on their freedom of political action, a system described as 'welfare state authoritarianism' (Breslauer, 1978).

## II Freedom: a consumer's view

Many top-down characterizations of democracy focus on what governments do and refrain from doing (see Chapter 11). Yet freedom is about the actions of individuals rather than states. Hence, there is a prima facie case for a bottom-up consumer's view reflecting the experience of ordinary people. But how much freer do ordinary individuals feel as a consequence of regime change? To find the answer, the New Europe Barometer has developed a battery of questions measuring freedom from the state for use in NEB surveys across Central and Eastern Europe and successor states of the Soviet Union.

*Much more freedom.* The New Europe Barometer index of freedom is radically different from an index of political participation, which is about such activities as voting and attending political meetings. In a civic culture, such activities are political virtues. However, Communist party-states denied freedoms and compelled participation in politics through incessant mobilization efforts. What was lacking was the freedom not to participate in politics.

Freedom requires the state to avoid interfering with the everyday lives of individuals, for example, remaining indifferent about whether people do or do not go to church or take an interest in politics. Since every respondent has lived under two different regimes, people are asked to compare the extent of freedom that they now experience in comparison with their experience under a Communist regime. Very few people reply that they don't know; this shows that they understand what freedom means. The replies produce a clear and consistent pattern (Figure 10.1)

- *Freer to decide for oneself whether or not to practise a religion.*
  The Communist system was distinctive in trying to make atheism the state religion; it failed to secure popular support. Poles reacted in an extreme fashion: an overwhelming majority were practising Catholics in order to show their commitment

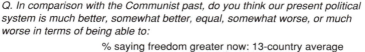

*Q. In comparison with the Communist past, do you think our present political system is much better, somewhat better, equal, somewhat worse, or much worse in terms of being able to:*

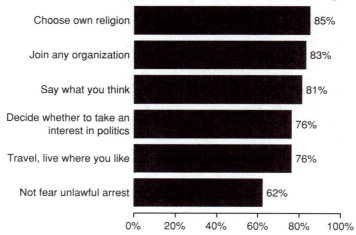

% saying freedom greater now: 13-country average

| | |
|---|---|
| Choose own religion | 85% |
| Join any organization | 83% |
| Say what you think | 81% |
| Decide whether to take an interest in politics | 76% |
| Travel, live where you like | 76% |
| Not fear unlawful arrest | 62% |

*Figure 10.1* Freedom then and now.
Source: Centre for the Study of Public Policy, New Europe Barometer 1993, including Belarus, Ukraine; New Russia Barometer, 1993.

to an anti-Communist institution. Across the region, the majority are indifferent, nominally professing a religion but not often going to church. Whatever their views, an overwhelming majority feel freer to decide for themselves about religion.

- *Freer to join any organization.*
  The suppression of organizations independent of the state is a hallmark of regimes with a totalitarian vocation. If people cannot join organizations of their choice, whether business, labour or social, then a civil society cannot emerge, and it is extremely difficult to organize public opposition to the party-state. The collapse of the Communist state has made five-sixths feel much freer to join whatever organizations they wish.

- *Freer to say what one thinks.*
  To control an individual's freedom of speech requires an elaborate system of informers routinely reporting to the state security police what people say. This apparatus collapsed with the party-state. Four-fifths of people in post-Communist societies feel freer today than before to say what they think.

- *Freer to to take an interest or no interest in politics.*
  In a system of totalitarian mobilization, political participation was compulsory. Very high election turnouts and a virtually unanimous vote for Communist candidates were indicators of the effort put into mobilization. For the three-quarters who now feel freer to determine their degree of interest in politics, freedom can mean *not* needing a Party card or repeating the party line to hold a job and the freedom to go to the park rather than the polling station on election day.

- *Freer to travel and live where you want.*
  Communist regimes severely restricted the right to travel to other countries and even to move from one city to another. Insofar as there are constraints on travel today, they tend to be economic, such as a lack of money for foreign holidays. All in all, three-quarters now feel freer to travel.

- *No fear of unlawful arrest.*
  In Stalinist times terror was important for securing mass compliance. De-Stalinization reduced its significance but the memory lingered, and that was sufficient to keep most people in line without repeatedly resorting to arrests for so-called political crimes. The collapse of Communism has made a positive difference in that three-fifths feel freer from the fear of unlawful arrest.

Responses to six questions about freedom show that on average 77 per cent feel freer than before to live without interference by the state. Among the minority who see no improvement, 18 per cent say that things have stayed much the same; such judgements appear to reflect the slackening of state controls over private life in the years shortly before the collapse of Communist regimes. Only 4 per cent see themselves as less free today than before. Subsequent NEB surveys show that the sense of increased freedom has remained strong even though the experience of Communist mobilization has receded into the past.

*Freedom from is not the same as freedom to.* Whereas democracy can be conceived as enabling people to 'interfere' with (that is, influence) what government does, freedom is about the government not interfering with many aspects of their everyday life. When citizens in post-Communist countries are asked whether they now feel they have more political influence on government than before, only one-third say that the change has increased popular influence, as against 49 per cent seeing no change, and

18 per cent saying that popular influence has actually worsened. Factor analysis confirms that there is no statistical relationship between freedom to influence government and freedom from government influence (Rose, 1995c).

An especially dramatic distinction between freedom and democracy can be found in Estonia and Latvia. The majority of Russian-speakers do not have citizenship and the right to vote in national elections. According to conventional theories of democracy, being denied the right to vote should make Russians there feel much less free than Baltic peoples, and the gap should be re-inforced by differences in national identities and current citizenship. But if freedom is separate from democracy, as the history of the Rechtsstaat suggests, then the readiness of Estonia and Latvia to allow Russian-speakers as well as their Baltic citizens to enjoy freedom from the state should not make the former feel less free.

A majority of Russian ethnics in the Baltics do not feel that the lack of citizenship and the right to vote makes them as unfree or disadvantage as when they were citizens of the Soviet Union. An average of 68 per cent of Russians in Estonia and Latvia report feeling freer now than when living within the Soviet Union. Moreover, in four areas – freedom to say what they think, join any organization, decide about religion and travel or live in another country – more than three-quarters of Russian-speakers in both Baltic societies feel freer from state interference. As long as Estonia and Latvia are governed by the principles of the Rechtsstaat, individuals without the vote can enjoy the freedoms of a civil society (see also Galbreath and Rose, 2008).

Many contemporary social philosophers and leaders of social democratic parties argue that if people are to feel free it is necessary for the state to provide generous social-welfare benefits and redistribute income to the poor through high levels of taxation. Some political scientists similarly assume that the state must 'buy' legitimacy. This implies that if new post-Communist regimes could not provide adequate social security during transformation, then democracy and freedom would be threatened with collapse.

East Germany offers a unique setting to test the links between social security and freedom. East Germans were uniquely transformed from being subjects of an oppressive political state offering the most generous social security benefits in the Communist bloc to being citizens of the Federal Republic of Germany. While the expanded German state has fully respected freedoms, in material terms transformation was not cost free. The East German economy was immediately under stress, because many large enterprises could not compete in a market economy. Generous West-German-financed unemployment benefits were not the same as the lifetime job guarantees of command economy.

When East Germans were asked to evaluate old and new regimes, the old social-security system was endorsed by 97 per cent compared to 24 per cent giving a positive rating to that of the Federal Republic (Figure 10.2). But when asked about freedom, 82 per cent of East Germans said they feel freer to say what they think in the Federal Republic, six times the proportion feeling free in the old system. Furthermore, 97 per cent now feel they have freedom of religion compared to 34 per cent before. Notwithstanding the decline in social security, almost twice as many East Germans endorse the new regime as the old. Moreover, gains in freedom have a greater influence on support for the Federal Republic than does the social security offered by the Communist regime (Chapter 12).

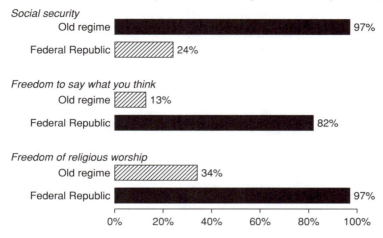

*Figure 10.2* East German evaluation of regime change.
Source: Rose, Zapf and Seifert (1993).

## III  A fundamental consensus

In a free society the great majority of questions asked in public-opinion surveys reveal differences of opinion about party preferences, political personalities and about how government ought to resolve major problems of the day. But to resolve these differences democratically requires a consensus about a small number of political fundamentals. This consensus must appear not only in the constitution but also in the minds of citizens.

A sense of freedom from the state is a fundamental value by which people discriminate between political regimes. From Central Europe to Siberia, the fall of the Berlin Wall and all that followed made a big difference to the enjoyment of freedom by hundreds of millions of people. This is true in every country. In Central and Eastern Europe and the Baltics, an absolute majority feels freer in all six areas. In Russia, Belarus and Ukraine an absolute majority of respondents feel freer in four of six areas; in the others, the median respondent sees no change (Table 10.1).

Because individuals judge freedom today against past experience, the current practice of government appears less important than the character of the old regime. Romanians are most likely to see big gains in freedom; across six areas 91 per cent feel freer today. This is less a positive endorsement of a new regime with many faults than it is a reaction to the despotic character of the preceding Ceausescu regime. Bulgarians rank high too in favouring the new regime against the old. Among Czechs subject to Soviet occupation in consequence of a brief period of freedom in the 1968 Prague spring, 87 per cent feel freer now than before. Even though Hungarians latterly enjoyed a less heavy-handed regime and the material benefits of 'goulash Communism', three-quarters feel the present regime offers more freedom than the old. Current political problems appear relevant as explanations of the lesser degree of freedom felt in Russia, Belarus and Ukraine. Nonetheless, across most areas of life an absolute majority in each post-Soviet country feels freer today than in the past.

*Table 10.1* More freedom in post-Communist countries

|  | Speech | Join org. | Travel | No fear of arrest | Interest politics | Religion | Average |
|---|---|---|---|---|---|---|---|
|  |  |  | (% feeling freer now than under Communist regime) |  |  |  |  |
| *New EU countries* |  |  |  |  |  |  |  |
| Bulgaria | 90 | 95 | 95 | 88 | 97 | 98 | 94 |
| Romania | 94 | 94 | 90 | 81 | 92 | 95 | 91 |
| Czech Republic | 84 | 90 | 96 | 73 | 84 | 94 | 87 |
| Slovakia | 82 | 88 | 88 | 62 | 80 | 96 | 83 |
| Lithuania | 87 | 90 | 68 | 66 | 89 | 91 | 82 |
| Estonia | 90 | 88 | 69 | 63 | 83 | 82 | 79 |
| Hungary | 73 | 81 | 76 | 59 | na | 83 | 74 |
| Poland | 83 | 78 | 75 | 71 | 69 | 70 | 74 |
| Latvia | 82 | 81 | 40 | 49 | 80 | 82 | 69 |
| Slovenia | 74 | 82 | 62 | 54 | 59 | 77 | 68 |
| *Post-Soviet countries* |  |  |  |  |  |  |  |
| Ukraine | 79 | 76 | 49 | 42 | 60 | 84 | 65 |
| Belarus | 73 | 74 | 48 | 37 | 57 | 87 | 63 |
| Russia | 73 | 77 | 47 | 29 | 62 | 83 | 62 |

Source: Centre for the Study of Public Policy, New Europe Barometer, 1993, including Belarus, Ukraine; New Russia Barometer, 1993.

A statistical analysis accounting for differences between those who feel freer today as against those who feel less free would be misleading because it would treat the appreciation of freedom as a variable. In fact, across diverse post-Communist societies there is a consensus recognizing the achievement of freedom. Because the proportion in the population feeling much freer is so high, a majority of old and young, educated and uneducated, and men and women all feel freer from the state. Even when there is a statistically significant difference between social groups, with younger, more educated and more prosperous people feeling slightly freer, it is a small difference in the size of the dominant majority, for example, between 80 and 84 per cent feeling freer in a given area.

Popular appreciation of freedom may be thought 'obvious'. But the point was not so obvious to analysts of the Communist bloc prior to the collapse of the system. Histories of autocratic rule were cited as evidence that national cultures created a collectivist mentality that was unconcerned with individual freedom. Communist regimes were credited with success because industrialization raised the material standard of living by comparison with the prewar era (see Chapter 3). However, whatever credit was given the Communist system for these achievements, it did not blind subjects to the regime's denial of freedom.

The readiness of people in diverse societies to appreciate their gains in freedom implies that the desire for freedom was not erased by two generations of Communist indoctrination. Moreover, the lengths to which individuals went to preserve an area of 'private space' in which they could say what they thought among friends of their own choice implies that totalitarian efforts to politicize the whole of social life were often counter-productive.

The regimes that replaced repressive Communist authorities have not been ideal. Everywhere citizens have complained about the ineffectiveness of government in dealing with the economic consequences of transformation. The fact that criticisms can be voiced publicly and frequently is evidence of greater freedom. Elections have offered people the chance to use their new freedom to vote the government of the day out of office – and this has often happened. Although weak political institutions are not positive *per se*, they can be an acceptable price to pay to achieve a greater good. As Joseph Schumpeter (1952: 288) emphasized, for people who do not want to be the objects of dictatorial efficiency, 'a lower level of government efficiency may be exactly what is wanted'.

# 11 Democratization backwards

No state, no Rechtsstaat, no democracy.

(Juan Linz, 1997)

The introduction of competitive elections in post-Communist countries has encouraged viewing transformation in terms of democratization, that is, a process in which a new regime progresses more or less steadily to the point at which it is consolidated as a democratic state. But events have shown that elections with multiple parties on the ballot are not necessarily free and fair. Thus, elections are a necessary but not a sufficient condition for the creation of a democratic state. In the words of John Stuart Mill, elections can create 'representative institutions without representative government'.

The rule of law is a necessary condition of achieving an accountable democratic regime (Linz, 1997: 120). In long-established democratic systems, the rule of law was institutionalized a century or more before the introduction of competitive elections with universal suffrage. Immediately after the collapse of Communism, political elites turned to elections to decide who governs, or at least, to give the veneer of legitimacy to an elite's hold on power. But an election does not guarantee that those elected will govern in accord with the rule of law. The successors of anti-modern regimes face the challenge of democratization backwards (Rose and Shin, 2001).

Whether new rulers see the weakness of the rule of law as a problem depends on whether they are trying to democratize – and leaders have headed in very different directions. The personalistic dictatorship of Turkmenistan has had little in common with the multi-party democracy of Estonia except that both were successor states of the Soviet Union. Ten new regimes of Central and Eastern Europe have achieved recognition as democratic states by the European Union while such post-Soviet regimes as Belarus and Uzbekistan are internationally recognised as very undemocratic.

To understand the dynamics of post-Communist regimes, we must examine how they differ from each other. Western scholars have responded to the palpable gap between the performance of new regimes and Western criteria of democracy by creating a plethora of categories involving democracy with adjectives. Regimes are seen as 'hybrid', 'delegative', 'illiberal', 'semi-democratic', a 'semi-dictatorship' 'pseudo-democracies' or 'disguised dictatorships' (see Schedler, 2006: 4ff). But qualifying the ideal of democracy with adjectives misses the point: the chief shortcoming of some post-Communist countries is not the absence of competitive elections but the absence of the rule of law.

# I Regimes in two dimensions

Many political scientists classify regimes along a single dimension, democratic or undemocratic according to the extent to which citizens can participate in elections. However, since governance is about the relationship between governors and governed, it is appropriate to characterize regimes in two dimensions. For governors to be held accountable, their actions must be bound by the rule of law. A lawless regime can manipulate elections in ways that are neither free nor fair, and if it is not accountable to the courts it can act arbitrarily. Taking the rule of law into account avoids what Terry Lynn Karl (2000: 95) has called 'the fallacy of electoralism', which 'privileges elections over all other dimensions of democracy'.

All elections are not the same: a ballot in which the winning party receives 99 per cent of the vote is not free, because there is no competition. An election in which election officials intimidate voters and manipulate the results is not fair. Countries that hold unfree or unfair elections are not defective democracies but autocracies, in which rulers rather than the people determine who governs. Their election results are not evidence of popular endorsement but of the ability of rulers to cow their subjects into submission. The gap between manipulated and actual support is illustrated by the vote for Communist parties before and after the abolition of the one-party state. In Soviet times more than 99 per cent of the electorate voted for the Communist Party. In the first competitive election in the Russian Federation in 1993, the Communist Party won the support of only 6 per cent of the electorate and 12 per cent of those who voted. In most of Central and Eastern Europe, Communist parties knew how unpopular they were; they did not even place their name on the ballot.

*The state as the starting point.* The defining characteristics of a state are that it has a monopoly of coercive institutions such as the police and army within a given territory. It claims the right to order subjects to pay taxes and risk their lives in military service. If it fails to meet these minimum requirements, it is no longer a state. North and South America are exceptional in being continents in which the boundaries of the great majority of states have been fixed for more than a century. Central and Eastern Europe are the opposite, since state boundaries have been in flux since the collapse of the Tsarist, Prussian and Habsburg empires at the end of the First World War. Six of the 10 post-Communist countries admitted to the European Union were not states when the Berlin Wall fell.

The rule of law is essential for the governance of a modern state. In a rule-of-law state the constitution not only sets out what governors can do but also what they cannot do – and it is enforced. When a regime accepts limitations on its powers, it is a Rechtsstaat in which law rather than might prevails. In such a regime, if governors disregard constitutional constraints or act outside the law, the courts can hold governors accountable. Governors cannot act arbitrarily, muzzling or jailing opponents. Bureaucrats are expected to administer public policies in accord with the law rather than act corruptly and to administer election laws fairly. A rule-of-law state does not have to be a democratic state. In Prussia, an early example of a Rechtsstaat, laws greatly restricted the right to vote and authorized censorship.

The rule of law is the foundation of democratic accountability. A government will only be accountable to its citizens through elections if governors are effectively constrained by the rule of law. An election is free insofar as a plurality of parties are able to compete. An election is fair insofar as parties compete on equal terms, for example, the regulations by which parties qualify for a place on the ballot are not written to favour the government; public officials do not intimidate opposition parties during the election campaign; the regime does not pressure the media to ignore the opposition; and there is no fraud in casting and counting votes. In many parts of the world, including successor states of the Soviet Union, the conduct of free and fair elections cannot be taken for granted.

A literal definition of democracy is 'rule by the people', but this does not give any indication about how the people can rule. The minimal definition is that of Joseph Schumpeter (1952: 271); in a democratic state there is 'free competition for a free vote'. Necessary conditions of a democratic state are that all adult citizens have the right to vote, elections are competitive and fair, and they decide which parties or individuals hold the principal offices in government. Broader definitions incorporate references to the freedom to form and join political parties and engage in public debate about how the country ought to be governed.

*Four types of regime.* To understand how states are governed we need to think in two dimensions. The first dimension – the accountability of governors to the rule of law – shows whether a state is modern. The second dimension – the accountability of governors to citizens through free and fair elections – is necessary if a modern state is also to be democratic. Combining these two attributes produces a fourfold classification of regimes (Table 11.1).

In Western nations an accountable democracy is the reference point for government, because it is what is familiar. Within these countries there are many historical studies about the development of democracy, or the need to reform its contemporary institutions to make them more democratic. Insofar as theorizing occurs, it involves conceptualizing democracy and the conditions for it to develop and become consolidated. Such theories can make a positive contribution to understanding dozens of democracies – but have little to say about the more than 100 countries that are not democracies.

In a constitutional oligarchy the rule of law is respected but elections do not decide who governs. Citizens are free to engage in political activity within legal limitations. Even if the right to vote is confined to a fraction of middle- and upper-class males, this group has the right to vote for competing parties in fair elections. However, the choice of governors remains in the hands of an elite or, in past centuries, at the discretion of a ruling monarch. Political tension arises when the elite is divided and one portion of the elite seeks to mobilize additional support by arguing in favour of expanding the right to vote.

In an unaccountable autocracy rulers ignore the law. If an unfair election is held that produces an unacceptable result, then, in the words of a character in a play by Bertholt Brecht, 'The government can dissolve the people and elect another'. As long

*Table 11.1* Democratic and undemocratic regimes

|  |  | RULE OF LAW | |
|  |  | Binding | Arbitrary |
| --- | --- | --- | --- |
| *ELECTIONS* | *All can vote* | Accountable democracy | Plebiscitarian autocracy |
|  | *Few, none can vote* | Constitutional oligarchy | Unaccountable autocracy |

as unaccountable power was limited to a circle around a despot, as in the court of Tsar Ivan the Terrible, its impact on distant subjects was limited. The twentieth century saw the creation of totalitarian regimes that went much further in the coercion of citizens. Whereas traditional autocrats showed little interest in many areas of social life, totalitarian regimes systematically and pervasively sought to control the whole of their subjects' lives. The totalitarian regimes of Hitler's Germany and Stalin's Soviet Union are no more, but North Korea, established in 1948, is older than two-thirds of the regimes in the European Union.

The will of governors is the dominant influence in a plebiscitarian autocracy. Governors know what they want and are not constrained by the rule of law. However, since elections are held, the government needs to organize a show of support. Opponents have a window of opportunity to mobilize protests against autocratic rule and competitive elections give them an incentive to bury differences in order to present a common front against an autocratic government. Even though election laws are unfair and the opposition may be subject to intermittent harassment, competitive elections make governors concede that there is a plurality of views about how the country should be governed. If a significant minority votes for the opposition, governors must treat this as a signal to introduce reforms to maintain their autocratic rule. From time to time the result of what was meant to be a predictable plebiscite goes wrong and an autocrat faces the choice of using coercion to remain in power or leaving office.

*The global pattern.* The extent to which accountable democracies are the dominant form of government in the world today can be estimated from ratings of two international non-governmental organizations that evaluate regimes. Freedom House evaluates the extent to which regimes give their citizens the political and civil rights necessary to hold governors accountable, such as the right to vote and to participate in free and fair elections (www.freedomhouse.org). Its standards are high enough to rule out blatantly unfair contests without penalizing new democracies in which inexperienced governors sometimes stumble when learning how to conduct free elections. Freedom House credits 123 regimes with holding free elections.

Respect for the rule of law is indicated by Transparency International's Perception of Corruption Index. It is compiled from expert assessments of the extent to which bribery influences a government's allocation of public resources. Financial corruption tends to correlate with disregard for laws that limit political power. In principle, every regime could be classified as law-abiding; in reality this is far from the case. Since the European Union requires its members to adhere to the rule of law, it provides a standard for labelling regimes as law-abiding. Among 27 EU member states Romania ranks lowest on the 10-point Perception of Corruption Index with an index score of 3.7. It is nonetheless well above a majority of regimes in the world today.

The chief obstacle to democratization today is not the absence of elections but the failure of governments holding elections to be bound by the rule of law. More than three-fifths of regimes fall below the minimum standard of regard for the rule of law (Figure 11.1). The largest category of states are unaccountable autocracies. If elections are held, governors make sure that the result shows what they want regardless of what the electorate wants. In institutional terms, some of these regimes are personal dictatorships, others are controlled by a military or civilian clique, and a few use a party to mobilize a show of popular support. Saudi Arabia is an extreme example of an absolute monarchy governed without elections.

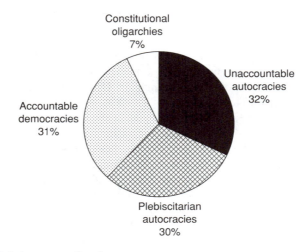

*Figure 11.1* Global pattern of regimes.
Source: Classification of 180 states according to whether an electoral democracy or not (Freedom House, 2007) and Perception of Corruption Index rating equal to or better than Romania (Transparency International, 2007).

Plebiscitarian autocracies constitute 30 per cent of all regimes. While there can be competitive elections, opposition parties face an uphill battle to compete with the party of power, since the conduct of elections is unfair and the law offers little protection from governors abusing the power of the state. A high level of corruption also denies the accountability of governors to the electorate. Latin America offers examples of this type of regime, in which elections can be held but the party of power normally controls the result.

Less than a third of regimes in the world today are accountable democracies. Institutionally, a majority in this category are parliamentary democracies, a smaller proportion are presidential systems, and some share power between a popularly elected president and an elected parliament. Most accountable democracies are in European states with modern economies. However, accountable democracies can be found on every continent. India is an outstanding demonstration of the possibility of a government being democratically elected even though most voters are poor and often illiterate as well.

Today, only 7 per cent of regimes are constitutional oligarchies in which public officials act in accord with national laws but without the need to be accountable to the electorate. For every one constitutional oligarchy there are more than four regimes that are plebiscitarian autocracies. Singapore is the best-known example. Its rulers boast of 'good' (that is, honest) government and its Transparency International rating is higher than the United States and than five-sixths of European Union member states. However, its leaders enforce laws that muzzle political criticism and opposition.

## II Evolution and disruption

By definition, the starting point for democratization is an autocratic regime. In the seventeenth and eighteenth centuries, the monarchs of Prussia and France began reforming the institutions that they had accumulated from feudalism, inheritance and conquest. A centralized bureaucracy subject to the rule of law was introduced. The first modern states were neither democratic nor democratizing. They were modernized in order to give their rulers more effective power over their subjects.

Accountable democracies have developed in three very different ways. The oldest, a minority, have evolved gradually and peacefully. A second group has proceeded by trial and error, introducing democracy and then relapsing into some form of autocratic rule before successfully re-introducing democracy. Third, post-Communist regimes are the leading example of democratization backwards, introducing competitive elections before the rule of law. Each category has tended to occur at a different period of time. Huntington's (1991) metaphor of a wave raises the possibility that the tide of democratization can reverse and generate 'de-democratization', as developments in post-colonial African states have demonstrated. But Huntington's focus on elections ignores the difference between regimes that introduce elections before the rule of law has been established rather than after. The metaphor of a wave is misleading, insofar as it ignores the fact that democratization does not flow like the tides of the ocean. A better nautical metaphor would be to describe a democracy as the result of the confluence of two streams of development, the rule of law and free and fair elections with universal suffrage.

*Evolution.* The old democratic regimes of England, the Netherlands and Scandinavia have evolved over the centuries. The rule of law was established first. This made it possible for assemblies that directly represented a very small portion of the population – aristocrats, landowners and other estates of the realm – to check the power of monarchs. To describe such assemblies as undemocratic is to project today's values backwards in time. To describe their development as a process of democratization is to impute twenty-first-century intentions to eighteenth- and nineteenth-century oligarchs.

Oligarchic rule-of-law regimes could evolve into democratic states through a process of competition between elites for power and influence. Parliaments representing elites in society claimed the right to hold the servants of the king accountable. The law recognized the right of individuals to organize political parties and to criticize government. The process that we now describe as democratization was often not the chosen goal of governors but a consequence of competition. At a given point in time, one group could press to expand the right to vote and the accountability of government to elected representatives in order to advance its particular interests and goals. The right to vote was gradually broadened until universal suffrage was achieved and government became accountable to a democratically chosen rather than an undemocratically constituted parliament.

*Trial-and-error democratization.* Gradual evolution requires that a regime is not disrupted by war or domestic upheavals. However, this has not been the case across most of Europe. Trial-and-error alternation between democratic and autocratic forms of government describes the dynamics of many Mediterranean and Central European states. To characterize those in this group as second-wave democracies is accurate insofar as democratic institutions have been established much later than in evolutionary democracies. However, this is not because they were late starters in attempting to democratize, but failed initially. For example, France introduce the rule of law early and introduced universal male suffrage a half-century before Britain. But since the French Revolution of 1789 it has had a succession of republics, monarchies and dictatorships led by generals. The current regime is the Fifth Republic.

Prior to 1914 Central and East European lands were an integral part of multi-national undemocratic empires. Lands that were part of the Habsburg or German Empire – what is now the Czech Republic, Hungary, Slovakia, Slovenia and much of Poland – were subject to a constitutional oligarchy. An unaccountable Russian Tsar ruled over other parts and Bulgaria, Romania and southern parts of what was once Yugoslavia had broken loose from an unaccountable Ottoman autocracy.

In the aftermath of the First World War new regimes were established with democratic institutions, reflecting what a contemporary historian described as 'the wish to be rid of tangible evils' (Bryce, 1921: vol. 2: 602). However, within a decade a process of 'de-democratization' began leading to the establishment of plebiscitarian or unaccountable autocracies. Mussolini seized power in Italy in the early 1920s. In Germany the democratic Weimar regime was replaced by a totalitarian regime in a quasi-constitutional *coup* after Adolf Hitler's Nazi Party won a plurality of votes in its 1932 election. In Austria an elected government was replaced by a dictatorship and subsequently absorbed into Hitler's Third Reich.

The states created in Eastern Europe initially held competitive elections in which a great multiplicity of parties won votes and seats in parliament, reflecting the multi-ethnic composition of the societies and the inexperience of the politicians. However, the weakness of the rule of law made it relatively easy to turn fledgeling new democracies into plebiscitarian or unaccountable autocracies. In Hungary, for example, the absence of a secret ballot meant that rural tenants could be intimidated by their landlords. In Poland General Pilsudski used his military position to dominate. By the mid-1930s, in every country in the region except Czechoslovakia elections were suspended or manipulated.

Defeat in and military occupation after the Second World War created the conditions in which accountable democratic regimes could emerge in Germany, Austria and Italy. In each country there were anti-Nazi politicians who had had experience of living in a Rechtsstaat prior to 1918 and of democratic elections for a few years afterwards. In reaction to the devastation created by their successors there was popular support for making a success of the new regimes. In Spain, Portugal and Greece, re-democratization was delayed until there was a consensus that an accountable democracy was preferable to a civil war.

*Democratization backwards.* The Communist legacy demonstrates the process of introducing competitive elections before the rule of law is fully institutionalized. Prior to the collapse of the Communist bloc, Russia had neither the rule of law nor competitive elections. The Tsarist regime was an extreme example of an unaccountable autocracy unchecked by an elitist parliament. After the 1917 revolution, a Constituent Assembly was elected by universal suffrage and Bolshevik candidates won no more than one-quarter of the vote. However, Red Guards soon used physical force to take over the Assembly on behalf of the Communists, and Vladimir Lenin began pursuing complete control without regard for the rule of law. The first competitive election in the Russian Federation was held in 1993, two months after the conflict between President Yeltsin and the parliament had been resolved by a shoot-out.

Central and Eastern European countries occupied by Soviet troops at the end of the Second World War had earlier experience of bureaucratic rule of law governance in the Prussian and Habsburg empires and this legacy survived to a substantial degree in interwar autocracies. Immediately following the end of the Second World War, competitive elections with universal suffrage were introduced (Rose and Munro,

2003). These elections produced coalition governments in which Communists occupied key positions. Backed by the presence of Soviet troops, Communist parties quickly seized control and by 1948 were building an anti-modern one-party state. By the time the Berlin Wall fell, these societies had experienced four decades of rule by a one-party regime governing without regard for the rule of law.

## III  Post-transformation regimes diverge

*Institutionalizing free and fair elections.* When it became clear in Central and Eastern Europe that Soviet troops would no longer use force to repress demands for change, subjects no longer had to pretend to support an unaccountable autocracy. When leaders of national Communist parties realized that they could no longer rely on Moscow's support, they were ready to hand over power to groups of anti-Communists and dissidents in order to establish, very belatedly, that they put their nationality ahead of loyalty to Moscow.

The first step was to call competitive elections to demonstrate publicly and conclusively that the one-party state was gone and to confer popular legitimacy on the new governors. Since 1990 free and fair elections have been institutionalized throughout Central and Eastern Europe. In marked contrast to the 'democratic centralism' of the Communist era, proportional representation has led to a large number of parties gaining seats in parliament and to coalition governments (see Chapters 14 and 15). Citizens can and do use their votes to turn the government of the day out of office. If only because of the problems of transformation, governing parties have lost office more frequently than in the older accountable democracies of Western Europe. However, there is little popular support for parties that challenge democratic institutions. Anti-democratic parties receive smaller shares of the vote than have been won by Jean-Marie Le Pen's National Front in France the late Jörg Haider's Freedom Party.

Leaders of new Central and East European regimes set as their goal the return to Europe; however, this rhetorical phrase could not overcome the legacy of having been 'away' for almost half a century. Moreover, the Europe that post-Communist regimes sought to join was not the same as before. It now consisted of accountable democracies. The European Union offered new regimes the opportunity to become integrated in this new and democratic Europe. To do so meant meeting the EU's standards for admission, which not only include holding free and fair elections but also enforcing the rule of law (Chapter 19). In May 2004 eight countries – the Czech Republic, Estonia, Hungary, Latvia, Lithuania, Poland, Slovakia and Slovenia – became members of the European Union. Bulgaria and Romania followed in 2007.

*Institutionalizing autocracies.* In the Soviet Union the Communist legacy was different. The idea of the Rechtsstaat had never taken hold in Tsarist times and the theory of socialist legality justified commissars exercising power without regard for human rights or life. By the time that Mikhail Gorbachev took office the totalitarian terror of Stalin's era had been exhausted but the much-vaunted 'liberalization' of the Soviet regime was not a step toward accountable democracy; it was a means of maintaining support for a post-totalitarian unaccountable autocracy.

In pursuit of the goals of glasnost (opening up) and perestroika (restructuring), Gorbachev licensed elections with very restricted choice: Communist Party members could compete against each other. Referendums intended to endorse these reforms were also introduced. However, the plebiscites intended to endorse Gorbachev's restructuring initiatives were followed by a political revolution leading to the break-up of the Soviet Union.

Elections in the 12 post-Soviet states frequently demonstrate the persistence of unfree and unfair practices from the Soviet era. Election results usually register what the government wants regardless of what the electorate wants. While unfair practices may not change who wins, they demonstrate that a regime does not respect the rule of law. There are variations in the extent to which elections are controlled by unaccountable autocrats or are plebiscites in which autocrats risk challengers producing an unwelcome result. In Turkmenistan the *Turkmenbashi* was elected president with 99.5 per cent of the vote in 1992 and 99.99 per cent of voters in a plebiscite subsequently endorsed extending his term for life. After his death in 2006, a quasi-competitive ballot gave more than 90 per cent of the vote to the acting president. In Belarus, Aleksandr Lukashenka initially won a competitive presidential election but in 1996 a plebiscite recorded 70 per cent endorsing a new constitution giving extensive powers to the president. During the 2006 election Lukashenka confirmed his status as an unaccountable autocrat by intimidating and jailing opponents.

Initially, Russian elections were competitive and could produce results against the Yeltsin government's wishes. In the 1993 Duma contest, the government's favoured party finished second; in 1996 President Boris Yeltsin received just above one-third of the vote in the first-round presidential ballot; and in the 1999 Duma election the Communist Party received more votes than the Kremlin's favoured party. The following year Vladimir Putin won just above half the vote in the first-round presidential ballot. However in the 2003 Duma election the Kremlin party came first and in the presidential election of 2004 the opposition parties put up only token candidates against Vladimir Putin, who was re-elected with 71 per cent of the vote. The closure of competition was underscored by the Kremlin party winning almost two-thirds of the Duma vote in 2007 and Putin's candidate, the unknown Dmitry Medvedev, winning 70 per cent of the vote in the 2008 presidential contest. The Office for Democratic Institutions and Human Rights (ODIHR) of the OSCE (Organisation for Security and Cooperation in Europe) refused to send observers to the 2007–8 elections because Moscow wanted to restrict its ability to observe the conduct of elections that were deemed unfair.

Because of the weakness of the rule of law, no post-Soviet regime can be described as a democracy or a constitutional oligarchy. Disregard for the law and unfair elections make the majority unaccountable autocracies. A minority hold elections that sometimes produce results that shock governors. Ukraine is the most striking example of a plebiscitarian autocracy. Notwithstanding a high level of corruption and intimidation of political adversaries, opponents of the 'party of power' have consistently won a significant share of the vote. In the winter of 2004, a series of competitive presidential elections and court decisions culminated in the victory of the opposition candidate for the presidency. While Moldova has had a high level of corruption, opposition parties have been able to contest elections and, if only because political elites are not united, there has been a degree of electoral competition. In Georgia too corruption has been tempered by electoral competition and popular demonstrations forced a president elected by fraudulent means in 2003 to cede power.

*Divergence of post-transformation regimes.* All 10 Central and Eastern European regimes now hold free and fair elections. Freedom House places eight of these regimes at the top of its democracy scale, equal to the oldest democratic states of the European Union.

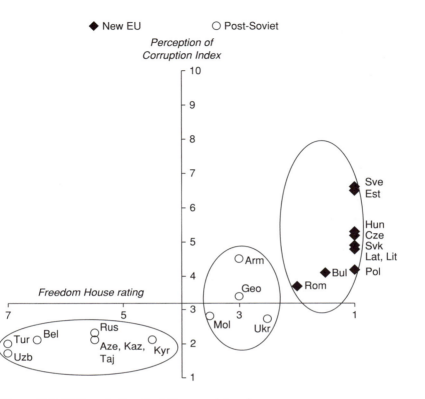

*Figure 11.2* Differentiating Post-Communist regimes.
Sources: Perception of Corruption Index (Transparency International, 2007); Freedom House rating (Freedom House, 2007).

The two laggards, Bulgaria and Romania, are ranked equal in democratic freedoms with Greece and South Africa respectively. By contrast, none of the successor states of the former Soviet Union has institutionalized free and fair elections (Figure 11.2). The Freedom House index divides these regimes into two categories, partly free or unfree. Four countries – Armenia, Georgia, Moldova and Ukraine – are classified as partly free because they hold competitive elections in which the outcome has deprived governors of their power, albeit sometimes by post-election disorder rather than after the prompt concession of defeat by governors. In two-thirds of post-Soviet regimes, elections cannot produce the 'wrong' result. Even if multiple candidates appear on the ballot, they are harassed by the state-security apparatus and denied access to the media. Freedom House labels these regimes as unfree.

Institutionalizing the rule of law has been a common challenge in every post-Communist regime, but the responses have been very different. In Central and Eastern Europe the primary problem has been corruption, in which elected and non-elected public officials have used their office for personal profit. As a consequence, these regimes have lower ratings on the Perception of Corruption Index than on the Freedom House index. Even more striking are differences in corruption between these 10 states. Slovenia and Estonia have ratings as good or better than the six Mediterranean countries that are now EU member states and four new EU countries are in the top quarter of Transparency International's international ratings. However, corruption in Poland, Bulgaria and Romania is even worse than in the worst Mediterranean countries. Nonetheless, corruption is not accompanied by a state police that infringes the liberties of citizens by arbitrarily arresting critics, censoring newspapers, closing down civil-society organizations or fixing elections.

The Soviet legacy results in all 12 post-Soviet regimes being very low on the Transparency International Index and most are in the bottom quarter internationally. On the 10-point scale, nine regimes cluster between 2.0 and 2.8. Uzbekistan is lowest; its rating of 1.7 is below Haiti and Nigeria. The oil-rich regimes of Azerbaijan and Uzbekistan have ratings below Sierra Leone and Albania. Moreover, corruption in the Russian Federation appears bad by absolute and relative standards; its index score is 2.3.

Corrupt administration co-exists with violations of the rule of law for political ends, for example, using the security services or tax authorities to intimidate or jail political opponents and undermine electoral competition. Amnesty International annually reports extra-legal violations of human rights in most countries of the Commonwealth of Independent States (www.amnesty.org). Furthermore, in Armenia, Azerbaijan, Georgia, Moldova and Tajikistan, the regime's claim to the monopoly of force has been challenged by armed forces from neighbouring countries and insurrection in Chechnya challenges the Russian regime. Where there is such armed conflict, the rule of law tends to be intermittent.

In the two decades since the fall of the Berlin Wall, countries long bound together in the Communist bloc have diverged. Figure 11.2 identifies three different clusters. A gulf has opened up between the new EU member states that regularly hold free and fair elections and post-Soviet regimes that do not. The latter differ only in the extent to which their elections are partly or wholly unfree. There is also a gap in the extent to which the rule of law is in effect. On the Transparency International Index, the mean score of countries in Central and Eastern Europe is 5.0. By contrast, the mean index score for post-Soviet states is 2.4. Soviet successor states have not failed to institutionalize democracy. From Central Asia to the borders of the European Union, they have succeeded in institutionalizing unaccountable autocracies.

# 12 The impact of a ready-made German state

The German question is too important to be left to the Germans alone.

(Klaus von Beyme)

If you can't take twentieth-century German history, stay out of Europe.

(Richard Rose)

The transformation of East Germany was unique. Instead of changing the regime within a state, it involved the disappearance of a state, the so-called German Democratic Republic (GDR). Instead of breaking up, as did the Soviet Union, GDR citizens and territory became part of the Federal Republic of Germany (FRG), which then had its capital in Bonn. Instead of having to create new institutions from scratch, East Germans experienced the impact of a ready-made state with democratic institutions and a market economy. German re-unification had major political implications for the whole of Europe and also for social science theories about the relative influence of culture, institutions and socio-economic differences on political attitudes. This justifies Klaus von Beyme's (1990: 183) claim about its importance. But given what happened when Germany sought expansion earlier in the century, there were also anxieties expressed by people, such as Margaret Thatcher.

The Berlin Wall went up in 1961 in order to stop the migration of East Germans to the Federal Republic in West Germany. For East Germans, the fall of the Berlin Wall in November 1989 led to the quadruple transformation of polity, economy, society and also state. It was unmatched by previous disruptions in twentieth-century German history, not least because it was bloodless. While the experience of escaping from Communist rule was shared with nations across the region, the consequences for East Germans have been unique. Elsewhere leaders of new regimes were challenged to create new institutions. By contrast, the Federal Republic supplied East Germans with the ready-made institutions of a stable and prosperous democratic state. This challenged East Germans to think and act differently than before.

In formal terms, transformation did not involve a change of regime, for the 1949 constitution of the Federal Republic made provision for the integration of the peoples and lands 'to whom participation is denied', that is, East Germany. Thus, re-unification was not a process of negotiation between two independent states, for the GDR could not claim parity with the Federal Republic. Its territories became five new *Bundesländern* (provinces) incorporated in the Federal Republic by a process analogous to the addition of states in the American union. The description of the process as *re*-unification was consistent with more than a century of efforts to create a German nation. It was also consistent with East German demonstrations in autumn 1989. The slogan 'We are the people', a claim for popular rights, was quickly augmented by the chant 'We are one people', a claim for re-unification. However, constitutional change could not guarantee the removal of 'the Wall in the head' that East Germans had developed in order to live within the confines of a regime with totalitarian aspirations.

To understand the significance of a quadruple transformation requires comparison across both time and space. The starting point is a comparison between East Germans and the peoples of neighbouring Communist countries of *Mitteleuropa* (Central Europe) before and immediately after transformation. This leads to a comparison of East and West Germans in a newly unified Germany. Given centuries of links between German-speaking peoples of Central Europe, the concluding section compares the impact of the fall of the Berlin Wall with Austria, which saw the departure of Soviet troops from Vienna and Eastern Austria in 1955. The pages that follow make particular use of 1993 surveys in East and West Germany (Rose, Zapf and Seifert, 1993).

## I  East Germans in the Communist bloc

The first article of the Constitution of the German Democratic Republic proclaimed that it was created as a socialist state of the German nation. Economically, militarily and politically, the GDR was an integral part of the Communist bloc. Within the bloc, there was widespread recognition, tinged with envy, of the relative material success of East Germany. When leftwing Germans lamented the economic plight of East Germans at a meeting of social scientists in Berlin in the early 1990s the Central and East Europeans present laughed in their faces. This is shown by comparing its living conditions with Poland and Czechoslovakia, which had territorial and population interchanges with Germany at the end of the Second World War; Hungary, a German-oriented Central European country; and the Soviet Union, the vanguard country of socialism (see Chapter 3).

*Living standards in the Communist era.* Soviet occupation forces in Central and Eastern Europe brought with them the Soviet model of building socialism. There were variations in its implementation, for example, the 'scripting' of unfree elections, but these were insignificant in comparison with the fundamental contrast between free and unfree elections.

In political and civil rights East Germans were subject to Communist constraints radically different from the Basic Law of the Federal Republic. In 1973, the first year in which Freedom House evaluated the political freedom of countries, East Germany was at the very bottom, at the same level as such very repressive countries as the Congo and Yemen and slightly lower than Communist-bloc countries such as Hungary and Poland. By 1986 Communist-style 'liberalization' raised East Germany's rating by half a point to the level of Czechoslovakia, where Soviet troops were also prominent.

In health, education and social welfare, all the countries of the former Soviet bloc showed significant improvements from their starting points as war-ravaged, relatively backward agricultural lands. Using health as a basic and readily comparable measure of wellbeing, in 1949 East Germans were the healthiest of the Communist-bloc countries. Infant mortality was a third less than in Poland. Similarly, the life expectancy of women was six years greater in East Germany than in Poland, and also higher than in any other Soviet-bloc country. Over four decades East Germans maintained their pre-eminence. By 1990 infant mortality was reduced to eight deaths per 1,000; in Czechoslovakia it was half again as great, in Poland twice as high, and in the former Soviet Union three times the East German level. The life expectancy of women improved in every country – but East German women still expected a longer life than women in Czechoslovakia, Hungary, Poland or the Soviet Union (see Tables 3.1, 3.2).

The nature of the non-market economy makes evaluating economic conditions difficult. Moreover, East Germans with relatives in the West could enjoy vicarious shopping, since relatives brought them West German consumer goods. A comparison of the economic situation of East Germans must therefore be taken with a large bag of salt. A World Bank comparison of per capita national product in Communist-bloc countries in 1989 (Marer *et al.*, 1992: 133ff) indicates, well beyond any margin of error, that East Germans were materially better off than citizens elsewhere in the Communist bloc. Depending upon the source, they had a living standard twice or three times as high as that of Poles, more than half again as high as Hungarians, and a sixth higher than in Czechoslovakia. Comparisons of car ownership support a similar conclusion (see Figure 3.1).

Vladimir Putin's experience as a young Russian KGB officer in Dresden in 1985 illustrates the gap between Soviet and East German economic achievements. When asked to compare life in Dresden with that in St Petersburg, Putin replied that it was much better, because 'We had come from a Russia where there were lines and shortages and in the GDR there was always plenty of everything. I gained about 25 pounds' (Putin, 2000: 70).

*Advantages of a ready-made state.* Everywhere except East Germany, the end of Communism faced governors with the challenge of creating new institutions. In the Baltic states *émigrés* could return with organizational skills they had acquired in exile, but the institutions for which they were suited were not there. Half a dozen years after the Berlin Wall fell Central and East European countries at best were only two-thirds of the way to creating the institutions of a market economy, and successor states of the former Soviet Union were further behind. By contrast, East Germans did not need to write a new constitution or currency. New institutions of state and market could be supplied, as it were, by copying what was in the Federal Republic.

The wholesale transference of ready-made institutions occurred with re-unification in October 1990, 11 months after the Berlin Wall fell. At the stroke of a pen, East Germans were no longer citizens of a Communist regime but of a leading European Rechtsstaat. Free and fair elections offered East Germans the opportunity to vote for all-German parties founded in the West or for a party seeking votes solely in East Germany. East Germans do not divide their vote the same as West Germans, but neither do American Southerners vote like non-Southerners, or English vote like Scots. More than three-quarters of East Germans vote for 'all-German' parties – a proportion similar to that of Scots voting for 'all-British' as distinct from Scottish parties. The one distinctive East German party, the ex-Communist Party of Democratic Socialists, was a regional party seeking special treatment from the national government rather than as an 'anti-regime' party, and it subsequently merged with a West German leftwing party.

The immediate integration of East Germany meant that East Germans became part of a society with European (that is, EU) standards almost a decade and a half before neighbouring ex-Communist-bloc countries. Within a German setting, comparisons between old and new Bundesländern are appropriate, since the German constitution commits the government to minimize inter-regional disparities in living conditions through the payment of social benefits such as pensions and unemployment benefits. The Federal Republic concurrently began spending large sums to bring the roads, buildings and other infrastructure of East Germany up to West German standards. It subsidized firms that could not compete with West German firms and it privatized state-owned enterprises in the hope that this would make them economically competitive.

Three years after re-unification, the Gross Domestic Product per capita, adjusted for differences in the cost of living between countries, showed Germans were far better off economically than other peoples of post-Communist Europe. Average purchasing power was more than double that of Czechs and treble that of Hungarians or Slovaks and four times higher than Poles. These differences were so great that allowing for inter-regional differences between East and West Germany would not alter the substantive conclusion: by sharing in the institutionalized welfare entitlements of a ready-made economy, East Germans have enjoyed a much higher living standard than peoples in other post-Communist societies. A decade later, when Czechs, Hungarians and Poles joined an enlarged European Union, the average income of East Germans, after adjusting for differences in purchasing power, was still half again to double that of their neighbours in countries that lacked the advantages of a ready-made state.

A cross-check on official statistics is provided by comparing a 1993 survey in East and West Germany with the New Europe Barometer survey of that year. When people were asked whether they had enough income to buy what their family needed, 86 per cent of East Germans replied that their income from the official economy was adequate, whether it took the form of wages or income-maintenance grants financed by taxpayers of the Federal Republic. This was virtually the same as in West Germany, where 91 per cent said their income was sufficient. By contrast, in post-Communist countries with economies still in transformation less than 1 in 3 could get enough from the official economy to meet their needs.

## II  Comparing Germans in a united Germany

The collapse of the Wall shifted the comparison of Germans from an international to an inter-regional framework. Whereas East Germans appear privileged in comparison with other Communist societies, their position vis-à-vis West Germans is fundamentally different, because of having been socialized in a Communist system rather than a free society. Equally significant, West Germans have faced the unique problem of integrating a population increase of more than one-quarter within a few years, a challenge unprecedented in Europe since the end of the Second World War.

*Division and its legacy.* Prior to the creation of two German states, the population had lived in the same state for more than three-quarters of a century and in 1949 both East and West Germans experienced very similar living conditions. Women in East Germany could expect to live one year longer than women in West Germany. However, by the time of German re-unification, life expectancy had increased by 11 years in West Germany as against only seven years in East Germany (see Table 3.2).

Economic statistics are not comparable for the period when East and West Germany had fundamentally different economic systems. The conversion of East German into West German Marks at the rate of 1 for 1 was a political decision made without regard to living standards. Moreover, the integration of East Germany into

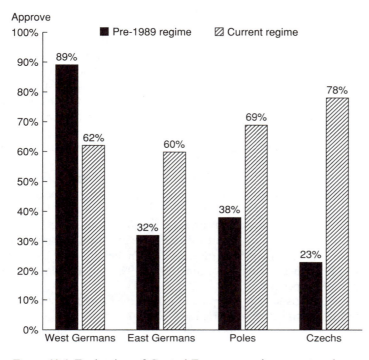

*Figure 12.1* Evaluation of Central European regimes, past and present.
Sources: Centre for the Study of Public Policy, New Europe Barometer, 1993; Richard Rose, Wolfgang Zapf and Wolfgang Seifert, *Germans in Comparative Perspective*, 1993.

the Soviet trading bloc meant that not only did fewer East Germans have cars than their Western cousins (Figure 3.1) but also that the quality was not comparable. This is illustrated by the collapse of the East German car industry after re-unification, as East Germans voted with their pocketbooks to abandon Trabis and Wartburgs for cars manufactured for sale in a market economy.

The fundamental political question in a society with a regime change is how people compare their old and new political systems. In East Germany, the basis for comparison is a Communist party-state and the Federal Republic. Even though institutions of governance have remained the same, the addition of five new Bundesländern has had a great impact too on West German society. Germans there were asked to evaluate the Federal Republic as it was before the turning point of 1990 and after re-unification.

Differences in context create differences in the evaluation of past regimes (Rose and Page, 1996). West Germans are virtually unanimous in positively evaluating the Federal Republic as it was before re-unification; 89 per cent are favourable (Figure 12.1). By contrast, only 32 per cent of East Germans were positive about their old regime. This is a reminder that the one-party state needed border guards ready to shoot to kill to keep a substantial portion of its population from escaping its repressive political system. The old regime's unpopularity was even greater than that of a Polish regime that had maintained martial law in the 1980s.

When East and West Germans are asked to evaluate the regime since re-unification, in arithmetic terms the answers are virtually identical; in both groups three-fifths are positive. However, because their pasts differ, the dynamics of opinion are radically different. Among East Germans, in comparison with the old regime the proportion viewing the Federal Republic favourably has almost doubled, thanks to the impact of a ready-made state. Among West Germans, however, the incorporation of East Germany into the Federal Republic has reduced approval by almost one-third (Figure 12.1). Although a majority remain positive, the percentage of West Germans positive about their political system in 1993 was lower than that of Czechs or Poles. Whereas for people who had recently been governed by Communists, a new regime struggling with transformation was preferable to the old, for West Germans whose political system was shocked by re-unification, more preferred the old regime to a regime that incorporated East Germans.

The legacy of the past also affects economic evaluations. Because of contrasts in context, 91 per cent of West Germans were positive about the country's social market economy before re-unification. Notwithstanding being relatively advantaged within the Communist bloc, only 36 per cent were positive about the GDR economic system. This reflects the familiarity that East Germans could gain with the market economy of West Germany through television and the visits of relatives. In neighbouring countries lacking integration with the West German economy, as of 1993, the old economy was endorsed by an average of 61 per cent.

While East and West Germans have participated in the same economic system since 1990, their subjective evaluations differ. Among East Germans 75 per cent gave a positive rating to the Federal Republic's system, nearly a third more than the 57 per cent of West Germans who did so. Due to the impact of a ready-made market economy, East Germans were also far more positive than Central Europeans about their new economic system. In the Czech Republic, Slovakia, Hungary and Poland, an average of 43 per cent were positive about the new economic system, a difference of 32 percentage points from East Germans.

When asked how long it would take before they had a standard of living with which they were content, 48 per cent of West Germans said that they were already content. Given decades of deprivation relative to West Germany, only 15 per cent of East Germans said that they were already content with their 1990s' living standards. While East Germans still felt the need to catch up with West Germans, the impact of re-unification has conferred economic advantages relative to others in post-Communist Central Europe. In 1993 only 3 per cent of New Europe Barometer respondents said that they were already content. Whereas 44 per cent of East Germans expected to be content with their standard of living in five years, in the neighbouring countries of the Czech Republic, Slovakia, Hungary and Poland, shortly after transformation only 14 per cent on average expected to be satisfied within five years.

## III  West Germans and Austrians compared

Germanic peoples have been a fact of political life in Central Europe for many centuries – but the division of Germanic peoples into states has followed a trial-and-error course, not least in the twentieth century. The creation of Austria as a separate state after the First World War was a byproduct of the collapse of the multinational Habsburg Empire and the very existence of the First Austrian Republic as a separate state was disputed by its citizens. Democratic institutions were subverted and in 1938 Austria was incorporated as a part of Hitler's Third Reich.

Like Germany, Austria was subject to four-power military occupation at the end of the Second World War. Soviet troops occupied eastern Austria, and Vienna, like Berlin, was under four-power occupation. American, British and French forces in western zones of the country could only gain access to the Austrian capital by going through Soviet-held territory. However, the outcome of four-power occupation was very different than in Germany. The 1955 peace treaty between the Second Austrian Republic and the occupying powers made Austria a neutral state that did not join NATO and Soviet forces were totally withdrawn. Since Czechoslovakia, Hungary and Poland had been independent since 1918, Austria had no territorial claims on countries in the Communist bloc.

As democracies with a market economy, the Federal Republic and the Second Austrian Republic have more in common with each other than either had with the East German Republic. While the collapse of the Iron Curtain had a big impact upon Austria as well as Germany, the significance was very different. Austria shares borders with Hungary, Slovenia, Slovakia and the Czech Republic and Vienna is closer to Croatia and Ukraine than to some other parts of Austria. The resulting free movement of goods, services and people has enabled Austria to resume historic ties with neighbouring countries formerly under Soviet domination. Whereas the Federal Republic has had to internalize the problems of the collapse of Communism through the integration of the former GDR, Austria has been a 'free rider' in the process of transformation. It has neither gained territory nor has it had to fund the transformation of a command economy into a modern market economy.

In social conditions, development in Austria has been similar to West Germany (Tables 3.1 and 3.2). However, politically, there is a fundamental difference: Austria was *not* disrupted by the collapse of Communism, whereas the politics of the Federal Republic has been greatly altered by re-unification. Thus, while West Germans can evaluate their regime separately before the collapse of Communism and today, this question is not meaningful to Austrians. Living in a stable system has made Austrians more positive about their current system of government than West or East Germans. In a 1991 New Europe Barometer survey, 79 per cent gave a positive assessment of the regime. This is 17 percentage points higher than the post-unification evaluation of West Germans. Even though re-unification greatly increased regime support among East Germans, it too remains lower than among Austrians (Figure 12.2).

The advantages of regime stability are also evident in the economic system. Before the fall of the Berlin Wall, West Germans were almost uniformly positive about the economic system; 91 per cent gave it a favourable rating. The shock of re-unification, however, caused the level of endorsement to fall to 57 per cent. In the absence of such a shock, no such fall occurred in Austria; 89 per cent of Austrians positively endorsed their economic system in the 1991 Barometer. East Germans are more positive about the Federal Republic's economic system than are West Germans. While the causes differ, three-quarters of East Germans as well as seven-eighths of Austrians similarly hold positive views of their economic systems.

Re-unification has shocked the economy of the Federal Republic. There have been big boosts in real wages and welfare payments to East Germans, but the costs of re-unification have been real too, given a legacy of non-competitive non-market industries and the billions invested in efforts to turn that economy around. The consequences of the fall of the Berlin Wall for Austria have been the opposite. Instead of having to incorporate the fall out of a command economy, it has enjoyed an

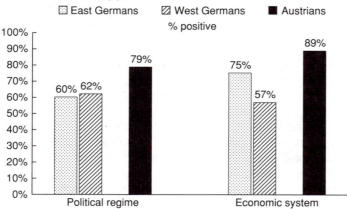

*Figure 12.2* Austrians and Germans evaluate regimes.
Sources: Austria: Centre for the Study of Public Policy, New Europe Barometer, 1991; Germany: Richard Rose, Wolfgang Zapf and Wolfgang Seifert, *Germans in Comparative Perspective*, 1993.

expansion of markets and trade with neighbouring countries no longer behind the Iron Curtain.

Immediately prior to re-unification, the living standard of the average Austrian, after adjusting for purchasing power parity, was about one-eighth less than of a German. The difference was sufficient to place Germany in the top group among OECD countries, whereas Austria was just below the middle. Since then, the Austrian economy has grown faster; between 1994 and 2004 its growth rate of 2.1 per cent per year was almost one-third greater than that of the post-unification German economy. The cumulative effect of such differences is a structural change in the two economies. The Organization for Economic Cooperation and Development (OECD) calculates that as of 2004, per capita income per head in Austria is now 8 per cent higher than in Germany. After taking into account differences in the cost of living in the two countries, the Austrian advantage rises to 11 per cent.

*Different combinations of advantages and handicaps.* While living in the GDR, East Germans were economically advantaged relative to people in other Communist countries. Yet these advantages came at a high cost. Like subjects of other Communist-bloc countries, East Germans had to live four decades in a repressive political regime. Even though East Germans were able to outpace Poland and Russia in socio-economic development, their living standards were well below that of the Federal Republic. Today, East Germans are uniquely privileged among the peoples of the former Communist bloc through the impact of becoming part of a ready-made state, the Federal Republic of Germany.

Throughout the Cold War era, citizens of the Federal Republic were privileged in living in a democratic Rechtsstaat and a prosperous market economy. This was achieved the hard way. Defeat in the Second World War not only imposed a moral burden on Germans but also a very substantial material burden; the reconstruction of post-1945 Germany took two decades. The collapse of the Soviet system enabled the Federal Republic to achieve the unity and freedom of Germany. However, the integration of two populations that had lived apart for four decades has been a difficult process. Among EU member states, West Germans are having to finance the transformation of a Communist system into an integral part of their state.

Austrians have benefited the most. After having shared in the military defeat of the Third Reich and four-power occupation, the country achieved independence without division in 1955. Vienna, unlike Berlin, was no longer patrolled by armies of four powers. Austria built a democratic Rechtsstaat on the basis of a consensus forged during 17 years of being dominated by Nazi and then Soviet forces. Concurrently, it created a prosperous social market economy. The fall of the Iron Curtain has brought economic and political benefits. Since neighbouring states have kept what they had sought for a century, political independence, they have no claims on the fiscal resources of Austria.

The complex sequence of events in Central Europe since 1945 rejects a simple deterministic explanation. The initial conditions were determined by the power of the Soviet Union and the United States. The position of East Germany and West Germany when the Berlin Wall fell in 1989 reflected decisions taken in the late 1940s; that of Austria reflected decisions taken between 1945 and 1955. These decisions set societies on different paths that became part of the inheritance of the Federal Republic after re-unification and of Austria after its neighbours became free to 'return to Europe'.

Change happened unexpectedly and abruptly. Machiavelli attributed inexplicable leaps in circumstances to *fortuna*. In modern German history *calamità* would be a more apt term, for many fateful events have been disastrous. The outcome of this process has left some people absolutely privileged, such as Austrians; some relatively advantaged, such as East Germans vis-à-vis peoples in other post-Communist countries; while West Germans have had to adapt to the price of re-unification.

# 13 Ex-Communists in post-Communist societies

Once an opportunist, always an opportunist.

(Anonymous, after Joseph Schumpeter)

Communist regimes are no more and party banners and membership badges are now hawked as souvenirs from Moscow to the Brandenburg Gate in Berlin. But what has happened to the tens of millions of people who were card-carrying members of a Communist Party before their Party collapsed? Do people who are now ex-Communists maintain Communist values?

Because the Communist Party was the only party during the political lifetime of activists, at the launch of the new democracies ex-Party members and dissenters from the Party were the only source of experienced politicians. Boris Yeltsin started out his political career working for the Party and then fell out with its leadership. New entrants to politics were by definition amateurs, whether coffee-house intellectuals or people trusted by their local community. The success of democratization in post-Communist countries has thus required the involvement of ex-Communists, for their numbers are too numerous and their political skills too great to be ignored. However, the combination of politicians who are too experienced in the ways of the old regime and those who are too inexperienced in dealing with political problems has encouraged popular scepticism and distrust.

The first round of free elections almost everywhere resulted in the repudiation of Communist parties, but the second round saw a revival of popular support for parties descended from the former ruling party. In Poland and Hungary, parties of ex-Communists won the largest share of the popular vote, and the Bulgarian Socialist Party has consistently remained a political force. The size of the vote for ex-Communist parties has often been too big to be ignored, but interpretation is ambiguous.

Insofar as Communist Party members were ideological true believers, then 'once a Communist, always a Communist'. However, insofar as Party membership was an opportunistic means for making a career, individuals should have no problem in dropping ideological baggage that is now a handicap. This follows from Joseph Schumpeter's (1952: 279) dictum that, in electoral competition, 'victory over the opponent' is the goal, and the production of programmes and ideologies is only incidental to this end. Just as a garment manufacturer is a profit-seeking businessman attuned to market opportunities, so a vote-seeking politician is dealing in votes, and must follow changes in fashion in the electorate. Such politicians can alter their behaviour in keeping with a change in the rules of the political game. Insofar as the large size of the Party meant that members were not a cohesive bloc but a 'catch all' coalition of people from all major sections of society, they could endorse inclusive slogans as vague as the 'third way' appeals of a Clinton or a Blair. In this model, people became Communists for the same reason that school teachers became Labour in County Durham or bankers become Democrats in American states dominated by that party: to get on in the world.

## I Alternative motives for joining the Party

Before seizing power, Communists could be perceived as a revolutionary coterie of true believers who dedicated their lives to propagating Marxism through deeds as well as words. This belief was shared by individuals as different as Lenin and J. Edgar Hoover. Ideological commitment was shown by the willingness of Communists to sacrifice everything for the Party, including their lives, the lives of others and historical truth.

After seizing power, Communist parties became 'organizational weapons' mobilizing support for the party-state. They sought to indoctrinate the mass of the population in Marxist-Leninist beliefs and to recruit millions of members to the Party. The intent was to integrate all major groups within society into the Communist way of working and thinking. However, the larger the Party membership, the lower the likely level of ideological commitment. In democratic societies many rank-and-file party members have a non-ideological attachment to a party. On such a reckoning, the transformation of Communist organizations from vanguard to mass mobilization parties meant the end of ideological commitment.

In the post-Stalinist era, revolutionary ideals were no longer necessary and could even be embarrassing when Party leaders embroiled in directing an anti-modern system responded to problems without regard to, or even in contradiction to Marxist-Leninist principles. The growth of government institutions in the Soviet Union created a tension between the Party, which based its authority on ideology, and government bureaucrats and technocrats, who justified actions on the grounds of expertise and effectiveness.

For party apparatchiks politics was no longer a calling requiring sacrifice but a job like any other. Apparatchiks lived from politics rather than for politics. A middle-aged official was at least two generations removed from the era of heroic struggle and a generation removed from the twists and turns of Communist politics from the Nazi–Soviet pact to de-Stalinization. The leadership's policy of 'proletarianizing' the Party meant that many activists depended solely upon the Party for their wellbeing, as it promoted them to a higher station in life than they could otherwise earn. Because power was as important as money in allocating privileges, the elite members in the nomenklatura enjoyed a better lifestyle than the masses. The Communist patronage system produced loyalty, but it also produced cynicism. In Central and Eastern Europe the ultimate insult was to say that a Party official actually believed the party line that he (it was rarely a she) was parroting.

Careerism and opportunism were important motivations for Russians to join the Party in the days of the Soviet Union. In this sense, Communists were no different from other people pursuing their self-interest. Three-quarters saw Party membership as a means of getting a job or promotion, and more than two-thirds saw Communists as people who had joined the Party to advance their own self-interest rather than the interests of society or of the working class (Table 13.1). Less than half saw Communists as motivated by ideals or the desire to help other people. A description of

*Table 13.1* Reasons Russians belonged to the Party

*Q. Which of these phrases do you think describes people who were formerly Communist Party members?*

|  | *Members* | *Non-members* (*% Russians agreeing*) | *Difference* |
|---|---|---|---|
| *Careerism, opportunism* | | | |
| To get job or promotion | 74 | 76 | 2 |
| Used Party for own purpose | 64 | 72 | 8 |
| Dishonest | 29 | 38 | 9 |
| *Altruism* | | | |
| Try to help other people | 55 | 43 | 12 |
| Idealists | 46 | 44 | 2 |
| *Other* | | | |
| Ordinary people, same as everyone | 73 | 66 | 7 |
| Intelligent | 55 | 46 | 9 |

Source: Centre for the Study of Public Policy, New Russia Barometer, 1995. Ex-Communists include individuals with Party members in the family, as their views are similar to those who were members.

Communists as intelligent is ambiguous, for a Party card could enable an individual to behave honestly or dishonestly, depending on the incentives of the moment.

The image of Party members is similar among those who belonged to the Party or had a family member in the Party and those who did not. This indicates a matter-of-fact attitude toward an institution accepted as a part of society, for better and for worse. Ex-Communists tended to have a slightly more favourable view of motives than non-Communists, but the striking fact is that across seven questions the average difference in opinions was only 7 per cent, and statistically insignificant on the big issues: the use of Party membership to get a job or promotion.

Insofar as idealists existed in Communist countries in the 1980s, they were dissidents from the party line, individuals who denounced the party-state on principle, even though it jeopardized their careers and could invite surveillance and restrictions that made their lives difficult. The chief difference between dissidents was whether they were licensed by the Party to voice disagreements or whether they held the morally stronger but politically weaker position of being outside the Party.

## II  What do ex-Communists think?

Many millions of former members of the Communist Party remain in their native country today; new regimes did not drive them into exile or strip Party members of their rights as citizens. This raises the paradoxical question: How Communist were Communists? To find an answer, the 1993 New Europe Barometer asked about Party membership in five Central and East European countries, the Czech Republic, Slovakia, Poland, Bulgaria and Romania and in spring 1995 in Russia. The variety of countries provides a robust basis for generalization, since the Communist Party's role was not the same in all of these countries.

People showed no hesitancy in answering a question about Party membership. Less than 1 per cent of Russians and in the Central and East European countries an average of 4 per cent gave no reply. In Russia 33 per cent reported that they or someone in their family had been a Party member, and in the five CEE countries it was an average of 34 per cent. As would be expected statistically, respondents saying that they were Party members were slightly less numerous than those saying another person in their family was a member. These figures are consistent with official statistics on Party membership.

Whatever the national context, the essential issue is: Do ex-Communists have different political values from their fellow citizens? The theory of Communists as ideologues predicts that people who were connected with the Party should differ greatly in fundamental values from fellow citizens who were not committed to the Party. But insofar as Party members were opportunists or simply assigned a Party card as part of its strategy of maximizing membership without regard to ideological commitment, then ex-Communists and non-Communists should be similar in their political views.

An assessment of the past is the starting point, since Party loyalties were formed through political socialization in a Communist regime. When asked, both Communists and ex-Communists are divided in their opinions on the old regime (Table 13.2). Differences between countries are greater than differences between Communists and ex-Communists within a country. In Russia, as many as 67 per cent spoke favourably of the old regime and in Hungary, the most liberal of the CEE Communist bloc, more than three-fifths did so. The relatively positive response in Slovakia undoubtedly reflects the conflation of the old Communist regime and the Czechoslovak state. By contrast, in the Czech Republic only 23 per cent were positive. Ex-Communists were usually only a few percentage points more likely to approve the old system.

When people were asked to evaluate the old command economy, a more positive picture appears. In six of the seven countries, many were favourable about the command economy, albeit with differences between the 79 per cent favourable in Russia and the 42 per cent among Czechs. Within each country, differences between Communists and non-Communists within a country are small.

Insofar as Communists identified their lives with the old regime, then they ought to be very negative about the regime that destroyed the Communist monopoly of power.

*Table 13.2* Ex-Communists and non-Communists evaluate regimes

|  | BUL | CZE | HUN | POL | ROM | SVK | NEB mean | RUS |
|---|---|---|---|---|---|---|---|---|
|  |  |  |  | *(% positive)* |  |  |  |  |
| *Approve Communist political regime* |  |  |  |  |  |  |  |  |
| Ex-Communists | 59 | 33 | 63 | 40 | 35 | 57 | 47 | 66 |
| Non-Communists | 49 | 18 | 54 | 37 | 29 | 48 | 39 | 67 |
| Difference | 10 | 15 | 9 | 3 | 6 | 9 | 8 | −1 |
| *Approve current political regime* |  |  |  |  |  |  |  |  |
| Non-Communists | 61 | 80 | 49 | 71 | 55 | 55 | 63 | 26 |
| Ex-Communists | 56 | 74 | 52 | 62 | 63 | 44 | 59 | 26 |
| Difference | 5 | 6 | 3 | 9 | −8 | 11 | −4 | 0 |
| *Approve political regime in future* |  |  |  |  |  |  |  |  |
| Non-Communists | 72 | 89 | 67 | 86 | 70 | 79 | 78 | 40 |
| Ex-Communists | 72 | 85 | 73 | 81 | 80 | 78 | 78 | 40 |
| Difference | 0 | 4 | 6 | 5 | −10 | 1 | 0 | 0 |

Sources: Centre for the Study of Public Policy, New Europe Barometer, 1993; New Russia Barometer, 1995. For Hungary: New Europe Barometer, 1995.

In fact, ex-Communists were not committed partisans, for they are about as likely as their fellow citizens to endorse the new regime (Table 13.2). In most countries surveyed, majorities of ex-Communists as well as non-Communists expressed a positive view of the new political system while in Russia there was agreement across party lines in being very negative about the first term of the Yeltsin administration. It is particularly striking that in Romania ex-Communists are even more likely than non-Communists to support the new regime, a comment on what it was like to be working for the party of Nicolae Ceausescu.

While journalists could always point to examples of ex-nomenklatura members (and non-Party members too) who struck it rich amidst the turbulence of transformation, inflation affected people regardless of their political past. When asked to compare their household's economic situation in the early 1990s with its situation under the previous regime, in every country a majority described it as worse than before. Such differences as there are between ex-Communists and non-Communists are either statistically insignificant or marginal. When asked to evaluate an economic system in transformation, non-Communists and ex-Communists tended to agree in giving it a negative rating.

Evaluations of what society will be like in five years could express hopes or fears, since the past is no guide to the future in a system in transformation. Expectations of the future showed no difference between ex-Communists and people who never had any Communist Party links (Table 13.2). Throughout Central and Eastern Europe big majorities in both groups are positive about the political future in comparison to the present. In Hungary ex-Communists are even more positive than non-Communists, reflecting self-confidence in their ability to seize opportunities whatever the political conditions. In Russia there was no difference in expectations between ex-Communists and non-Communists. In addition, big majorities are optimistic that the introduction of the market will bring benefits before too long. In short, the key part of the 'ex-Communist' label is 'ex' or even 'never was'.

## III Abandoning undemocratic alternatives

In a democracy the job of the opposition is to oppose – and as long as opposition does not mobilize support for undemocratic alternatives then the regime is secure. In post-Communist countries undemocratic alternatives were not confined to textbooks of political theory: they could be taken from the country's recent past, in which both Communist rule and non-Communist dictatorships had featured. In the early 1990s it was thus an open question how much support there was for autocratic as well as democratic alternatives to the government of the day.

Among ex-Communists as well as non-Communists, support for a return to Communist rule has been limited. When asked point blank, less than 1 in 5 NEB respondents endorsed doing so; in Russia less than 2 in 5 did so (Table 13.3). Equally striking, there was no substantive difference in views between ex-Communists and non-Party members. For example, in the Czech Republic 89 per cent of Party members and 96 per cent of non-members rejected this alternative.

Positive evaluation of the Communist regime is not the same as support for a return to the status quo ante. Across Central and Eastern Europe, the majority, 55 per cent, was definitely anti-Communist, disapproving of the old political regime and not wanting it back. The second largest group, 26 per cent, felt nostalgia, being positive toward

*Table 13.3* Communist ties and support for alternative regimes

| | BUL | CZE | HUN | POL | ROM | SVK | NEB mean | RUS |
|---|---|---|---|---|---|---|---|---|
| | | | | (% agree) | | | | |
| *Favour return to Communist rule* | | | | | | | | |
| Ex-Communists | 29 | 11 | 26 | 17 | 12 | 18 | 18 | 36 |
| Non-Communists | 22 | 4 | 18 | 18 | 13 | 15 | 13 | 30 |
| Difference | 7 | 7 | 8 | −1 | −1 | 3 | 5 | 6 |
| *Approve dictator ruling in place of parliament* | | | | | | | | |
| Ex-Communists | 44 | 15 | 18 | 33 | 28 | 22 | 27 | 55 |
| Non-Communists | 46 | 17 | 22 | 36 | 37 | 25 | 31 | 46 |
| Difference | −2 | −2 | −4 | −3 | −9 | −3 | −4 | −9 |

Sources: Centre for the Study of Public Policy, New Europe Barometer, 1993; New Russia Barometer, 1995. For Hungary: New Europe Barometer, 1995.

the old regime but not wanting to see it restored. Reactionaries favouring the old regime and wanting it back made up only 12 per cent of respondents in Central and Eastern Europe. The few remaining disapproved of democratic pluralism so much that they saw the return of an unsatisfactory Communist regime as the lesser evil.

There has been greater support for a dictator replacing parliament than for a return to Communist rule. However, this alternative was rejected by more than two-thirds of Central and Eastern Europeans in 1993. The small difference in views between ex-Communists and those who had never belonged to the Party was actually due to non-Communists being on average 4 percentage points more in favour of a dictatorship (Table 13.3).

The position of the Party and the state has been different in Russia. The Communist Party of the Russian Federation has retained its links with the past – but this has not been to its electoral advantage. In the 1996 presidential election Boris Yeltsin campaigned as an anti-Communist against a Communist opponent, Gennady Zyuganov, who won almost the same share of the vote as Yeltsin in the first-round ballot. When push came to shove, those who rejected both candidates in the first round came down in favour of Yeltsin by a margin of 7 to 3, thus giving him the absolute majority needed to retain the presidency. Vladimir Putin has given priority to the role of the state rather than that of the Party. Serving the party-state as a KGB intelligence officer was different from serving it as a Party apparatchik. Electorally, he has marginalized the role of the Communist Party by building a 'catch all' party, United Russia.

Transformation is about breaking the link with the past and generational change gradually attenuates knowledge of the past, as those who were old enough to have been recruited into the Party of the party-state die off and an increasing proportion of the population is too young to have been indoctrinated with Communist ideology at school.

Age does make a difference in the desire for the return of a Communist regime. Consistently, the oldest generation is the most reactionary politically while those under the age of 30 are least supportive of a return to the old regime. In Russia, for example, more than half of those old enough to remember the Second World War say they would like to see the Communist regime back; by contrast, less than a sixth of the glasnost generation want to see their newly opened society once again controlled by commissars. Moreover, when the views of Party members and non-members are broken down by generation, in each generation older Party members are more likely to approve of the Communist regime.

However, generational change is slow-moving. If one simply waited for endorsement of Communism to die out in the literal sense, then it would take until the second quarter of the twenty-first century for this to happen. But such a view is mistaken, for it does not take into account the motives that led many people to become Party members. In a country in which a Communist regime controlled all the major resources of society, such as housing, and access to shops selling privileged goods, joining the party in power was the way to get ahead. Refusing to join the Party led to a loss of opportunities. The collapse of Communist party-states put an end to that Party's monopoly of privileges.

It is not necessary to wait for the turnover of generations for significant changes in attitudes to occur. Transformation and its aftermath have been big shocks for all ages in society. Even if older people are unable to start a new career, they can see their children and grandchildren enjoying opportunities that they could never have hoped for. Analysis of New Europe Barometer surveys shows that older as well as young people are not set in their ways. Even though differences between generations remain, all ages become more positive when there are positive political developments and all ages become more negative when there are negative developments (Mishler and Rose, 2007).

Big changes on the supply side of politics have helped bury Communist parties too. Institutional transformation meant that it no longer paid to be a Communist, for the Party no longer had privileges to dispense. Furthermore, if ex-Communists want to make money and live well they do not need to proclaim Marxist shibboleths; they could sell cars, go into real estate or peddle influence based on personal connections accumulated in nomenklatura days.

Ex-Communists who compete in elections have demonstrated the aptness of the old dictum: 'Once an opportunist, always an opportunist'. Throughout Central and Eastern Europe, Communist activists purged themselves of past associations by abandoning the name of the old party, while using its assets to build a new party criticizing transformation from a populist, social democratic and/or nationalist perspective. The idea of a one-party state has been abandoned. In its place former Communists invoke the economic security that some people felt the old order offered, albeit at a price. In consequence, by the mid-1990s parties launched by former Communists were winning votes and in Poland and Hungary forming the government by ousting the anti-Communist winners of the first free elections.

The adaptability of ex-Communists to electoral competition presented the Socialist International, an international association of social democrats, with an awkward choice: it could either accept parties formed by former Communists as members or it could grant membership to new parties formed by people who had proven their social democratic values under the old regime by being dissident critics of the party-state. The argument for accepting the former was that they were often winning votes and office; the case for the latter was that they had much better credentials as democrats and as socialists. In the event, the Socialist International responded in Bulgaria, Hungary and Poland by granting membership to a party of ex-Communists that wins lots of votes and a party of committed social democrats that does not. In doing so it has thus confirmed that the attachment of ex-Communists was not to advancing an ideology but to advancing themselves.

# Part IV
# Elections after transformation

# 14 Parties without civil society

To say that voters are free to decide who to vote for is meaningful only in the sense that everyone is free to start another textile mill.

(Joseph Schumpeter)

The liberal theory of democracy is demand-driven: voters decide what they want and politicians compete to supply their wishes. By contrast, a realist theory is supply-driven: elites decide which parties appear on the ballot and voters choose from the menu that the elites supply. Both supply and demand are combined in Joseph Schumpeter's theory of democracy as duopolistic competition. Elections are reduced to a choice between a party in government and an opposition out of power. If satisfied with what government is doing, voters can endorse the In party, and if dissatisfied they can dismiss it by voting for the Out party. But for this to happen, elites must organize political parties.

In Western Europe organizations representing major interests in civil society, such as chambers of commerce, trade unions, agricultural and ethnic associations, were active in promoting democratization. As the right to vote was broadened, political parties were established in association with civil-society organizations. Political socialization in farmers' organizations, trade unions, church schools and ethnic associations created loyalties among people who did not have the right to vote. European socialist parties were often organized as a part of the campaign to ensure all working-class men the right to vote. Parents often transmitted group and party loyalties to their children before they were old enough to vote. These links created the basis for stable parties and durable party identifications.

In the regimes that filled the void created by the collapse of the Communist party-state, there was an urgent need to hold competitive elections to confirm that the old regime was truly gone. So fast and unexpected was the collapse of Communist regimes in autumn 1989 that there was no time to find out what people wanted. Nor could elites look to the institutions of civil society to organize parties, because Communist regimes denied the right of civil society to exist. The regimes only tolerated trade unions, business associations, media and cultural organizations that were controlled by Communist commissars.

In conditions of great uncertainty elites first had to agree the rules of an electoral system. There was overwhelming agreement that every citizen age 18 or older should have the right to vote and that there should be a parliament to hold the government accountable. In the light of past experience, Central and East European politicians did not want a president who might become a dictator. By contrast, post-Soviet states favoured a strong president with centralized powers.

To represent an unknown number of diverse views and interests, there was agreement on proportional representation (PR) to elect many or all Members of Parliament. Since proportional representation awards seats in parliament according to a party's share of the vote, even when voters endorse a particular candidate on a party's list, votes for all its candidates are added up to determine how many seats the party gets. Thus, before the first free election could be held, elites also had to organize parties.

## I Organizing parties from scratch

Politicians wanting to organize parties have two broad alternatives: to create parties based on historic social divisions or to create new institutions with fresh appeals. Parties organized to represent durable divisions within civil society have stamina: in France, Germany and Austria many parties have persisted from one regime to the next. However, the legacy of four decades of Communist rule left great discontinuities. When Soviet forces advanced across Eastern Europe, they were accompanied by political commissars. Non-Communist political leaders from the prewar era were threatened with exile, deportation, imprisonment or execution. For example, in Bulgaria Nikola Petkov, leader of the chief opposition party to the new regime, was arrested in 1947, charged with treason, and hanged. In Czechoslovakia the Communist takeover was sealed in 1948 when Foreign Minister Jan Masaryk was found dead after being taken into custody. Popular-front governments with Communists in key positions were established, and non-Communists were quickly eliminated.

Differences of opinion could be debated within the Communist Party and, with the decay of the Party's totalitarian zeal, dissident opinions could sometimes be voiced outside its ranks. However, while dissidents were allowed to speak they were not allowed to form competing organizations. The Polish Solidarity movement was a great exception, but its activities were repressed by martial law and it could not appear on a ballot until 1989. Many dissidents associated party politics with Communist-style repression, hypocrisy and corruption. In the words of Václav Havel, leader of the Czech dissidents, 'Parties are for [Communist] party members; the Civic Forum is for all' (quoted in Olson, 1993: 642).

To create a party requires organization by political entrepreneurs. Former Communist activists were the most experienced political entrepreneurs. Their Party ties were both an asset and a liability. Communists had skills useful in party organization and networks extending across many institutions. But especially in Central and Eastern Europe, identification with the old regime was a liability, because only a small fraction of the electorate wanted to return to the past. In such circumstances, many Communist Party workers left party politics while those who remained in party politics have joined in freshly named parties. In Hungary, the leader of the Socialist (that is, ex-Communist) Party, Gyula Horn, campaigned against an ineffectual conservative government with the slogan, 'Let the experts govern'. In Bulgaria the Socialist (that is, ex-Communist) Party has maintained itself through patronage networks.

While anti-Communist movements could maintain unity in the face of a common enemy, dissidents had no experience of organizing mass movements. They were 'more like tribes than parties, being held together by friendship ties and opposition to the Communist regime' (Lomax, 1995: 185f). Often, dissidents did not share a common positive set of beliefs. Free elections created a quandary for politicians. The choice was no longer between the Communist Party and their critics, a conflict that could be framed in the 'language of philosophic and moral absolutes, of right against wrong, love against hate, truth against falsehood' (Garton Ash, 1990: 51f). Instead, elections involved competition among a wide range of non-Communist, anti-Communist and ex-Communist groups.

When civic movements sought to develop a party for post-Communist politics, they failed. This was spectacularly demonstrated in Poland. Solidarity leader Lech Walesa won only 40 per cent of the vote in the first presidential election ballot and by 1993 Solidarity was an also-ran party. In Czechoslovakia the linked Czech and Slovak protest movements, Civic Forum and Public Against Violence, cooperated successfully in contesting the 1990 election, but both parties disappeared before the 1992 election that led to the break-up of the state.

Political amateurs outside politics during the Communist regime have been a third source of party leaders. Abstention from politics under the old regime enabled amateurs to offer a fresh approach to national issues and many claimed they would act for the good of all. However, goodwill is insufficient to maintain a political party. Amateurs quickly had to learn how to manage differences of opinion about how the common good is defined or else leave the arena of democratic party competition.

To participate in the new politics, political elites had to create organizations that would be legally recognized as parties by the national election commissions; recruit candidates and agree their order on the party list; file nomination papers to gain a place on the ballot; conduct a nationwide election campaign; and raise money to pay for all these activities. All this had to be done under great pressure from the electoral calendar. Virtually every party contesting the first election was created just a few months before the vote was called.

Election laws have made it easy for groups to register as parties and qualify for a place on the ballot. In every post-Communist country dozens of new parties have been formed in celebration of freedom. However, many have been 'sofa parties', for their membership would not fill all the furniture in a room, let alone fill a ballot box with votes. In Romania, even though there were fewer than ten weeks between the adoption of an election law and the 1990 parliamentary election, 60 parties nominated lists of candidates. However, 51 parties did not win a single seat and the average vote of these losers was only one-seventh of 1 per cent.

## II  Appealing in many dimensions

Parties can appeal on the basis of policies reflecting the interests of distinctive groups, such as farmers or an ethnic minority. In conditions of high uncertainty, it can be an advantage to focus on a well-defined social or political group. In a proportional-representation system, the target group does not need to be large, for as long as the party gets enough votes to clear the threshold for being allocated seats, usually no more than 5 per cent, it can sit in parliament and may even become a partner in a coalition government. However, in the absence of institutions to mobilize support from specific interests, such an appeal may fail to win enough votes to qualify for seats in parliament or face a low ceiling on its support.

By contrast, a party can make a 'fuzzy-focus' appeal for votes on the grounds that it will defend a vaguely defined national interest or its leader is trustworthy and competent. Slogans such as 'Let's go' or 'Vote for a brighter future' do not give any indication about the intended direction of future change. Like an indeterminately shaped ink blot, fuzzy-focus parties can encourage voters to see in them what they want. A group calling itself the People's Party leaves open what sorts of people it appeals to and competitors do not want to oppose it on the grounds that they are anti-people. Vladimir Putin's United Russia party is an example of a fuzzy-focus party. A fuzzy-focus party has the potential to gather a large share of the popular vote; however, there is no core of support to guarantee it electoral support if its leader proves untrustworthy or incompetent.

Free elections have demonstrated the truth of the old political adage: 'There is only one way to stand still, but there are many ways to go forward'. The many parties competing in post-Communist elections include those of anti-Communists and of ex-Communists, parties that hark back to pre-1945 cultural traditions, parties that emphasize current economic interests, whether social democratic or free market and new parties proclaiming green values or appealing for votes on the grounds of their leader's personality.

*Multiple dimensions of party competition.* A system is defined by the way in which its constituent parts are combined in relation to each other; thus, a party system is defined by the dimensions on which parties compete. The simplest model of structured competition is that of competition along a single dimension defined by economic interests and labelled left versus right. However, in a system with more than half a dozen parties, there is no reason to expect competition to be restricted to a single dimension. Left and rightwing parties can co-exist with parties appealing on the basis of religion, as in Northern Ireland; parties can be differentiated by language and ethnicity, as in Canada; or even more dimensions, as in Belgium, where parties differ along lines of language, religious and economic interests. Within a system, some parties can place themselves outside these dimensions by making a fuzzy-focus appeal. If all parties do so, then electoral competition will be completely unstructured and there is likely to be a lot of volatility in voting from one election to the next.

To determine how electors see party competition, the New Europe Barometer asks people to identify, from a list of six dimensions, the one or two that they think best fits their country (Figure 14.1). A big majority of electors see party competition occurring along a multiplicity of dimensions. Altogether, 75 per cent have no difficulty in identifying two dimensions, 18 per cent say they don't know how parties differ, and only 7 per cent see parties as competing along a single dimension.

In the eyes of the electorate, party systems of new European democracies are fragmented, for there is no agreement on what party competition is about. Distinctions between left and right are not the only differences that matter: distinctions between association with or opposition to the Communist regime, or being a party of personality or of ideas are equally important. In 9 out of 10 countries, no dimension of party competition is named by as much as half of the electorate. In five countries – the Czech Republic, Slovakia, Romania, Slovenia, and Estonia – at least one-quarter name three different dimensions as important and in Hungary and Lithuania five different dimensions of competition are identified as important by at least one-fifth of the electorate. Over all, four different dimensions of party competition are seen as salient by about one-third of voters.

For 33 per cent, the choice at the ballot box is between parties with policies and parties with personalities. This does not reflect a reversion to the interwar appeal of

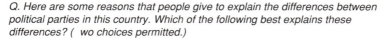

*Q. Here are some reasons that people give to explain the differences between political parties in this country. Which of the following best explains these differences? ( wo choices permitted.)*

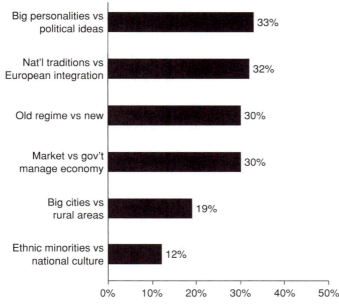

*Figure 14.1* Dimensions of party competition.
Source: Centre for the Study of Public Policy, New Europe Barometer, 2001.

dictatorship by a strong man but of new parties embracing the personalistic appeals of American-style election campaigns. Even if a party's leader is not especially personable, public-relations techniques can exploit the inevitable television prominence of a leader. For example, in the first Hungarian election, the German advisers of one party even flew in a hairdresser from Germany to give their candidate a makeover.

The term 'charismatic leader' is often misused as a description of any party leader who wins an election. Strictly speaking, the term describes a leader with a following so strong that he or she can overturn the established institutions of a regime. Lenin was such a leader, and so too was Charles de Gaulle. In post-Communist societies, only Vladimir Meciar of Slovakia could claim to have used his appeal to break up a political regime, the federal state of Czechoslovakia. This ex-boxer was a major figure in the Slovak movement, Public Against Violence; he left it in 1991 to found a nationalist party, the Movement for a Democratic Slovakia. His campaign for greater powers for Slovakia snowballed into the break up of the Federation into two independent states. In Russia Vladimir Putin has done the opposite: he has used his personal appeal to 'tighten up' rather than break-up the institutions of the Russian Federation. By producing a resounding election victory for his successor and claiming the constitutional office of Prime Minister for himself, Putin has shown an aptitude for institutionalizing his personal appeal.

Post-Communist countries differ in whether the head of state, the President, is popularly elected. Where this occurs, as in Bulgaria, Poland and Romania, the requirement for the winner to have an absolute majority of the vote normally results in a large number of independent as well as partisan candidates in the first ballot and the second-round victory going to the candidate who can appeal to a coalition of partisan and independent voters. Presidential ballots show the limits of personal appeal. In Poland, for example, the Solidarity leader, Lech Walesa, was forced into a second-round run-off to win his first presidential contest; in 1995 he won only one-third of the first-round vote and lost in the run-off; and in 2000 he finished seventh with only 1 per cent of the vote.

Voters see political ideas as the alternative to political beauty contests, but there is no agreement about the most important dimensions of policy that differentiate parties (Figure 14.1). A distinctive feature of Central and East European politics is the importance given by the electorate to a party's endorsement or rejection of the previous regime. Some parties emphasize the positive achievements of the past, for example, stable prices and full employment, and claim they can achieve these benefits without the costs that the old regime imposed. Other parties attack the past regime as anti-modern, suppressing individual and national freedom and depressing economic growth. While parties and politicians associated with the Communist regime may not want to boast of this fact, competitors with anti-Communist credentials do have an incentive to highlight this when competing with parties that lack such an appeal.

Transformation was both backward-facing and forward-looking and this too provides grounds for party competition. It meant the recovery of independence from domination by the Soviet Union and created the opportunity for Central and East European states to become members of the European Union. When the NEB survey analyzed here was conducted, negotiations for membership were well advanced. An incidental consequence was that this encouraged nationalist politicians to charge that EU membership would threaten national traditions. The contrast between European and traditional parties was seen as important by almost one-third of NEB respondents, and deemed important in every country.

Whether the government or the market should be most important in making economic decisions differentiates parties throughout Europe. It has a special salience in societies experiencing the transformation of a command into a market economy. It is thus striking that less than 1 in 3 of post-transformation citizens see the economy as a major dimension differentiating parties. In addition 1 in 5 see differences between urban and rural interests as a dimension of party competition. Political and cultural dimensions of party competition are mentioned twice as often as economic differences.

For most of history, the peoples of Central and Eastern Europe lived in multinational states. However, the Holocaust and devastation of the Second World War reduced the size and variety of minority populations. The fall of Communist regimes increased ethnic homogeneity with the break-up of Communist states along ethnic lines. Of 10 Central and East European countries, six came into existence after the fall of the Berlin Wall. The limited size of ethnic minorities today has meant that parties appealing to such groups gain few if any seats in parliament. In Estonia and Latvia, where Russians constitute more than one-third of residents, polarization between majority and minority ethnic parties does not occur because most Russian ethnics do not have Baltic citizenship or the right to vote. Across the region, relatively few citizens see ethnic differences as a major source of differentiation between parties.

The uncertainties of competitive elections and the ease of placing parties on the ballot have led to all sorts of novel parties appearing on the ballot. For example, in Poland a Beer Lovers party won seats at the first free election and in Estonia a Royalist party did so. However, none of these novel parties has managed to secure a durable position in its party system.

In 1990 the general principle – free elections 'can delegitimate just as easily as they legitimate new political regimes' (White, 1990: 285) – had particular salience. Given the twentieth-century history of Central and Eastern Europe, there were grounds for anxiety that parties would gain votes by offering to deal with the problems of transformation by replacing a democratic with an autocratic regime. In the event, the appearance of undemocratic parties on the ballot has shown the weakness rather than the strength of their popular appeal. Parties of the radical right receive few votes. In Romania, virulent nationalist and radical right parties win upwards of one-eighth of the vote. In Hungary the Justice and Life Party, founded by an anti-Semitic rightwing leader, Istvan Csurka, has failed to attract a significant electoral following. In no Central or East European country has an anti-democratic party won the quarter of the vote that Vladimir Zhirinovsky's extreme nationalist party took in the December 1993 Russian parliamentary election.

## III Counting and weighing parties

The starting point for the post-transformation party systems was the creative destruction of the party-state. Disoriented politicians launched parties with many different appeals; not surprisingly, their efforts often met with little success. Citizens were disoriented, for instead of being compelled to endorse a one-party regime they were suddenly free to vote for a party that actually represented their views – if only they could figure out which party that might be.

*A proliferation of parties.* The transformation of politics has been accompanied by the multiplication of parties (Figure 14.2). However, the more parties there are on the ballot at a given election, the less the average vote for a party. Moreover, since some parties do better than average, others do worse or fail to win seats in parliament.

Between 1990 and 2007, 53 parliamentary elections were held in 10 Central and East European countries and almost 300 succeeded at least once in gaining 1 per cent or more of the vote or two seats in parliament (Figure 14.2). The average country has therefore had 29 parties in its party system. Poland has had the most parties, 35. President Lech Walesa described party competition there as 'excessively democratic' (quoted in Webb, 1992: 166). In Russia, even more parties, 37, have won at least 1 per cent of the vote in Duma elections. Due to complex electoral laws affecting the registration of parties, Hungary has had the 'fewest' parties, 20. By comparison, in the same period only four parties have won at least 1 per cent of the American presidential vote; in Britain seven parties have done so; and in Sweden, with proportional representation, nine parties.

Many parties form electoral alliances in order to maximize their chances of gaining enough votes to clear the proportional representation threshold to qualify for seats. Because an alliance appears on the ballot as a single party, the above tally actually understates the number participating in elections. In Poland, for example, 35 parties joined together to fight the 1997 election under the banner of Solidarity Electoral Action

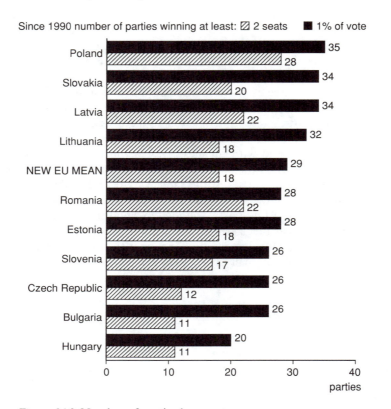

Since 1990 number of parties winning at least: ▨ 2 seats  ■ 1% of vote

*Figure 14.2* Number of parties by country.
Source: Richard Rose and Neil Munro, *Parties and Elections in New European Democracies*, 2009, parliamentary elections 1990–2007.

and it won the most seats in that election. However, the alliance was a very temporary convenience; it broke up before the following election.

A more stringent criterion for counting parties is to recognize only those that win seats in parliament, since without any MPs a party cannot try to hold government accountable. Proportional representation thresholds of up to 5 per cent and higher still for alliances of parties consign parties with a small percentage of votes to political limbo. Since parliaments in post-Communist countries have fewer members than the British Parliament, any party winning at least two seats can be counted as a parliamentary party. The requirement of two seats is necessary to avoid treating 'one-person bands' as if they were political parties. In an Estonian parliament with 101 seats and less than 1 million electors, 18 different parties have won seats. In the region, 18 parties on average have achieved representation in parliament and everywhere there has been double-digit representation (Figure 14.2). In Poland as many as 28 parties have won seats in the *Sejm*, while in Hungary only 11 parties have won parliamentary seats.

The Russian Duma election of 1995 is an extreme example of competition between parties. A total of 43 parties competed for proportional representation seats. Because only six parties won enough votes to clear the 5 per cent threshold to qualify for seats, more than 30 million Russians wasted their votes on 37 parties that failed to gain representation in the Duma. In the single-member districts electing half of the Duma seats by first past the post, an average of 11 candidates contested the median district and upwards of two-thirds of votes were cast for candidates who did not win seats.

The ironic consequence of generations of one-party rule is that party competition in Central and Eastern Europe is now more fragmented than in Western Europe. Since parties have frequently been created, merged, split or dissolved, the number at any one election is less than the total number of parties competing in at least one election since 1990 (cf. Chapter 15). Nonetheless, the average number of parties winning votes is much higher than in the West European idea of multi-party competition, where less than half a dozen parties are likely to win seats. At the average Central and Eastern Europe election, 11 parties win at least 1 per cent of the vote and seven parties win seats.

Since parties differ in their electoral strength, they should be weighed as well as counted; this is recognized in the commonplace but vague distinction between big and small parties. Winning half the seats in parliament clearly qualifies a party as big. However, if one party consistently wins more than half the seats, it is not just another competitor but the dominant party in the system. One-party dominance has existed for periods of time in countries with competitive elections, such as Italy and Japan; however this is no longer the case and it is neither evident nor welcome in post-Communist countries that have become new EU democracies.

No one party is dominant in any of the 10 countries of Central and Eastern Europe today. The average vote for the largest party at the most recent national election is 32 per cent while in Latvia the party coming first averages only 20 per cent (Figure 14.3). The strength of the leading party at the most recent Polish election is not a sign of one-party dominance. In six elections five different Polish parties have been the

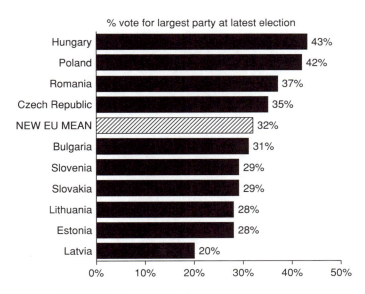

*Figure 14.3* No single party dominates.
Source: Calculated from Richard Rose and Neil Munro, *Parties and Elections in New European Democracies*, 2009, for latest election as of summer, 2008.

biggest party at least once but three did not survive to fight the most recent election. In first-round ballots for the Romanian presidency, Ion Iliescu won the most votes four times, but this was not because he represented a dominant party, for Iliescu ran in the name of three different parties. In Hungary, big parties have kept big through electoral alliances.

Since votes are spread unevenly between parties, there could be two-party competition if the two largest parties won enough votes so that one or the other could be sure of leading the government. However, this does not happen in CEE countries. Voters disperse their preferences so widely that no two parties can claim the duopoly of votes assumed in Schumpeter's theory of accountable democracy. At the most recent CEE national election, the two largest parties together averaged less than three-fifths of the popular vote and in half the countries barely half the vote or less. Thus, the combined vote for 'third' or 'minor' parties approached or exceeded that of the two largest parties. Even when two parties together have more than half the seats, if they are rivals then neither is likely to form a coalition with the other. In such circumstances, the leading party in a coalition often needs at least two more parties as partners in order to form a government. The presence of many parties on the ballot competing on a multiplicity of different grounds is thus a recipe for electoral confusion and uncertainty.

# 15  A floating system of parties

> Building a party system appears to be a necessary condition for consolidating demo-
> cracy and governing effectively.
> 
> (Scott Mainwaring and Tim Scully, *Building Democratic Institutions*)

Democracy requires leaders to be accountable as well as elected. Accountability is exercised by citizens voting for or against the governing party on the basis of its past performance. But in order for this to happen, the party system must be institutionalized,
that is, the same parties must compete at one election after another. People cannot
vote for or against a party nor can politicians be held accountable if a party has
disappeared from the ballot before the end of a parliament. When the same parties
compete at one election after another, then differences in the parties' share of the
vote reflect individuals floating between parties. However, when political elites form
new parties or split or merge from one election to the next, this creates a floating
party system.

Although transformation has offered voters a choice of many parties, the fact that
parties float on and off the ballot from one election to the next is an obstacle to accountability. In post-Communist countries the deficit in accountability is especially severe
because of the weakness of the chief alternative means of accountability, civil-society
institutions.

Institutionalization is a process that needs time to arrive at a stable equilibrium in
party competition. When the first competitive elections in half a century were held,
neither politicians nor voters were sure about what parties stood for, how much or
how little support they could expect, or what they would do if elected. The party names
that appeared on the ballot at the first post-Communist elections were not the labels
of political organizations with strong roots in society. They were *proto-* or *pre*-parties
with uncertain prospects of development.

The first free election showed politicians how much or how little popular support
they had. It created three categories of parties: those with enough votes to be confident of winning a significant number of seats in the future; those with fewer votes
and seats but enough to have an asset to offer as a partner in an electoral alliance or
merger; and those well below the threshold required to win seats in parliament. The
rational-choice hypothesis is that in subsequent elections the number of parties should
fall until a stable supply replaces a floating system of parties. Ambitious politicians
will abandon hopeless parties, thus removing them from the ballot and rather than
create new parties join larger parties that win seats. Smaller parties will merge to make

sure they have enough votes to win seats and improve their chances of participating in the formation of coalition governments. The result of rational responses to feed-back from the electorate will be a prompt reduction in the number of parties.

As the supply of parties becomes institutionalized, the volatility of voters should also decrease. After the first election, electors can see the difference between voting for a party that wins seats and wasting their vote on parties that do not and switch to parties that have a presence in parliament. As parties establish a record in office or a profile in opposition, voters can identify with a party that matches their broad political outlook. New parties no longer have the credibility to tempt voters to float to their support nor are voters forced to float by the disappearance of parties. Changes in electoral behaviour are confined to movement between established parties. The outcome should be a stable equilibrium in which each party's vote alters marginally from one election to the next but the number and names of parties in the system remain the same.

## I  Discontinuity in the supply of parties

The first condition for institutionalizing a party system is that laws that set the terms of party competition should not alter radically, for example, changing from a proportional representation to a first-past-the-post electoral system. Notwithstanding initial uncertainty about electoral systems, the first election institutionalized support for whatever rules were adopted by creating hundreds of Members of Parliament with an interest in maintaining the system that had given them office. While there have been frequent changes in parties and government since, new MPs are as ready as their predecessors to maintain the rules by which they have won their seats. Those with the biggest grievances – leaders of parties that fail to win any seats in parliament – are in the weakest position to force change.

In the rule-of-law regimes of Central and Eastern Europe, election laws have been subject to relatively few and minor amendments. The most noteworthy changes have involved raising the threshold of votes required to win seats under proportional representation. This has been justified on the grounds of avoiding a parliament with 'too many' parties. For example, in Poland there was initially no threshold for a party to qualify for a PR seat; to curb a proliferation of parties a 5 per cent threshold was introduced for one party's qualification and a higher threshold for an alliance of parties. In successor states of the Soviet Union, in contrast, election laws have been re-written so that winners of the first election have little likelihood of subsequent electoral defeat. In Russia Vladimir Putin has eliminated liberal and pro-market parties from the Duma by raising the threshold for gaining seats to 7 per cent, and has made it harder for opposition politicians to appear on the ballot at a presidential election. In other parts of the Soviet Union, changes in the law and in the administration of the law have produced elections that are neither free nor fair.

*A floating choice of parties.* Since the fall of the Berlin Wall, every Central and East European country except Lithuania has held five or six elections. The institutionalization hypothesis predicts that the number of parties fighting national elections should fall at each successive election. However, this has not happened.

In founding elections in Central and Eastern Europe, in the median country 11 parties took 1 per cent or more of the vote and in Poland 18 parties did so. Before the second election an average of three parties dropped out; however, the effect was counterbalanced by more new parties entering the lists. In the extreme case of Estonia 10 new parties appeared on the ballot. The third round of elections showed movement in the opposite direction; an average of seven parties dropped out of competition while half that number of new parties formed. In the fourth round, the average number of parties dropping out was greater than that of the new parties appearing. However, in the fifth round of elections, the number of new parties was greater than that of parties disappearing. Hence, there is no trend toward the institutionalization of the supply of parties.

Nor has there been a substantial decline in the percentage of wasted votes cast for parties that fail to win seats because they fall below the proportional-representation threshold to qualify for doing so. In the first round of free elections, an average of 9.9 per cent of votes cast were wasted by going to parties that won no seats. At the second election the entry of many new parties more than doubled the size of wasted votes to an average of 20.3 per cent. In Poland the price paid for reducing the number of parties in the *Sejm* was that more than one-third of votes were wasted. At the third election wasted votes dropped to 13.4 per cent on average. At the fourth and fifth elections, 10 per cent of the vote was wasted, slightly more than at the first round of elections. In five countries the share of the vote wasted has risen between the first and the most recent elections and in five countries it has fallen. Thus, voters exhibited no clear tendency to concentrate their votes on larger parties.

The result of the continuing turnover of parties from one election to another is that a majority of Central and East European parties have contested only one election (Figure 15.1). In addition, more than one-fifth of all parties have fought only two elections. Instead of the supply of parties stabilizing, new European democracies have institutionalized floating party systems. Only 19 parties have fought in all national

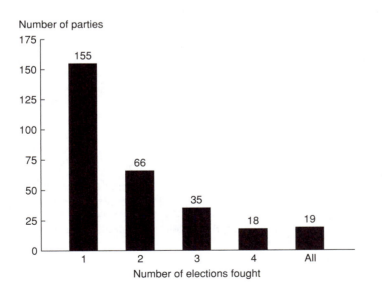

*Figure 15.1* Number of elections fought by parties.
Source: Richard Rose and Neil Munro, *Parties and Elections in New European Democracies*, 2009, parliamentary election results for 10 new EU member states, 1990–2007.

elections since 1990, while more than nine-tenths have not. In the extreme case of Latvia, where the first free election was not held until 1993, no party competing then has remained on the ballot at every subsequent election. In Poland 35 parties have won votes in at least one election, but only two have fought in all six of its elections and neither has averaged as much as 10 per cent of the vote. The turnover of parties is particularly striking given state subsidies to political parties to fight elections and maintain an organization and the additional resources available to parties in parliament and in government.

Russia has had 37 parties win at least 1 per cent of the vote and along with Slovakia has had the most parties, 22, to fight only one election. The two Russian parties that stand out because they win seats at every election are the Communist Party and the Liberal Democrats of Vladimir Zhirinovsky. The tightening up of the rules of electoral competition has reduced wasted votes by reducing the number of parties fighting elections. In 2007 only seven Russian parties won at least 1 per cent of the vote, compared to 18 doing so in 1995 (Rose and Mishler, 2008).

## II Persisting volatility

The entry and exit of parties from electoral competition creates supply-side volatility that adds to changes that arise because of voters floating between parties that persist. Voters whose party is no longer on the ballot are forced to behave differently and new parties attract some supporters from existing parties. The extent of electoral volatility depends not only on the number of parties that float on and off the ballot but also on the size of the vote that they leave behind or attract. The turnover of parties so small that they win no seats generates far less volatility than the disappearance or entry of a party that attracts a lot of votes.

Changes in party support can be measured by an Index of Electoral Volatility. It sums, without regard to the plus or minus sign, changes between two elections in the share of the vote that each party receives, including parties that only contest one election. Because changes in vote shares increase the vote for some parties while reducing the vote for others, floating votes have a double impact. At a maximum, the Index can reach 200 per cent between the final one-party election of a Communist regime and the first free election. However, in a system in which all parties were fully institutionalized and electors behaved the same from one election to the next, the Index of Volatility would be 0. If only three parties contest a pair of elections and the vote of one goes up 6 per cent, the vote of another goes up 4 per cent and a third goes down 10 per cent, then the Index is 20 per cent. If a party that won 20 per cent drops out, thus pushing up the vote share of other parties by the same amount, Index of Electoral Volatility is 40 percentage points. Since the Index reflects the net change in votes between parties, it does not take into account changes occurring when voters switch in opposite directions between a pair of parties, as their movements cancel each other out. Panel surveys of voters in the 1990s found that such movements were substantial (Tworzecki, 2003: 293).

The overwhelming failure of founding parties to institutionalize themselves is demonstrated by electoral volatility between the first and most recent national elections (Figure 15.2). Everywhere the Index is above 100 per cent and averages 162 per cent, a figure that reflects a shift of support between parties of more than four-fifths of the total vote. In Latvia the complete change in the parties contesting its founding

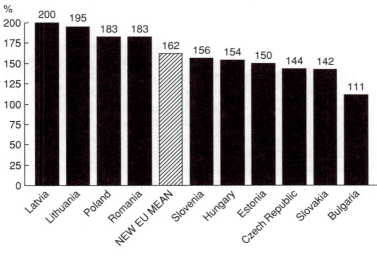

Index of Volatility between founding and latest election

*Figure 15.2* Electoral volatility, 1990–2007.
Source: Richard Rose and Neil Munro, *Parties and Elections in New European Democracies*, 2009.

Note: For calculation of Volatility Index, see text.

election and the 2007 contest produces an Index score of 200. Volatility in the Czech and Slovak republics cannot be explained by the break-up of Czechoslovakia, for in Poland and Romania, where the state has remained intact, volatility has been higher still. The lower volatility in Bulgaria has been due to the continuing strength of the Bulgarian Socialist Party.

Although volatility is often used to characterize contemporary election results in Western Europe, the degree of change there is far less than in post-transformation countries. Between 1990 and the most recent national elections, the Index of Volatility in the 15 European Union countries averaged 43 per cent, little more than one-quarter that in post-transformation countries. Volatility has been relatively high in France (74 per cent) due to a major regrouping of parties in the National Assembly election of 2002, and in Italy (71 per cent) due to changes in the electoral system and the supply of parties. However, in both countries it is well below the least volatile post-transformation country. Given that one-fifth of German voters today had been part of the East German electorate prior to 1990, the low level of volatility in Germany, 29 per cent, is particularly striking. It is a consequence of institutionalized West German parties winning the bulk of the vote there (see Chapter 12).

Between the first and second elections, the Index of Electoral Volatility was high, an average of 113 per cent. A major cause of high volatility was the collapse of anti-Communist movements that had fought the founding election as a single party. The lack of support from civil-society institutions is illustrated by comparing volatility between the first free elections in Central and Eastern Europe with those in West European countries that re-introduced democratic elections after the Second World War. Notwithstanding 12 years of Nazi domination in Germany and seven in Austria, parties with origins in the late nineteenth century re-emerged after 1945. Thus, the Index of Volatility in Austria was 24 per cent and in Germany 52 per cent and in post-fascist Italy the Index was 46 per cent. In the first free elections in Spain and Portugal in the 1970s the Index of Volatility was 25 per cent in each country, less than one-quarter that of the average Central and East European country in the early 1990s.

If a big shift in votes between the first and second election is the price that party politicians pay to learn what kind of parties will attract voters, then the Index of Volatility should fall at each successive election. However, this has not happened: the Index of Volatility has remained high. Between the second and third elections, it averaged 101 per cent and in the extreme case of Poland, volatility rose to 130 per cent. Between the third and fourth elections, the average value of the Index of Volatility rose to 109 per cent, and for the following pair of elections it averaged 97 per cent and reached 144 per cent in Slovakia. Thus, almost two decades after the first free elections in Central and Eastern Europe, there remains a floating system of parties.

In Russia, volatility between the first Duma election and the 2007 election, 140 per cent, is slightly below the CEE average, because of persisting support for Communist and Liberal Democratic parties. Electoral volatility rose at successive elections until 2007, when it dropped to 66 per cent as a consequence of Vladimir Putin establishing United Russia as the dominant party of power (Rose and Mishler, 2008). In other post-Soviet states, the stabilization in party support can be an indicator of the institutionalization of unfree and unfair elections.

## III  Elite behaviour creates volatility

Electoral volatility reflects both supply and demand. Supply-side volatility is structural: when elites close or create a party this alters the structure of party competition. Changing the choice of parties on the ballot forces supporters of parties that disappear to behave differently and any vote attracted by a new party reduces the vote share of the existing parties. By contrast, demand-side volatility reflects individual voters moving between existing parties. In well-institutionalized, established party systems, demand-side volatility, often described as electoral swing, is the primary source of volatility and it is low. In Britain, for example, the party system is so well institutionalized that the Index of Volatility was only 12 per cent between the 2001 and 2005 elections and 27 per cent in the landslide election victory of Tony Blair in 1997.

The greater the importance of demand-side effects on volatility, the more this reflects fickleness among voters, while the greater the importance of supply-side volatility, the more this reflects the actions of political elites. The relative importance of supply- and demand-side volatility can be determined by disaggregating the Index of Party Volatility into its two component parts. The first step is to calculate supply-side volatility resulting from actions of the elite, that is, parties disappearing from the ballot and new parties emerging. Insofar as these parties have little popular appeal, supply-side volatility will be low. The extent to which volatility reflects demands of voters is indicated by volatility in the support for parties that fight successive elections.

Supply-side changes are the primary cause of electoral volatility. Four-fifths of the overall volatility in the vote between the first and the latest elections is due to the changes in the supply of parties by political elites (Figure 15.3). In eight of the 10 CEE countries, supply-side changes in parties contribute more than 100 percentage points to the Index of Volatility. The volatility induced by supply-side changes has been above

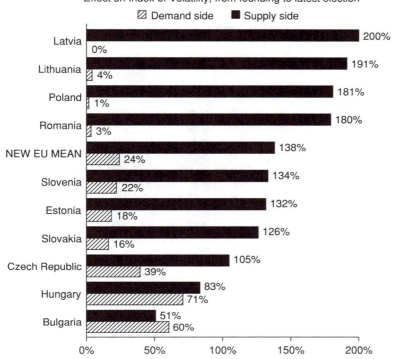

Effect on Index of Volatility, from founding to latest election

☑ Demand side  ■ Supply side

| | |
|---|---|
| Latvia | 200% / 0% |
| Lithuania | 191% / 4% |
| Poland | 181% / 1% |
| Romania | 180% / 3% |
| NEW EU MEAN | 138% / 24% |
| Slovenia | 134% / 22% |
| Estonia | 132% / 18% |
| Slovakia | 126% / 16% |
| Czech Republic | 105% / 39% |
| Hungary | 83% / 71% |
| Bulgaria | 51% / 60% |

*Figure 15.3* Supply and demand effects on volatility.
Source: Richard Rose and Neil Munro, *Parties and Elections in New European Democracies*, 2009.

Note: For the calculation of the Volatility Index and an explanation of supply and demand in this context, see text.

180 per cent in Lithuania, Poland and Romania, and in Latvia it has been total. The large amount of supply-side turnover in parties has kept demand-side volatility low, since voters cannot float between parties that are not consistently present on the ballot, Only in Bulgaria, where founding parties have persisted with many ups and downs, is demand-side volatility higher.

The evidence rejects the assumption that political elites will reduce the supply of parties as they find out which win votes and which do not. From one election to the next, there has been no decline in the average level of supply-side volatility (Figure 15.4). Between the first and the second elections, volatility resulting from the exit and entry of parties was 72 per cent and it was 69 per cent between the fourth and fifth elections. In each pair of elections since the founding election supply-side effects have had more impact on the vote than have demand-side fluctuations. Insofar as the Index of Volatility has altered, it is due to a reduction in the readiness of voters to switch between parties that persist from one election to the next. Between the first and the most recent pairs of elections, demand-side volatility fell by six points. In consequence, the volatility induced by a changing supply of parties has actually been growing in relative importance.

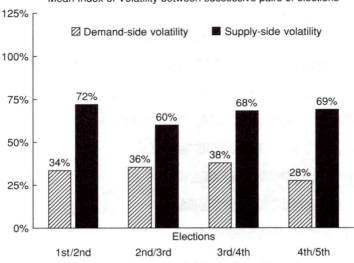

*Figure 15.4* No downward trend in supply-side volatility.
Source: Richard Rose and Neil Munro, *Parties and Elections in New European Democracies*, 2009.

Note: Parliamentary election results from 10 new EU countries, 1990–2007.

The continuing volatility in the supply of parties is in stark contrast to patterns in established democracies. For a generation after the Second World War, party systems of Western Europe combined consistency in the supply of parties and stability in the response of voters (Rose and Urwin, 1970). In the generation since, that stability has been under pressure on the demand side, as greater prosperity, education, secularization and new lifestyles have weakened the established loyalties of voters. Electoral volatility in Western Europe is driven by changes in electoral demands. Whereas in nine out of 10 CEE countries a high degree of volatility reflects changes in the parties that the elites supply, in three-quarters of the 15 older EU countries, the primary cause of such volatility as there has been between 1990 and 2007 is due to voters floating between established parties. Whereas West European electorates can hold parties to account by reaffirming or withdrawing their support from one election to the next, in Central and Eastern Europe this is not possible as long as political elites supply a floating system of parties.

# 16 Voters without trust

Elections buttress the regime – not by legitimising it but by prompting the Soviet population to show that the *illegitimacy* of its 'democratic practice' has been accepted.
(V. Zaslavsky and R. Brym, 'The Functions of Elections in the USSR')

In a country of millions of people, democratic government must be representative government and representation is based on the assumption that voters trust the party they vote for to reflect their views. Trust is generated by what individual politicians do and by their association with trusted civil-society organizations such as churches or trade unions. When these conditions are met, the party system is institutionalized, there are few floating parties, and few floating voters.

But what happens if voters distrust parties? In such circumstances an election may be democratic in the sense of offering voters a free choice between competing elites. However, when the choice offered is between distrusted alternatives, then voters can only be negatively represented. They can vote to turn a very unsatisfactory government out of office in hopes of being governed by a party that they distrust less. However, this can lead to an electoral process in which there is a rotation of rascals, as one distrusted party succeeds another.

The starting point for the electorate in a transformation society was the experience of the democratic centralism of a party-state in which centralism was much more evident than democracy. Socialization by the Party was carried on by the top-down efforts of Party apparatchiks in schools, youth organizations and at work. Socialization against the Party was carried on at the bottom of the hour-glass society. It started with parents cautioning children not to trust authorities. However, there was no escape from contact with untrustworthy institutions. Elections were held, as Zaslavsky and Brym (1978: 371) note, to demoralize subjects by forcing them to make a hypocritical show of compliance. Instead of producing Marxist-Leninist ideologues, the party's efforts produced cynicism and distrust.

Communist party-states created what the Czech dissident (and subsequently president) Václav Havel termed the 'politics of anti-politics'. The legacy also contributed to a sense of negative party identification; individuals can be clear about which party they will never vote for even if they are uncertain about which party, if any, they favour.

When a free election is held, many citizens are cross-pressured. On the one hand there is widespread distrust of political parties. This implies that even if people do vote, they will not have any commitment to the party that they vote for. However, citizens who distrust political parties can nonetheless hold political values. These values may be associated with ideologies that parties claim to represent, such as the market, social democracy or environmentalism. However, given a floating system of parties, there can be a gap between what parties represent and the political values of the electorate.

## I A legacy of distrust

The Communist legacy of distrust in institutions is particularly salient for political parties. In Central and Eastern Europe an average of 74 per cent of the electorate actively distrusts political parties (Table 16.1). The only difference between countries is in the degree to which parties are distrusted. More than five-sixths of citizens actively distrust parties in Poland and Bulgaria, and in four countries distrust in parties is higher than in Russia.

The alternative view of parties is not trust but scepticism. Sceptics are uncertain in their views of parties. When offered a seven-point scale measuring trust in parties, sceptics choose the mid point rather than expressing a trusting or distrustful view. Sceptics are significant because in principle experience may alter their views and if political developments were positive, sceptics could become trusting. However, sceptics constitute only one-sixth of the CEE electorate on average. Nonetheless, sceptics are more numerous than the 10 per cent who trust parties and in Poland and Bulgaria trust falls to 3 and 6 per cent respectively. The chief difference in attitudes is not between those who trust and distrust parties, but between those who actively distrust parties and those who are sceptical (see Mishler and Rose, 1997; 2001).

*Fleeting preferences.* When an election is called, the first decision an individual must make is whether or not to vote. A majority of electors do go to vote but their choice is often transitory. Between elections, when there is no immediate pressure to choose a party, people are often completely detached from parties. This is shown by the results of New Europe Barometer surveys. The standard question asked is what party a person would vote for if an election were held that week – and this is normally a time

*Table 16.1* Distrust in parties high

*Q. To what extent do you trust political parties to look after your interests?*

|  | Trusts % | Sceptical % | Distrusts % |
|---|---|---|---|
| Poland | 3 | 10 | 87 |
| Bulgaria | 6 | 10 | 84 |
| Romania | 9 | 11 | 80 |
| Slovakia | 10 | 14 | 76 |
| NEW EU MEAN | 10 | 16 | 74 |
| Latvia | 10 | 16 | 74 |
| Estonia | 7 | 20 | 73 |
| Slovenia | 10 | 19 | 71 |
| Czech Republic | 15 | 15 | 70 |
| Lithuania | 10 | 21 | 69 |
| Hungary | 16 | 25 | 60 |
| Russia | 10 | 14 | 75 |

Source: Centre for the Study of Public Policy, New Europe Barometer, 2004; New Russia Barometer, 2005. Trusts: chooses, points 5–7; Sceptical, point 4; Distrusts, points 1–3.

when an election is not imminent. To encourage a sense of privacy, respondents are asked to mark their party preference on a ballot and place it in an envelope. Insofar as voters have more than a fleeting inclination to favour a party, they should have a party preference in the years between elections as well as on election day.

The fleeting nature of party support in Central and Eastern Europe is shown by the fact the biggest group in the electorate consists of people who have no party preference between elections. Across Central and Eastern Europe, 39 per cent of electors cannot name a party they favour and in Slovenia almost half could not do so. In nine out of 10 countries, people without a party preference outnumber the 22 per cent favouring the most popular party in their country. In the New Russia Barometer survey in January 2005 the contrast was even greater. Three-fifths could not name a party they would vote for and only 14 per cent said they would vote for United Russia, which at the Duma election two years later received the support, if only fleetingly, of 41 per cent of the registered electorate.

*Distrusting voters predominate.* Electors not only distrust parties as a group but also identify particular parties that they would never vote for. An NEB survey found that in Romania, 95 per cent could identify a party they rejected and 90 per cent did so in Poland. In Hungary, 70 per cent identified a party they firmly rejected and in Slovenia, 54 per cent (Rose and Mishler, 1998). In Hungary the parties rejected were closely associated with the old Communist regime; in Poland an unsuccessful anti-Communist governing party; and parties representing ethnic minorities, such as the party of ethnic Turks in Bulgaria and Hungarians in Romania. Thus, far more electors can name a party that they would never vote for than can name a party that they favour.

Ballots make no provision for people to cast a vote against a party, for example, by placing a minus sign next to its name and having this mark subtracted from the total vote of the party they dislike. In Russia prior to the second-term electoral reforms of President Putin the ballot offered the option of voting against all parties. However, it did not identify which particular party a voter was most against, for example, the Communist Party or a free-market party. For want of anything better, an elector is confronted with a choice between up to a dozen parties that he or she is likely to view with scepticism or distrust.

Because the vote of every individual is equal, an election cannot register the degree of commitment or distrust of individual voters. Individuals who cast a negative vote and apathetic electors whose voting is a fleeting choice have their votes counted just the same as those who are positively committed to the party they voted for. Nor can non-voters be characterized as alienated votes. Most people who do not vote at a given election are usually absent for transitory reasons, such as illness or being on holiday.

Attempts to project the American concept of long-term party identification onto people who have seen their party system transformed by a change in regime are doubly inappropriate. CEE party systems are radically different from the United States, where parties are strongly institutionalized. The Democratic and Republican parties have each been in existence for more than 150 years. An individual can thus vote for the same party throughout his or her lifetime and parents can pass their party identification on to their children before they are old enough to vote. The unsuitability of the concept was inadvertently demonstrated by a survey in Russia in May 1998, between two Duma elections (Miller and Klobucar, 2000). It asked people to choose a party identification from a list of 14 parties nominally active at the time of the survey. However, by the time the Duma election was held 18 months later, nine of the parties listed did not appear on the ballot and a majority voted for parties that did not exist at the time the inter-election survey was conducted.

When the New Europe Barometer asks people whether they identify with any political party, only 19 per cent say that they do. Across Central and Eastern Europe, the percentage who do not identify with any party is as high as 94 per cent in Romania, 93 per cent in Russia and 91 per cent in Poland. The minority identifying with a party is highest in Bulgaria and Hungary, yet even then 62 per cent of Bulgarians and 64 per cent of Hungarians do not identify with a party. Since proportional-representation electoral systems require voters to cast a ballot for a party, the failure of the great mass of people to identify with a party is particularly striking.

The most common measure of party preference in Europe is a question asking: *If an election were held this week, which party would you vote for?* This is not a test of party identification but of an individual being willing to show transitory support. While the question was asked when an election was not imminent, 61 per cent of NEB respondents did choose a party, a figure similar to turnout at national elections. The percentage choosing a party varied from 76 per cent in the Czech Republic to 53 per cent in Slovenia.

The principal division in post-transformation societies is between distrusting voters and distrusting non-voters (Figure 16.1). The largest group overall, 44 per cent of the electorate, are distrusting voters who can name a party that they would vote for but do not trust parties. This is the largest group in all but one of the Central and East European countries; in the one exception, Slovenia, distrustful non-voters are even more numerous. In no country is the civic ideal of voters trusting parties and having a party preference even approximated. Distrusting voters outnumber trusting voters by a margin of more than 5 to 1. In Russia the dissociation from parties is even stronger: trusting voters were only 6 per cent of respondents in the fifteenth NRB survey.

*Q.  o what extent do you trust political parties to look after your interests?*
*Q. In this envelope is a ballot with the names of political parties. Please put a cross on the pink ballot by the name of the party that you would vote for if an election were held this week.*

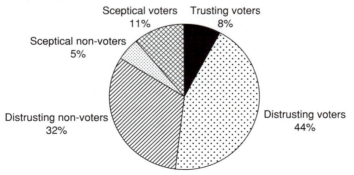

*Figure 16.1* Trusting voters the exception.
Source: Centre for the Study of Public Policy, New Europe Barometer, 2004.

Note: Trust as defined in Table 16.1. Voters and non-voters classified by their party preference if an election held this week.

## II  Political values without parties

The low level of attachment to political parties in post-transformation societies is not proof that citizens lack political values. Instead, it may reflect a mismatch between what parties supply and the demands of electors. After all, people do not need prompting from political parties to develop values and the politicization of everyday life in Communist times was a stimulus to individuals to sort out in their own minds what they thought of the values advocated by Communist apparatchiks. After a decade of living in post-transformation societies people can develop political values similar to those found in established democracies.

*Broad outlooks.* In a cross-national survey people cannot be asked to choose from a common list of parties, but they can be asked to indicate their political outlook, if any, from a broad range of world views. These outlooks stand for principles relevant to many issues of public policy, such as support for markets, national traditions or the environment. They are thus more relevant to governance than question-begging prescriptions that government should do what the people want. Whereas democratic values are meant to be consensual, political outlooks differ in ways immediately relevant to party competition, because they indicate which side people will favour in disputes about issues of public policy.

Barometer surveys offer respondents three outlooks consistent with economic cleavages: pro-market, social democratic and Communist. A fourth alternative, national traditions, evokes Lipset and Rokkan's (1967) emphasis on the politics of national defence against foreign and global influences. A green outlook has particular relevance because Communist regimes degraded the environment. In addition, respondents have the chance to say they have other values or no recognizable political outlook.

The largest group, 31 per cent, rejects all outlooks associated with a political ideology (Table 16.2). In Russia, where for generations the party-state used its institutions to promote Marxist-Leninist ideology, 42 per cent were unable to endorse any

*Table 16.2* Broad political outlooks

| Q. Which broad political outlook are you most inclined to favour? | None % | Market % | Social dem. % | Comm. % | Nat'l trad'n % | Green % | Other % |
|---|---|---|---|---|---|---|---|
| Poland | 51 | 8 | 19 | 4 | 9 | 5 | 5 |
| Hungary | 42 | 10 | 13 | 2 | 6 | 16 | 10 |
| Bulgaria | 41 | 19 | 19 | 10 | 2 | 4 | 4 |
| Romania | 38 | 23 | 23 | 4 | 6 | 4 | 1 |
| Slovakia | 36 | 13 | 25 | 11 | 8 | 5 | 3 |
| NEW EU MEAN | 31 | 21 | 22 | 5 | 9 | 8 | 4 |
| Slovenia | 25 | 30 | 21 | 1 | 6 | 12 | 5 |
| Latvia | 23 | 34 | 17 | 1 | 8 | 15 | 1 |
| Lithuania | 19 | 31 | 28 | 4 | 9 | 5 | 4 |
| Estonia | 19 | 22 | 22 | 2 | 17 | 13 | 5 |
| Czech Republic | 13 | 23 | 32 | 7 | 14 | 6 | 5 |
| Russia | 42 | 17 | 8 | 16 | 4 | 6 | 6 |

Source:  Centre for the Study of Public Policy, New Europe Barometer, 2001; New Russia Barometer, 2005. Due to rounding, here and elsewhere percentages may not add up to exactly 100.

political outlook. The replies are a caution against generalizing to the population as a whole the values held by political elites. They are also an incentive to political elites to organize fuzzy-focus parties that leave open what their substantive policy priorities are.

Insofar as Central and East Europeans do endorse any outlook, the most favoured alternatives are the market and social democracy. The market is endorsed by an average of 21 per cent and social democracy by an average of 22 per cent. Those in favour of the market are most numerous in Slovenia, Latvia and Lithuania, and tied for first in Bulgaria, Romania and Estonia. Elsewhere support for social democracy is marginally higher. It would be misleading to describe the whole of the electorate as divided along ideological lines separating pro-market and social democratic outlooks, for together these groups include an average of only 43 per cent of the electorate.

Cradle-to-grave indoctrination impressed Communist subjects, but not in the compliant manner sometimes assumed. Instead, in Central and Eastern Europe only 5 per cent today describe their outlook as Communist and in four countries only 1 or 2 per cent do so. The proportion calling themselves Communist is far less than the nominal members of national Communist Parties in the old regime. Many Party members were not believers but held a Party card because it offered material advantages without requiring ideological conviction (see Chapter 13). Russia is the exception, for self-styled Communists outnumber social democrats by a margin of 2 to 1. However, only one-sixth of Russians endorse this outlook, a figure consistent with the weak showing of the Communist Party at Russian elections.

National traditions have limited salience; they characterize the outlook of only 9 per cent of Central and East Europeans. With the exception of Estonia, there is little difference between new states founded after the collapse of Communism and countries where a national revolution occurred much earlier. Commitment to green values is limited to 8 per cent across the region. The capacity of electors to form values in the absence of political parties is illustrated by the above-average levels of green respondents in Hungary, Estonia and Latvia, where no green party won seats at the most recent election.

Offering the category of 'other' allows people to mention an outlook that was not proffered, such as that of Christians. The category can also capture outlooks important within a single country but generalizable across the region, for example, the position of ethnic Turks in Bulgaria. In the event, only 4 per cent named an outlook other than those offered in the NEB survey.

*Collective or individual responsibility?* Even though individuals may not be committed to a political party or outlook, every family has an interest in securing their welfare through health care, education and security in old age. The balance between individual and collective responsibility for delivering welfare services is a major political issue in every modern society.

Popular demand for collective action by the state implies popular trust in the integrity and effectiveness of public institutions. Communist regimes were committed to the collective provision of welfare to the complete exclusion of private provision. However, their anti-modern character made many subjects distrustful of the state and encouraged reliance on resources independent of it. Transformation removed a distrusted regime but distrust has lingered, making people more inclined to rely on their own resources than those of the state. Moreover, in post-transformation societies there are opportunities for individuals to turn to non-state institutions for education, health care or social security.

Rejection of Communist rule is not evidence of the rejection of welfare from the state. Nor does endorsement of the state provision of welfare imply rejection of democratic governance. Established European democracies spend a substantial portion of their Gross National Product on the collective provision of health care, education and social security. This is particularly true of social democratic Sweden and the social state of the Federal Republic of Germany, political systems that many post-transformation citizens would like to emulate (see Table 1.1).

To identify preferences for the state or individuals to take responsibility for their welfare, the New Europe Barometer asks respondents a battery of questions about major influences on welfare. Even though many people do not identify with any political party or outlook, almost everyone has an opinion about whether the individual or the state should be responsible for welfare; only 5 per cent on average reply don't know.

On every question new Europeans differ in their preference for state or individual guarantees of welfare (Table 16.3). Given a choice between making incomes more equal or individual achievement determining earnings, people divide into two halves. Replies to a question about whether individuals or the state should be responsible for material wellbeing show no statistical difference between those endorsing each alternative. Likewise, there is no significant difference in those believing that enterprises are best run if state-owned or when run by private entrepreneurs. Given the upheavals of transformation, it is understandable that more people prefer a job that is secure even if not well paying to a well-paid job that is not so secure. Nonetheless, one-third of CEE respondents endorse the more risky and individualist alternative.

People tend to be consistent in the views that they hold about who should be responsible for welfare. A statistical analysis of responses finds that the four questions in Table 16.3 reflect a common underlying attitude. On this basis, Central and East Europeans can be grouped into three categories:

*Table 16.3* Collectivist versus individualist attitudes

*On this card are contrasting opinions about public issues. Please state with which alternative you are more inclined to agree.*

|  | % Agree |
|---|---|
| Incomes should be made more equal, so there is no great difference | 50 |
| OR |  |
| Individual achievement should determine how much people are paid | 50 |
| Individuals should take responsibility for themselves and their livelihood | 51 |
| OR |  |
| The state should be responsible for everyone's material security | 49 |
| State ownership is the best way to run an enterprise | 51 |
| OR |  |
| An enterprise is best run by private entrepreneurs | 49 |
| A good job is one that is secure even if it doesn't pay very much | 67 |
| OR |  |
| A good job pays a lot of money, even if it is not so secure | 33 |

Source: Centre for the Study of Public Policy, New Europe Barometer, 2004.

Note: A factor analysis of the questions in Table 16.3 plus a question about views on taxing and spending found the four questions in the table formed the first factor, accounting for 34 per cent of the variance, with loadings ranging from .71 to .57. A second factor, accounting for an additional 20 per cent of the variance, consisted of the single question about taxing and spending.

- *Collectivists* (43 per cent favour three or four collectivist alternatives). In this group are people who favour such things as making incomes more equal, state ownership of enterprises and state guarantee of material security and prefer a secure job with lower pay to a well-paid but less secure job. Collectivists are the largest group in CEE societies, albeit a majority only in Hungary.
- *Individualists* (33 per cent favour three or four individualist alternatives). Post-transformation societies offer individuals opportunities to better themselves (Chapter 9). These include earning more money by accepting risks, making individual provision for welfare, higher earnings for some, and private enterprise. In every post-transformation society there is a substantial bloc who prefer individual responsibility for welfare. However, only in the Czech Republic is this group in the majority.
- *Ambivalent* (24 per cent endorse two collectivist and two individualist alternatives). Because individuals do not reason with ideological rigour, almost one-quarter of Central and East Europeans are of two minds about whether the state or individuals should have the primary responsibility for welfare. For example, an individual can be in favour of private ownership of enterprises but prefer a low-paying job with greater income security or favour greater equality of income but be prepared to take responsibility for their own welfare. While this group is not the largest in any society, it is politically critical, for those who are ambivalent constitute the median group in eight of 10 Central and East European countries.

Respondents can be placed on an individual-collectivist scale according to the number of times that they endorse each type of question and a multiple regression analysis can account for 24.5 per cent of the variance in how individuals place themselves on this scale. In particular, people who are more educated and higher in social status are more likely to endorse individualist values. Central and East Europeans who are more educated, have a higher social status, are younger and male are more likely to favour the individual provision of welfare, while older, less educated, of lower status and women are more likely to favour state provision of welfare. Economic circumstances influence values too: people who have fewer consumer goods or are negative about their future economic conditions tend to favour collective values, while those who are better off tend to be individualist. As expected, the minority who trust political institutions are more likely to endorse collectivist values, but those who feel freer now are more likely to favour individual approaches.

The readiness of people to articulate ideas about what the state ought and ought not to do indicates that there is, as it were, a party system in the heads of voters. However, it has yet to be realized in electoral competition because of the inability or unwillingness of political elites to supply parties that have the trust of voters.

# Part V

# Time matters

# 17 Learning to support new regimes

> The new political class, and society as a whole, have to learn how to build up and run a democratic system. This will be a new experience and a long learning process.
>
> (Elemer Hankiss, Hungarian sociologist, 1990)

Theories of democratic consolidation assume that time matters. It takes time for inexperienced leaders to learn that governing is different from leading protest demonstrations. It also takes time for citizens to learn which of their hopes and fears of a new regime are justified and which are not. Consolidating popular support is a process in which citizens learn from the performance of a new government what 'real existing democracy' is actually like – for better and for worse.

The overnight fall of the Berlin Wall radically altered the way in which hundreds of millions of Europeans could learn about democracy. Instead of vicariously learning what democracy meant from clandestine listening to foreign radio broadcasts, people could listen to debates involving competing party leaders. However, when the first free elections were held in 1990, people could only have hopes of what transformation would bring. After almost two decades, regimes are no longer new. Citizens have learned what post-transformation regimes are like.

What people learn depends on what they experience, and post-Communist elites have differed greatly in the institutions that they have supplied. In Central and Eastern Europe politicians quickly adapted to electoral competition and so did voters, frequently voting the government of the day out of office. In successor states of the Soviet Union, the pattern has been different: uncompetitive and unfree elections have been the rule. In Belarus, Aleksandr Lukashenka has established a dictatorship behind an electoral facade. In Ukraine, elections have been competitive but governments have been quarrelsome at best and corrupt and brutal at worst. In Russia, President Putin has replaced the unpredictability of the Yeltsin years with an order that restricts civil and political liberties.

The democratic ideal is that a new regime consolidates popular support by delivering what voters want. However, the real choice facing people in countries such as Poland, the Czech Republic and Bulgaria is not between an idealized democracy and their current regime; it is between what is there today or one or another form of undemocratic rule for which their national history offers precedents. The New Europe Barometer shows the extent to which experience has altered support for new regimes from the hopeful days of the early 1990s to the time of entry to the European Union. Since the NEB covers post-Soviet as well as new European Union member states, it can also show the extent to which the passage of time has led people to support autocratic regimes.

## I  Evaluating alternative regimes

In a new regime, competition for political support is not so much competition between political parties as it is between democratic and undemocratic systems. When asked what democracy means, people born in Communist-bloc countries emphasize three themes: the freedom to do and say what you want; the choice of government by competitive elections; and a welfare state. The first two themes are found in almost every definition of democracy. The addition of welfare policies such as a guaranteed minimum income differs from the association of freedom and the free market espoused by Ronald Reagan and Margaret Thatcher. However, it is consistent with European ideas of a social democratic or social market state.

In the Communist era, the compliance of subjects with the dictates of the regime encouraged some to believe that subjects of repressive regimes did not care much for democracy. To test this, the New Europe Barometer asks where people would like their political system to be on a scale ranging from a complete democracy to a complete dictatorship. Throughout the region, democracy is strongly endorsed as an ideal. Altogether, 86 per cent give it a favourable rating, and the remainder are divided between those with a neutral view, 9 per cent, or a small group regarding a dictatorship as ideal, 9 per cent. Moreover, the largest group, 35 per cent, give democracy the highest possible rating, 10 on the 10-point scale (Figure 17.1). The only difference between CEE countries is the size of the majority endorsing democracy as an ideal. A total of 93 per cent of Hungarians are positive about democracy and so are 90 per cent of Romanians. Even where enthusiasm is least high, Russia, 75 per cent nonetheless endorse democracy as an ideal, 15 per cent are neutral, and only 10 per cent regard dictatorship as ideal.

However, new regimes have not, or at least not yet, succeeded in supplying the political institutions that their citizens want. While giving three cheers for democracy as an ideal, citizens are barely willing to give two cheers for the way their political system operates today. These views are a reminder that even if Freedom House gives a regime its top rating it may still have many faults in the eyes of its citizens. In 6 of 10 CEE countries, more than half rate their political system as democratic and in four, a plurality rates their regime as democratic and the median citizen sees it as halfway between a democracy and a dictatorship. In Russia only 42 per cent see the regime as democratic, 33 per cent see it as a dictatorship and the remainder are neutral.

There is a substantial gap between what people would like their new system of government to be and what it actually is Whereas 86 per cent of CEE citizens view democracy as the ideal form of government, only 53 per cent regard their current system as relatively democratic. The gap is greatest in Romania and in Belarus, where less than half those who would like a democratic system of government think that this is what they now have. There is also a big gap in evaluating the ideal state and the state of Russia today (Figure 17.1).

Dissatisfaction with the new regime produces distrust but it need not mean that citizens want to replace an imperfect democracy with an undemocratic alternative. To test this, the New Europe Barometer asks people about a variety of alternatives that are historically relevant in the region, ranging from rule by the military to a return to Communist rule.

Q. On a scale in which 1 means complete dictatorship and 10 means complete democracy:
   (a) Where would you like our political system to be?
   (b) Where would you place our country at the present time?

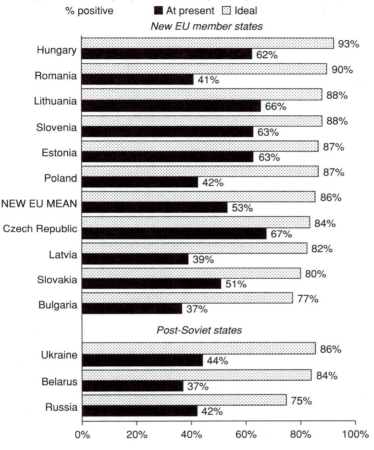

*Figure 17.1* Comparing democracy real and ideal.
Source: Centre for the Study of Public Policy, New Europe Barometer, 2004; New Russia Barometer, 2008.

Note: Percent positive: a reply of 6 to 10 on a 10-point scale.

Even though the army is more trusted than other institutions of post-Communist government, more than nine-tenths of citizens do not want a military dictatorship. This is consistent with the self-image of the military. It was subordinate to the Communist Party in the old regime and this remains the case today. In CEE countries, the military is oriented more toward participation in NATO activities than toward intervention in domestic politics and in Russia, it competes with other groups within the state for money and the political favour of the Kremlin (Figure 17.2).

Where a Communist regime was imposed by Soviet force, there is least support for a return to Communism. For example, in the Baltic states, even though Russian ethnics constitute a substantial minority of the population, nine-tenths reject going back

*Q. Our present system of government is not the only one that this country has had. Some people say that we would be better off if the country was governed differently. What do you think?*
   *(a) Army should rule*
   *(b) Return to Communist rule*
   *(c) Get rid of Parliament and elections and have a strong leader*
     *who can quickly decide everything?*

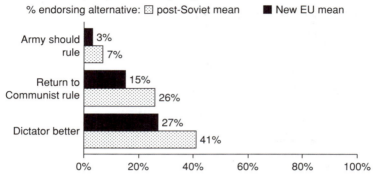

*Figure 17.2* Rejection of undemocratic alternatives.
Source: Centre for the Study of Public Policy, New Europe Barometer, 2004; New Russia Barometer, 2008.

to the Communist system and in Central and Eastern Europe as a whole, more than five-sixths reject a return to Communism. In post-Soviet countries, a larger minority is in favour of a return to a system that made the country a great power but even in Russia only 28 per cent hold this view, as against 72 per cent opposing a return to a Communist regime. Attitudes toward the Communist regime reflect nostalgia for a past that is gone rather than a demand for Communist rule in future: twice as many Russians speak favourably of the old system as would like it to return (Munro, 2006).

The alternative regime endorsed by the largest minority is a dictator who quickly decides everything without regard to democratic institutions. In CEE countries, an average of 27 per cent favour this and 41 per cent in post-Soviet societies. However, there are substantial differences between countries. In the Czech Republic, seven-eighths are against a dictatorship and three-quarters of Romanians, who experienced a very despotic Communist regime. On the other hand, almost half of Poles were so fed up with their government in 2005 that they endorsed a dictatorship. It would be a mistake to infer from Vladimir Putin's popularity that Russians want to be ruled by a dictator; by the end of his time in office only 18 per cent held this view. In Belarus, however more than three-fifths endorse the statement that it is better to have a strong leader who can rule without parliament, as do two-fifths in Ukraine.

Consistent with the Churchill hypothesis, a majority of citizens in every Central and East European country invariably rejects each undemocratic alternative. The only difference is in the size of the majority that disapproves. In the Czech Republic and Hungary, 75 per cent reject all three undemocratic alternatives and across the ten CEE countries, an average of 66 per cent do so. The pattern is different in post-Soviet countries: 74 per cent of Belorussians endorse at least one undemocratic alternative as do 49 per cent of Ukrainians and 35 per cent of Russians.

The political impact of undemocratic attractions is dissipated when there is no agreement about which is the best alternative to replace the current regime. There can also be disagreements among citizens about who would make the best dictator, and also disagreement within the political elite. In sum, while citizens are critical about the democratic achievements of their new regime, undemocratic alternatives have a limited appeal.

## II Paths of change

The logic of consolidating a regime is that the trend over time is crucial. Whatever the initial level of support, it should increase as the fact of persistence gradually increases its acceptance as 'the only game in town' (Linz, 1990; Rose, Mishler and Munro, 2006: Chapter 9). Theories of democratic consolidation also assume that support for undemocratic alternatives should fall. But this is not the only path that can be taken. The passage of time can lead to the consolidation of a repressive autocracy as subjects become resigned to accepting it even if its subjects do not like the 'game' that their ruler plays.

The NEB measure of support for the current regime does not assume that all post-Communist regimes are democratic and this is palpably not the case. Instead, immediately after asking for an evaluation of the old regime, people are asked to evaluate the current system of governing on a scale that runs from minus 100 to plus 100; it has the incidental advantage of providing a neutral alternative, 0. This enables respondents to express the degree to which they are positive or negative about their regime. Because the NEB has repeated the same key questions in each round of surveys since 1991, there are copious trend data about popular support.

When the NEB began asking Central and East Europeans to evaluate their new regime, the problem of transforming a command into a market economy was very evident. Nonetheless, when first interviewed an average of 59 per cent were positive about their new regime. In the Czech Republic and Romania, where the previous regimes had been unusually repressive, escaping their evils was sufficient to encourage more than two-thirds of citizens to give the new system a positive evaluation. On the other hand, in Latvia, where Russian residents had special grievances, barely two-fifths were initially positive about the new regime.

The passage of time has tended to consolidate support for new European democracies, with a majority of citizens in every country now responding positively when asked to evaluate the current regime. In the NEB survey shortly after EU enlargement, an average of 61 per cent expressed a positive view and an additional 9 per cent were neutral. Thus, those in favour of the new regime outnumber those with a negative appraisal by a margin of 2 to 1. However, national trajectories of support have varied. Support for the new regime has risen by more than 20 percentage points in Estonia, Lithuania and Slovenia and it has remained steady and high in the Czech Republic and in Hungary. However, since 1991 support has fallen significantly for the new regimes of Bulgaria and Romania. This critical view has been shared by the European Union, which delayed their entry for almost three years after the 2004 NEB round.

Consistent with the theory that time rather than democratization matters most for the consolidation of regimes, the biggest gains in support have occurred in post-Soviet states, where democratization has made least progress (Table 17.1). In 1992 only 14 per cent of Russians favoured their new regime and between one-quarter and one-third were positive in Ukraine and Belarus. From such low starting points, the alternatives were a complete collapse or a big increase in popular support. In Russia, support has

*Table 17.1* Trends in support for the current regime

Q. *Where on this scale would you put our current system of governing with free elections and many parties?*

| | 1991 | 1992 | 1993 | 1995 | 1998 | 2001 | 2004 | Change |
|---|---|---|---|---|---|---|---|---|
| | | | *(Current regime: % approving)* | | | | | |
| *New EU countries* | | | | | | | | |
| Estonia | na | na | 55 | 69 | 62 | 69 | 76 | 21 |
| Lithuania | na | na | 47 | 34 | 39 | 46 | 71 | 24 |
| Slovenia | 49 | 68 | 55 | 66 | 51 | 75 | 70 | 21 |
| Czech Republic | 71 | 71 | 78 | 77 | 56 | 76 | 70 | −1 |
| Hungary | 57 | 43 | 51 | 50 | 53 | 76 | 65 | 8 |
| NEW EU MEAN | 59 | 60 | 57 | 60 | 54 | 61 | 61 | 2 |
| Poland | 52 | 56 | 69 | 76 | 66 | 66 | 53 | 1 |
| Slovakia | 50 | 58 | 52 | 61 | 50 | 39 | 52 | 2 |
| Latvia | na | na | 41 | 43 | 35 | 53 | 52 | 11 |
| Romania | 69 | 68 | 60 | 60 | 66 | 50 | 52 | −17 |
| Bulgaria | 64 | 55 | 59 | 66 | 58 | 59 | 51 | −13 |
| *Post-Soviet countries* | | | | | | | | |
| Russia | na | 14 | 36 | 26 | 36 | 46 | 84* | 70 |
| Belarus | na | 35 | 29 | 35 | 48 | 47 | 75 | 40 |
| Ukraine | na | 25 | 24 | 33 | 22 | 31 | 70 | 45 |

Sources: Centre for the Study of Public Policy, New Europe Barometer 1991–2004. New Russia Barometer: 1992–2008. *Data is from 2008 survey.

risen under Vladimir Putin, reaching 84 per cent by the end of his second term as president. In Ukraine support for the regime abruptly doubled in early 2005 as a consequence of the Orange Revolution. Expressions of support are even higher in undemocratic Belarus.

Consistent with the positive trend in support for the current regime, there has been a downwards trend in the endorsement of a dictator replacing the new regime. Approval of a dictatorship fell in 9 out of 10 CEE countries by an average of 9 percentage points and by as much as 33 per cent in Lithuania and 28 per cent in Bulgaria. Poland has been the only country where the minority supporting a dictatorship has been consistently high. In three post-Soviet states, endorsement of a dictatorship has fallen by 10 percentage points or more, and in Russia from 36 per cent favouring a dictatorship in 1998 to 18 per cent in 2008, albeit it still remains above the level of new EU member states. Endorsement of a return to Communist rule has been consistently low in new EU member states, but fluctuated up and down in Russia, Ukraine and Belarus.

## III Confident democrats

A regime is consolidated when the mass of the population, whatever their preferences for forms of rule, accepts that no other regime will replace it and each new generation is socialized to take it for granted. This happens not only in democratic regimes but also in undemocratic regimes such as Singapore and Saudi Arabia. However, there is a big majority of post-Communist citizens old enough to know that the current regime is *not* the only way in which the country can be governed and this provides grounds for an expectation of further regime change.

In the years immediately after the fall of the Berlin Wall there was no assurance that new regimes or even states would survive. The break-up of Czechoslovakia was a peaceful 'velvet' divorce, but the fighting among successor states of Yugoslavia was a palpable reminder that bloodshed can accompany political transformation. Among post-Soviet countries, the Baltic states regained independence with only a dozen lives lost, but from Moldova to the Caucasus, force has been used to change state boundaries.

With the passage of time, the memory of past regimes and state boundaries fades. The idea of the restoration of the Austro-Hungary monarchy or the pre-1945 boundaries of Germany is inconceivable. The persistence of a regime becomes a matter of fact. In such circumstances, whatever the expectations and hopes at the start of transformation, people have had to adapt to the regime that they faced. Adaptation does not require a new regime to deliver a high level of economic growth. It is a reflection of a regime's capacity to show its citizens that, like it or not, it is here to stay and it is futile to expect it to go away.

To determine the extent to which people think their regime could change, the New Europe Barometer asks how likely or unlikely it is that parliament could be closed down and competing parties abolished. When the question was first asked in the ten countries of Central and Eastern Europe in the early 1990s, an average of 37 per cent thought this might happen, and in Poland as many as 56 per cent thought an end to representative government possible. With the passage of time, the proportion thinking regime change possible has fallen sharply. Only 13 per cent of new EU citizens now think another regime might take power (Table 17.2). In no country does as many as one-fifth see a fresh transformation of the polity possible and in Hungary only 3 per cent do so.

*Table 17.2* Little expectation of regime change

*Q. Some people think this country would be better governed if parliament was closed down and all parties were abolished. How likely do you think this is to happen in the next few years?*

| | 1991 | 1992 | 1993 | 1995 | 1998 | 2001 | 2004 | Change |
|---|---|---|---|---|---|---|---|---|
| | | | *(% saying suspension likely, might happen)* | | | | | |
| *New EU countries* | | | | | | | | |
| Poland | 56 | 60 | 53 | 62 | 10 | 11 | 19 | −37 |
| Latvia | na | na | 28 | 32 | 37 | 15 | 19 | −9 |
| Slovakia | 47 | 33 | 35 | 34 | 28 | 19 | 15 | −32 |
| Slovenia | 30 | 19 | 56 | 17 | 15 | 6 | 14 | −16 |
| Romania | 32 | 27 | 30 | 13 | 30 | 11 | 14 | −18 |
| Estonia | na | na | 41 | 16 | 21 | 16 | 13 | −28 |
| Bulgaria | 30 | 34 | 37 | 26 | 9 | 9 | 13 | −17 |
| NEW EU MEAN | 37 | 33 | 37 | 27 | 20 | 11 | 13 | −24 |
| Czech Republic | 39 | 36 | 28 | 20 | 20 | 7 | 10 | −29 |
| Lithuania | na | na | 37 | 27 | 15 | 11 | 9 | −28 |
| Hungary | 25 | 24 | 29 | 25 | 10 | 9 | 3 | −22 |
| *Post-Soviet countries* | | | | | | | | |
| Ukraine | na | 43 | 49 | 42 | 25 | 42 | 22 | −21 |
| Russia | na | na | 61 | 26 | 23 | 30 | 21* | −40 |
| Belarus | na | 40 | 49 | 36 | 27 | 22 | 17 | −23 |

Sources: Centre for the Study of Public Policy, New Europe Barometer 1991–2088. New Russia Barometer: 1991–2007a. *Data is from survey in April 2007.

Even though parliament and competing parties are less important in post-Soviet states, there has also been a big shift in the acceptance of these institutions as a fixed feature of the political landscape. The proportion of Russians thinking it possible that parliament and parties could be abolished has fallen from three-fifths just before the 1993 shoot-out between President Yeltsin's forces and those of the Russian parliament to one-sixth. In Belarus and Ukraine those thinking representative institutions could be done away with has halved.

Across Central and Eastern Europe, confident democrats are far more numerous than confident authoritarians. Combining individual views about whether parliament could be suspended with their assessment of whether this would be welcome or not identifies:

- *Confident democrats* (69 per cent). This group consists of people who do not think parliamentary elections could be abolished and would not approve if this happened.
- *Anxious democrats* (5 per cent). Those disapproving of an end to parliament but worried that it could happen. In the early 1990s they could be regarded as vigilant defenders of new regimes. Today, such vigilance is hardly required.
- *Dejected authoritarians* (16 per cent). Demoralization characterizes those who would like to see representative institutions abolished but think it unlikely to happen. This makes it harder for such individuals to be mobilized in support of demands for a new regime.
- *Hopeful authoritarians* (10 per cent). People who believe that parliamentary elections could be suspended and would approve this happening are an isolated minority in every CEE country.

In Russia, Belarus and Ukraine, more than three-fifths were confident that the regime would remain the same and did not want any change in their institutions and thought it unlikely to happen. By the end of Putin's term as president, dejected Russians who wanted to see an end to representative institutions outnumbered those who were hopeful that this could happen.

A combination of confident democrats and demoralized opponents creates a strong bulwark against regime change in new EU democracies. Any demagogue seeking to mobilize the demoralized to 'do something' about their new regime faces a problem of credibility, even among those who might welcome autocratic rule.

## IV  Consolidation: For better and for worse

Political support reflects both current circumstances and future expectations. If future expectations are positive, this encourages an expectation of the consolidation of support for the current regime.

Expectations of the political future are invariably more positive than current evaluations. In the eight Central and East European states admitted to the EU in 2004, an average of 75 per cent have a positive view of what they expect their regime to be like in five years' time. The 11-point increase is limited because of a substantial level of approval earlier in the decade (cf. Figure 17.3, Table 17.1).

In Bulgaria and Romania, barely half the citizens supported the regime in 2004 when it was being considered for EU entry. Doubts were shared by EU representatives and the two countries were not admitted then. However, the shortcomings of the two polit-

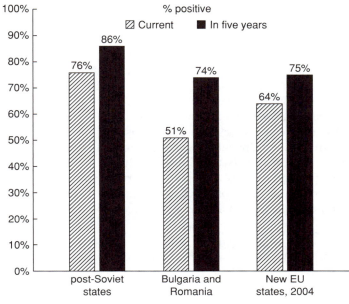

Q. Where on this scale would you put our current system of governing with free elections and many parties?
Q. Where on this scale would you put our system of governing five years in the future?

*Figure 17.3* Support for the regime now and in future.
Sources: Centre for the Study of Public Policy, New Europe Barometer, 2004; New Russia Barometer, 2008.

ical systems encouraged advocates of their admission to argue that early admission of the two countries would 'lock in' democratic governance, as happened following the admission of Spain, Portugal and Greece soon after abandoning dictatorship. This hope was shared by Bulgarians and Romanians: three-quarters were positive about what their regime would become in five years, an increase of almost half over their current evaluation. The EU came to the same conclusion; the two countries were admitted in 2007.

In post-Soviet countries, expectations of the future have been even more positive (Figure 17.3). In Ukraine, 89 per cent were positive about the future of the regime immediately after the Orange Revolution. In Belarus, positive views of the regime in five years were expressed by 82 per cent. In Russia, 88 per cent are now positive about the future. If these expectations are met, then the three regimes are moving from a situation of preponderant popular support to virtually consensual support – albeit for autocratic regimes.

As post-Soviet societies illustrate, future expectations can favour a regime whether or not it is seen as becoming more democratic. When people are asked how democratic they expect their regime to be in five years, big majorities expect it to become substantially more democratic than at present, and this is true whatever the current evaluation of the regime. Across Central and Eastern Europe, the percentage seeing their current regime as democratic in five years rises to 83 per cent.

In post-Soviet states, views of the future differ. In Ukraine, there was optimism immediately after Viktor Yushchenko's election victory; 80 per cent believed the regime would be democratic in five years. Events since have made such a view appear overly optimistic. In Belarus, people are less optimistic; only 53 per cent thought the regime would be democratic in five years. In Russia, there is substantial uncertainty. At the end of Putin's presidency 42 per cent thought the country would be democratic in five years, 38 per cent didn't know what to think, and the remaining 20 per cent were either ambivalent or negative about the prospect of Russia becoming democratic in future.

The gap between the democracy that most post-Communist citizens regard as ideal and the reality of their current regime has not led to frustration and mass protests, as political scientists once theorized. In adapting to transformation, even dissatisfied Central and East Europeans can welcome the new regime as a lesser evil compared to a Communist past. Moreover, the gap between popular aspirations and what leaders supply can create a positive tension, encouraging idealists to press for reforms to make an acceptable system more democratic (Rose, Shin and Munro, 1999). NEB evidence shows that a significant fraction see this as likely to happen. However, in successor states of the Soviet Union, given the choice between adapting to the regime as it is or becoming frustrated democrats, most appear willing to go along with the powers that be.

# 18  Adapting to Russia-style normality

> Normal has two meanings: the way things *are* and the way things *ought to be*. The expectation conveyed in the latter is often dashed by the reality of the former.
>
> (Janine Wedel, 1992)

The word normal is ambiguous in English. It can refer to acting in accord with a desirable standard of behaviour, a norm, or it can refer to the way the average person behaves. However, in an anti-modern society such as Russia's, behaviour that was *normalno* was often not how people ought to behave. In societies in which everyone behaves as they ought to, there is no difference between the two meanings of normal and everyday activities are predictable. However, where this is not the case, as in Wedel's (1992: 16) study of Poland under martial law, there is a tension between what is normatively desirable and what was normal in life under Communist repression.

The Soviet regime was a society in which the more or less predictable actions of the regime were not regarded as meeting popular norms of how government ought to behave. When Vladimir Shlapentokh wrote *A Normal Totalitarian Society* (2001: xi), he described his approach to studying predictable behaviour in Soviet society as comparable to the non-judgmental approach a herpetologist adopts in studying snakes.

The transformation of the Soviet Union into the Russian Federation repudiated Soviet standards of normality that had previously been taken for granted. It created a void until new institutions and norms could be established. In Central and Eastern Europe this was filled by the invocation of European norms, whatever this term was supposed to mean. However, even though Russians at the start of transformation endorsed some values that are also widespread in Europe, such as freedom and Christianity (Figure 1.2), they were not part of everyday Soviet life. To describe the society's norms as 'post-Soviet' calls attention to what was being left behind, but it does not identify what society is like today.

The political inertia of transformed institutions has exerted a steady pressure on Russians to accept what the Kremlin supplies as normal, and the longer the new regime remains in place, the greater the pressure on its subjects to adapt to it (Rose, Mishler and Munro, 2006: Chapter 9). Two decades after the abrupt launch of glasnost and perestroika, Russians have had lots of time to learn what is now normal. The turnover of generations has resulted in the median NRB respondent having spent almost half his or her adulthood as a citizen of the Russian Federation rather than a Soviet subject. Yet the turnover of generations is not necessary for people to adapt to transformation

(Mishler and Rose, 2007), and the capacity of Russians to adapt leaves open the nature of the norms to which they have adapted.

## I What do Russians mean by normality?

The ambiguity of contemporary Russian life is expressed in the hybrid characterizations that are used to describe it. Compound labels applied by Westerners combine European norms and deviations from them, such as calling the system 'partly free', a form of 'managed pluralism' or 'predatory capitalism'. Compound labels can also be used by Russians. For example, Vladimir Putin's deputy head of administration has characterized the regime as a 'sovereign democracy', implying that foreigners have no right to evaluate the government of Russia.

The recognition of social norms is necessary for individuals to adopt the routines that make everyday life predictable. Therefore, New Russia Barometer XIV included a battery of questions asking to what extent people associated seven social conditions for which government has a recognized responsibility with the idea of a normal society. Unlike questions about abstract concepts such as capitalism or democracy, Russians had no problem in understanding the idea of a normal society; on average only 1 per cent said they did not have any opinion. Nor did people have any difficulty in deciding how important or unimportant each was. There was virtual unanimity that all of the attributes addressed are either essential or important to life in a normal society:

| | |
|---|---|
| Opportunities to improve your living conditions | 99% |
| No inflation | 99% |
| No fear of crime | 98% |
| Everyone can find a job | 98% |
| Welfare services will help the needy | 98% |
| Can live without government interfering | 96% |
| Public officials treat everyone fairly | 96% |

The only difference is whether a person considers a given condition as essential or important – and big majorities think each is essential. A total of 85 per cent believes having opportunities to improve living conditions and being without fear of crime are essential; more than four-fifths regard it is essential that everyone can find a job and there is no fear of inflation; and 72 per cent believe freedom from government interference and state provision of welfare are essentials of a normal life.

The Russian ideal of a normal society is not one in which the state is all-powerful or very weak; it is a society in which there is freedom and an effective state. This ideal has significant parallels with another word frequently invoked in Russian political discourse, order ( *poryadok*). In-depth interviews by Ellen Carnaghan (2007: 156ff) emphasize that Russians do not think of order in the colloquial 'law-and-order' sense of gun-toting Americans but in the Weberian sense of a Rechtsstaat, in which the state is effective in meeting its responsibilities. For Russians, disorder (that is, unpredictable novelty) began under Gorbachev and intensified during the Yeltsin administration. President Putin has taken advantage of this by frequently justifying his actions as promoting order in society.

The characteristics of the Russian idea of a normal society are similar to those citizens in a Western society have. However, the ambiguity of the term 'normal' is a caution that what may be normal in both the idealistic and the everyday sense in a Western society is not necessarily so in Russia, as people may regard the way in which Russian society functions as very different from how it ought to function.

## II Becoming normal

For a decade after the start of transformation, Russian society was in turbulence. Boris Yeltsin's first term concentrated on the destruction of the Soviet system; however the imposition of a new constitution and economic system was not followed by the creation of a normal pattern of life. The economy was not normal; in 1998, 63 per cent of those in employment had had their wages paid late or not at all in the previous 12 months. Yeltsin's second term was marked by his chronic illnesses, erratic behaviour and unpopularity with the public, climaxing in his surprise resignation in December 1999. When Vladimir Putin (2000: 212) became president, he declared, 'Russia has reached its limits for political and socio-economic upheavals, cataclysms and radical reforms'. Putin explicitly promised to introduce political stability – and in his terms he succeeded. In the 2007 New Russia Barometer survey, a retrospective judgment of Boris Yeltsin gave him a mean rating of 2.7 on a 10-point scale of approval, while Putin's mean approval rating was 7.2.

*The trend.* Like democratization, normalization is a process rather than a goal that can be achieved over night. A reduction in turbulence is a pre-condition for life to become normal, but does not make a post-transformation society normal.

The New Russia Barometer began monitoring the extent to which life was becoming normal in January 2000, with a question designed to determine whether people saw their life as not at all normal, a little normal, fairly normal or definitely normal. At that time seven-eighths saw life as not at all or only a little normal. Only a deviant few described Russian life as definitely normal (Table 18.1).

There has been an unsteady but positive trend since 2001 toward the normalization of Russian society. By the start of President Putin's second term, the minority seeing society as definitely or fairly normal had risen to a quarter of the population. However, more than two-thirds still saw it as only a little or not at all normal. The proportion seeing Russia as more or less normal has now increased to the point that by 2008 the median group consists of 32 per cent viewing society as fairly normal and,

*Table 18.1* Trends in viewing life as normal

| Q. Do you think Russian life today is that of a normal society? | | | | | | | |
|---|---|---|---|---|---|---|---|
| | 2000a | 2001 | 2003a | 2004 | 2005 | 2007a | 2008 | Change |
| | % | % | % | % | % | % | % | |
| Definitely | 2 | 9 | 15 | 10 | 10 | 19 | 32 | +30 |
| Fairly | 11 | 13 | 25 | 18 | 26 | 27 | 32 | +21 |
| Normal | 13 | 21 | 40 | 28 | 36 | 46 | 64 | +51 |
| Only a little | 54 | 50 | 40 | 45 | 49 | 40 | 26 | −28 |
| Not at all | 33 | 29 | 20 | 27 | 15 | 14 | 10 | −23 |
| Not normal | 87 | 79 | 60 | 72 | 64 | 54 | 36 | −51 |

Source: Centre for the Study of Public Policy, New Russia Barometer.

even more striking, an equal percentage see society as definitely normal. Those viewing life as only a little or not at all normal have fallen by more than half and only 1
in 10 now sees society as not at all normal.

A multiplicity of influences affects the extent to which Russians see their society
as normal. (For details, see the multiple regression analysis in Rose, (2008a: 79). It
accounts for 16.6 per cent of the variance between individuals in their assessment of
how normal Russian life is.) Given the responsibility of government for maintaining
conditions in which normal life can flourish, political performance matters. Those
who see government as promoting order are substantially more likely to see society
as normal and by 2007 this was true of 61 per cent, as against 27 per cent seeing no
change and only 1 in 8 seeing order as worsening. Likewise, those who see government offering more protection for the poor are also more likely to see society as
normal. Although most Russians feel that it is normal for public officials to treat them
unfairly, those in the minority who feel they are treated fairly are also more inclined
to judge society as normal. Having positive expectations of the political and economic
future is associated with people seeing society as normal.

How Russians relate to others also affects how society is evaluated. Those who tend
to trust other people are more likely to see it as normal. So too are the minority with
a relatively high social status. However, the positive effect of social status is partially
offset by the negative effect of education: better-educated Russians are less likely
to see society as normal. This can reflect the devaluation of education as against
market-oriented 'smarts' as well as educated people having higher standards of what
a normal society ought to be.

The ambiguity of normality is illustrated by the fact that experience of corruption
does not alter popular judgments. Russians who report paying a bribe to public officials
are just as likely to see their society as normal as those who receive services to which
they are entitled without paying a bribe. Notwithstanding the theoretical importance
of economic conditions, neither destitution nor unemployment has any significant
influence on whether Russians see their society as normal, nor does the possession of
consumer goods.

*Expectations.* At the start of transformation there was very widespread uncertainty
about its long-term consequences. When the New Russia Barometer asked in spring
1994, how long it would be before people thought they would be satisfied with the
political system, 65 per cent said they did not know. Similarly, 64 per cent were uncertain whether they would ever be satisfied with the economic system.

By 2001, when the NRB began regular monitoring of how long it would take for
Russian society to become normal, people divided into five groups (Table 18.2). The
largest group (50 per cent), was uncertain, thinking it difficult to say whether Russian
society would ever become normal and this was augmented by an additional 9 per
cent who said the society would never be normal. More than one-quarter thought it
would take at least half a dozen years for the society to become normal. At the other
extreme, 9 per cent thought Russian society was already normal and an additional 5
per cent thought it could become so in a few years.

Uncertainty has since fallen and optimism grown. In 2001, 14 per cent thought the
country was already normal or would be normal in five years. This expectation turned
out to be an under-estimate for, by 2008, more than twice as many thought that Russia
was definitely normal. In addition, almost one-third see Russia as becoming normal
within a decade and pessimists believing it will never become normal are now a small

*Table 18.2* When society will become normal

| Q. How long do you think it will be before Russia becomes a normal society? | | | | | | | |
|---|---|---|---|---|---|---|---|
| | 2001 % | 2003a % | 2004 % | 2005 % | 2007a % | 2008 % | Change |
| Already normal | 9 | 15 | 10 | 10 | 17 | 29 | +20 |
| 1–5 years | 5 | 10 | 12 | 8 | 11 | 11 | +6 |
| 6–10 years | 27 | 34 | 33 | 31 | 22 | 20 | −7 |
| Never | 9 | 11 | 11 | 8 | 9 | 6 | −3 |
| Difficult to know | 50 | 30 | 34 | 42 | 41 | 34 | −16 |

Source: Centre for the Study of Public Policy, New Russia Barometer.

minority. The proportion of Russians uncertain about whether society can ever become normal has fallen to one-third.

If current expectations are realized, a quarter-century after Mikhail Gorbachev opened the Pandora's box of reforms that triggered transformation, most Russians will be living in what they see as a normal society. The chief influences encouraging the belief that society can become normal in the next decade are much the same as those leading people to regard it as normal today. Expectations of the future, a positive view of government performance and current social status combine to encourage optimism about the achievement of post-transformation normality.

## III Obstacles to normality

Although Russians have positive expectations of the future, there remain major obstacles to society becoming normal. Russians are well aware of this. When the New Russia Barometer asks people to identify major obstacles to normal life, hardly any Russian is a don't know.

*Government the biggest obstacle.* The failure of government to enforce laws or to obey its own laws, as made manifest by corruption, is seen as the biggest obstacle to the normalization of Russian society (Table 18.2). This is not so much a demand for government to get tough in dealing with street criminals, as it is a demand for the government to set a good example by getting its own officials to follow the rule of law. This view is re-inforced by one-third of Russians seeing the behaviour of the Kremlin as a major obstacle to Russia becoming normal.

The concept of a normal society covers the economy as well as the polity: almost half see low wages and unemployment as obstacles to Russia becoming normal. This is a reminder that many Russians do not expect the wealth created by revenue from oil and gas exports to trickle down and produce a property-owning democracy. Instead, they see many fruits of the energy boom as enriching a predatory oligarchy that siphons off much of the country's wealth in a corrupt manner. However, this does not mean that the transition to the market is itself blamed for abnormal conditions, a view held by only 13 per cent. Moreover, only 2 per cent regard the introduction of democratic institutions as a major obstacle to normal life. This implies that when 'democracy' is blamed for the country's problems people are referring to the abnormal way in which its sovereign democracy operates.

Q. *What do you think is the biggest obstacle to Russia becoming a normal society? And the second biggest?*

Obstacle named as biggest or second biggest, %

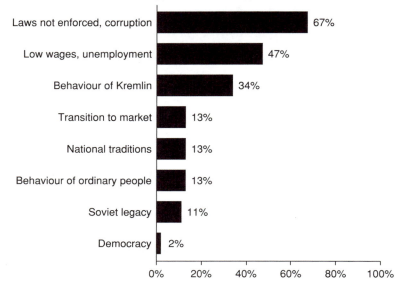

*Figure 18.1* Obstacles to Russia becoming normal.
Sources: Centre for the Study of Public Policy, New Russia Barometer, 2005. The items come from New Russia Barometer, 2004: Behaviour of ordinary people, Soviet legacy and Democracy.

Russians reject the cultural hypothesis that the country's past is a major obstacle to the post-transformation society becoming normal. Only 13 per cent see national traditions or how ordinary people behave as major obstacles to achieving normality as they (and as Europeans) define it today. Equally striking, although many Russians are aware of problems arising from the Soviet legacy, only 11 per cent see the Soviet past as a major obstacle to normalization. Past failings are acknowledged as a problem but not as a permanent curse.

In short, the chief obstacle to the normalization of society is not Russian customs but the performance of the Russian state. It has failed to make its own officials abide by rule-of-law norms and failed to manage the economy so that most people have a steady wage, and do not need to juggle a portfolio of resources in order to cope with transformation and its aftermath.

*Adapting to what is.* The euphoria that was created by the start of Russia's transformation is no more. The unpredictable shocks of transformation are now part of the past too. Today, Russian society is in its post-transformation phase: what happens next year is not expected to be radically different from what is happening this year. The longer Russia continues on its current path, the more distant society becomes from what it was when the Federation was launched and the more the path taken is likely to be accepted as normal, if only in the sense of that is the way that things are.

In the past decade most Russians have adapted to post-transformation society. When asked in 1998 whether they had done so, the largest group, 45 per cent, said they would never adapt, while only 29 per cent reported said that they had adapted. There was also a group in the middle that was trying to adapt. However, when the same question was repeated a decade later, 66 per cent have now adapted to the new system, and 20 per cent expected to do so in the near future. The proportion of 'social refuseniks', asserting that they will never adapt, has dropped from nearly half to 1 in 7 (Figure 18.2).

The adaptability of Russians shows the limitation of theories that postulate that cultural norms persist unchanging, whether from the Tsarist era or from Soviet times. Re-socialization *out* of Soviet norms can be just as important in producing support for the regime as socialization into those norms was in an earlier era. Adaptation has occurred not only among those too young to have grown up in the Soviet system but also among those who were initially socialized by its institutions. Two-thirds of Russians between 30 to 59 in age have already adapted and so have three-fifths of Russians age 60 or older.

The expectation of normalization is a bulwark against radical rejection of the current regime. Even though there are major features of life that Russians do not like, the passage of time has begun to make acceptable, on a matter-of-fact basis, a regime that offers people some (though not all) the freedoms and some (but not all) the material benefits that people would like. Order and predictability *à la Putin* is a second-best solution, but Russians prefer it to the risk of another cycle of transformation.

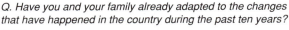

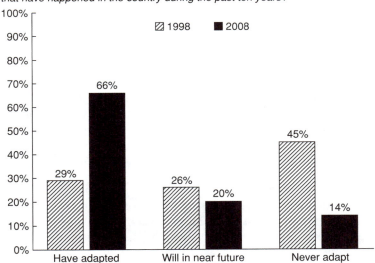

*Figure 18.2* Russians have adapted to transformation.
Source: Levada Centre nationwide surveys, October 1998; March 2008.

# 19  An evolving Europe

Europe is experiencing an unusual time. Here you have half a continent, cut off from its roots nearly half a century ago, that now wishes to return.

(Tadeusz Mazowiecki, Prime Minister of Poland, 1990)

The fall of the Berlin Wall marked the start of the return to Europe of more than 100 million Central and East Europeans who had been absent during half a century of war and Soviet occupation. But it was not Europe as before. After the Second World War, Western Europe was transformed by the conscious rejection of European traditions that had led to two great wars in the lifetime of its leaders. Dictatorships were replaced by democratic regimes, economic stagnation was replaced by economic growth and mass affluence, and peace was secured through the NATO military alliance. The European Union, founded with six members in 1957, created institutions for promoting the economic and political integration of its member states.

On the other side of the Iron Curtain, the Soviet Union used a combination of political commissars and Red Army strength to integrate almost half the continent into a Communist bloc led from Moscow. It explicitly rejected such European values and institutions as the market, the rule of law and democracy. Soviet institutions created an alternative model. While the collapse of the Communist bloc gave Central and East Europeans the opportunity of returning to Europe, it did not provide a similar sense of direction in post-Soviet lands. It left a legacy of ties between leaders of the Russian Federation and other Soviet successor states. These links have now been institutionalized under Moscow's leadership in the Commonwealth of Independent States and by Russia moving troops into Georgia.

The expansion of the European Union to include many democracies bordering post-Communist lands offered countries escaping from Communist rule an attractive goal: membership. But before they could become members, new regimes had to establish their credentials for exercising democratic governance. Concurrently, post-Soviet elites had to decide how much to draw on what was normal in the Soviet past, what was normal in Western Europe and what was distinctive in their current national circumstances.

## I  Europe as pull and push

The transformation of Central and Eastern Europe not only ended dependence on Moscow; it also created new forms of interdependence. The situation was familiar to older politicians who had lived through the 1930s and 1940s, when national govern-ments unsuccessfully sought to balance their country between Nazi Germany and Stalinist Russia. The novelty was that interdependence now offered the opportunity to become a modern twenty-first-century European state. To achieve this goal, new regimes needed economic institutions as a foundation for a dynamic market economy and they needed military security to deter another invasion of their territory by a stronger power. The World Bank and the International Monetary Fund provided economic assistance and NATO offered military security. In 1999, the Czech Republic, Hungary and Poland became members of NATO under American leadership and in 2004 the other seven CEE countries now in the European Union were admitted to NATO. Since member-ship in NATO is not a requirement for membership in the EU and four of the EU's first 15 members did not belong to NATO, it is not considered further here.

Above all, fledgeling regimes in countries that were small in population and sur-rounded by larger neighbours needed a political framework that offered opportun-ities for cooperation for mutual benefit and the assurance that they were not left to fend for themselves in an uncertain world. The European Union provided just that. As was said of post-Franco Spain: 'If Spain is the problem, Europe is the solution' (quoted in Rose, 1996: 261). In 1991 the governments of what were then Czechos-lovakia, Hungary and Poland met at Visegrad, Slovakia to begin discussions about seeking membership in the European Union. Their initiative was subsequently followed by half a dozen other countries.

*Meeting the Copenhagen criteria*. Although any country in a broadly defined con-tinent can apply for membership in the European Union, admission is not available on demand. A country must undergo a lengthy scrutiny to determine whether it meets the EU's standards of democratic governance and its application must then be endorsed by all the existing EU member states. Just as the European Union was not built in a day, so a government cannot achieve EU membership overnight. It took more than a decade of discussions for eight post-Communist countries to be admitted to the European Union in 2004.

At its 1993 Council of Ministers meeting in Copenhagen, the EU set out five mem-bership criteria that applicant countries should meet: democratic institutions, the rule of law, respect for human and minority rights, a functioning market economy and an effective public administration. The criteria are broad but not empty of meaning. For example, Communist regimes had not tried to meet the first four criteria and also failed to achieve an effective bureaucratic administration.

In principle, the Copenhagen criteria were goals that CEE regimes wanted to meet as part of the process of expunging the anti-modern legacy of their predecessors. However, the legacy of the past meant that this aspiration was not easily met. The European Union offered money, training and technical assistance to raise standards of govern-ance. It was also prepared to push applicant countries to change their behaviour where it was judged inconsistent with EU standards. For example, discussions with Slovakia did not commence until after its autocratic leader, Vladimir Meciar, lost the 1998 elec-tion and was replaced by parties unequivocally committed to democratic governance.

On occasion, there was conflict between the EU's criteria and the particular prac-tices of national governments, leading to complaints from applicants that the EU was seeking to impose conditions that infringed their national independence. The conflict was most evident in Estonia and Latvia, where laws required residents to know the state's official language in order to become citizens, a requirement that the great bulk of Russian residents could not meet. The Baltic states argued that this was justified in the circumstances of Soviet occupation; the EU pushed governments to liberalize their laws on citizenship to meet its minority-rights standards. However, it did not require the abandonment of language tests. In Poland and the Baltic states, there was a fear that a completely open market would result in Germans and Scandinavians, having much deeper purses than their own citizens, buying large amounts of their national land. Concessions were negotiated to mitigate this risk. Existing member states were anxious that their national labour forces, already experiencing high levels of unemployment, would be put under additional pressure by an influx of workers from Central and Eastern Europe. These states secured restrictions on the free movement of labour from the low-wage countries of Eastern Europe.

Deciding whether national governments met the Copenhagen criteria involved lengthy political discussions between applicants placing the most positive gloss on their achievements and sceptical European Commission officials. There is an alternative to asking Eurocrats to evaluate how a country is governed: it is to ask the people who live there. The New Europe Barometer has done just that; its questionnaires include a multiplicity of questions in which citizens evaluate the performance of their government on each of the Copenhagen criteria. The replies discussed below cover the NEB survey immediately following the admission of eight CEE countries to the European Union – the Czech Republic, Estonia, Hungary, Latvia, Lithuania, Poland, Slovakia and Slovenia – plus Bulgaria and Romania, which were admitted three years later. Cyprus and Malta were admitted to the EU in 2004, but since neither was part of the Communist bloc, they are not covered by NEB surveys. For comparative purposes, the following analysis also includes Russian data.

Conducting free and fair elections is a pre-condition for a country being considered for EU membership. CEE countries had demonstrated their commitment to electoral democracy well before Brussels began evaluating their application. However, commitment to the rule of law, including human rights, has been more problematic. When CEE citizens are asked their perception of corruption among public officials, everywhere less than half think that most officials are honest. The size of the minority viewing officials positively varies greatly from Slovenia, where 47 per cent think most officials are not corrupt, to 12 per cent in Bulgaria (Table 19.1).

Fairness in dealing with citizens is an integral feature of an impartial bureaucracy; it is defined by applying the law in the same way to citizens in similar circumstances. However, in every applicant country, less than half its citizens expect people like themselves to receive fair treatment from government. The percentage expecting fair treatment varies widely, from 46 per cent in the Czech Republic to 19 per cent in Hungary and Bulgaria.

Human rights issues tend to involve a limited number of people, whether marginal members of society abused by the police, or ethnic minorities systematically discriminated against. Because NEB surveys represent the whole of a country's population, the evaluation of human rights is from the perspective of the majority of citizens rather than potentially affected minorities. In most new EU member states most citizens think that their government does respect individual human rights. In Hungary as many as 76 per cent regard their government as doing so, while the proportion falls to 30 per cent in Romania.

Because EU entry makes a country part of a single European market it is necessary to have a functioning market economy. This criterion was introduced in recognition

*Table 19.1* Public evaluation of the rule of law

*Q. How widespread do you think bribe-taking and corruption are among public officials in this country?*
*Q. Do you think people like yourself are treated fairly by government?*
*Q. How much respect do you think this country's government has for individual human rights?*

|  | *Majority not corrupt* | *Fair treatment (% positive)* | *Respect human rights* |
|---|---|---|---|
| Slovenia | 47 | 39 | 67 |
| Estonia | 39 | 31 | 62 |
| Hungary | 36 | 19 | 76 |
| Czech Republic | 31 | 46 | 42 |
| Latvia | 27 | 25 | 53 |
| NEW EU MEAN | 27 | 28 | 54 |
| Poland | 26 | 21 | 62 |
| Slovakia | 20 | 25 | 51 |
| Lithuania | 18 | 22 | 45 |
| Romania | 15 | 28 | 30 |
| Bulgaria | 12 | 19 | 47 |
| Russia | 18 | 30 | 33 |

Sources: Centre for the Study of Public Policy, New Europe Barometer, 2004; New Russia Barometer, 2008: respect for human rights, 2005.

of the dysfunctional nature of post-Communist economies during transformation (Chapter 8). Given variations in living conditions within the older EU member states, no particular level of Gross Domestic Product is specified. Given differences in political ideologies within the EU, it is left open whether the economy functions according to social democratic, liberal or social market principles.

Paradoxically, the first sign that markets are functioning is that firms that could only survive in a command economy, such as producers of equipment for the Soviet military-industrial complex, go out of business, and inefficient state enterprises stop hoarding labour. Both measures increase unemployment and lead to the contraction of the economy as officially measured. The second sign of a market economy beginning to function is that official statistics of Gross Domestic Product register steady and substantial economic growth. This is not only important for raising living standards but also indicates that the official economy is beginning to incorporate activities that people had previously been undertaking in the unofficial shadow economy.

The speed with which market conditions were introduced varied substantially and so did the extent of subsequent economic growth (cf. Figures 8.2 and 19.1). In Poland shock therapy produced a sharp downturn in 1991 but an equally quick recovery launching a period of sustained economic growth in the following year. In Slovenia the turnaround occurred a year later. Thus, by the time that Poland entered the European Union its economy had grown by more than half since its low point and the same was true of Slovenia. By contrast, the turning point was not reached in Bulgaria and Romania until 1998 and in Lithuania until 1999. Countries where governments were slow to respond to the imperatives of transformation have paid a price: their economies have grown much less than the earliest reformers. At the time of entering the EU, the official

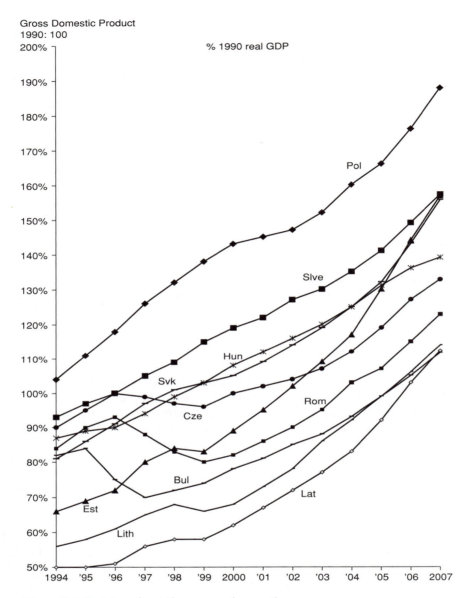

Gross Domestic Product
1990: 100

*Figure 19.1* Post-transformation economic growth.
Source: EBRD, *Transition Report*, 2001, 2007; 2006 figures are based on estimates, 2007 figures are forecasts.

economies of Latvia and Lithuania had yet to regain the GDP with which they had been credited in 1990.

The New Europe Barometer indicator of a functioning market economy is whether people can earn enough from working in the official economy or from their pension to meet their basic needs (see Chapter 8). At the time of the EU enlargement in 2004, only 35 per cent of CEE households said that they could do so. Slovenia was exceptional in that more than half of households received enough money from their first job to meet their needs. Bulgaria was at the other extreme: the market economy only enabled 15 per cent to get by on the basis of their official economy earnings.

By relying on a portfolio of economies, a clear majority of households managed not only to avoid destitution but also to begin furnishing their households with a variety of consumer durables that West Europeans had long taken for granted. Ownership of major consumer goods is not only satisfying to households but also useful as an indicator that families have sufficient discretionary income to purchase goods that are nice to have but not necessary to avoid destitution. By the time of EU enlargement in 2004 an average of 95 per cent of households had a modern colour television set, 54 per cent a car and half had a video cassette recorder or had updated to a DVD set. While these goods are not distributed evenly throughout society, most households have enough discretionary income to enjoy at least two of these 'good' goods and only 4 per cent had none.

A striking feature of these bottom-up assessments of democratic governance is that no country is consistently evaluated as the worst in Central and Eastern Europe (for details, see Rose, 2008b). Instead, each country appears to be rated higher on some Copenhagen criteria and worse on others. For example, the Hungarian government has the most positive evaluation in terms of respect for human rights while it falls to the bottom in terms of fair treatment of citizens. The Czech Republic ranks highest for the fair treatment of individuals but is next to bottom as regards respect for human rights. The government of Slovenia is exceptional in consistently receiving a favourable evaluation from its citizens. In a complementary way, there is a tendency for Bulgaria and Romania to be near or at the bottom in comparative rankings. The European Union took this view too, delaying the admission of these two countries until 2007.

The decision about whether to admit a country to the European Union is a political rather than a statistical calculation. Differences between the most and least successful Central and East European applicants did not restrict EU enlargement. Instead, the existing member states decided that all were 'good enough' for membership. In making this judgment they were not only relying on current evidence but also on the prospect that admitting countries would strengthen the reform of their political and economic institutions, as had been the case a generation earlier, when Spain, Portugal and Greece achieved EU membership within a dozen years of replacing dictatorships with democratic regimes.

## II  Turning away: post-Soviet states

The transformation of the Russian Federation began in a radically different context: the collapse of the Soviet Union. This event was described by Vladimir Putin in his 25 April 2005 State of the Union speech as 'the greatest geopolitical catastrophe of the century'. Because the Communist Party of the Soviet Union had integrated diverse territories of the Tsar in a formally federal Soviet Union of 15 republics from the Russian Federation to Uzbekistan, the republics were in position to break away as independent states when Mikhail Gorbachev's attempts at restructuring got out of hand. However, because the Soviet population and the command economy were integrated across the borders of republics, the break-up of the USSR left many cross-national ties in place.

*Russia's history outside Europe.* The sprawling Russian Federation reaches across four continents; it has land borders with 14 countries and is close by water to five more. In Europe it has land borders with Norway, Finland, Estonia, Latvia, Belarus and Ukraine; Kaliningrad borders Lithuania and Poland; and the Russian Federation shares the Black Sea with the Turkish fleet. In Central Asia the Federation has land borders with Georgia, Azerbaijan and Kazakhstan and the Caspian Sea is a common border with Iran and Turkmenistan. In the Far East it has land borders with the People's Republic of China, Mongolia and North Korea, and it is narrowly separated by water from Japan and from the American state of Alaska.

Throughout its history Russia's interest in Europe has tended to be defensive, and with good reason, given successive invasions from Napoleon, Imperial Germany and Nazi Germany. The Tsarist practice of expanding eastward to the borders of Mongolia and China meant that many of the republics incorporated into the Soviet Union were remote from Europe in every sense. For example, Central Asia lands are on trade routes to China, they have substantial Muslim populations and border Muslim countries such as Iran. For such states there was no question of a return to Europe, for they had never been part of a European state-system.

Peter the Great founded St Petersburg in order to create an opening to Europe and since then some Russian intellectuals have looked to European models of national development, whether in state administration (Prussia), culture (France) or industry (England). However, their views were strongly rejected by Slavophiles who stood for traditional political and social institutions. The founding generation of the Soviet Union looked to Karl Marx and other Europeans for inspiration, but Joseph Stalin and his successors did not. Europe, however defined, was seen as a competitor. Nikita Khrushchev expressed this outlook in a declaration to Western diplomats in 1956: 'As for capitalist states, it doesn't depend on you whether or not we exist. Whether you like it or not, history is on our side. We will bury you.'

The collapse of the Soviet Union did not undermine the pride of Russians in being Russian. Moreover, it created a state in which ethnic Russians were four-fifths of the population, making Russians much more dominant than they had been in the Soviet Union. Ethnic minorities in the new state are fragmented. Vladimir Putin has played on national pride. In an early address as President, he rejected 'the mechanical copying of other nations' experience'. Russia's experience, for better or for worse has been different from Europe; thus 'Russia has to search for its own path to renewal' (Putin, 2000: 212). One of his deputies, Vladimir Surkov, went further, arguing, 'I often hear that democracy is more important than sovereignty. We don't agree with this. An independent state is worth fighting for. It would be nice to run away into Europe, but they won't accept us there.' (quoted in Rose and Munro, 2008: 52). Thus, the developmental path of the government of the Russian Federation has been different from that of Central and East European states.

*Russia's choice today.* Russia's size and significance has gained it a place at what has become the G8 meeting of world leaders from four continents. The boom in oil prices, combined with Russia's vast energy reserves, has not only created vast amounts of foreign earnings but also given Russia a new role in international affairs. President Putin has used Russia's energy exports to pursue a 'divide and dominate' strategy in relation to European states dependent on Russian energy. This strategy has benefited from the inability of EU member states to respond with a common strategy.

In principle, the Russian Federation could apply to join the European Union. If this were to happen, its system of governance would come under scrutiny, and by the Copenhagen criteria, found wanting. It does not meet the minimum condition for membership, holding free and fair elections. On rule-of-law criteria, Russia falls below the minimum of new member states in corruption and in fair treatment of its citizens, and is rated by its citizens as almost as bad as the worst new EU member state in respect for human rights (Table 19.1). Dmitry Medvedev, like Vladimir Putin a lawyer before becoming Russia's president, has told foreigners, 'Russia is a country where people don't like to observe the law. It is a country of legal nihilism.' (Barber *et al.*, 2008).

To test support for arguments of Russian intellectuals who see Europe as a way of 'civilizing' or 'democratizing' the country, the New Russia Barometer regularly asks people whether they see the country's future as linked more with Europe or with the successor states of the Soviet Union. To allow for widespread popular ignorance of the European Union, the question refers to Western Europe. This allows Russians to distinguish 'good' Western Europe from the United States, which is not always viewed as good.

By a majority of 2 to 1, Russians see the country's future linked with other CIS states rather than with Western Europe (Figure 19.2). The two alternatives are not seen as an either/or choice, as was the case in the Cold War era. The median Russian sees the country's future as being more with CIS countries than with Europe. However, among those with a definite opinion, support for CIS ties is four times that for Western Europe. The preference for the Commonwealth of Independent States is consistent with family histories. Far more Russians have relatives in Soviet successor states to the east than in Baltic states or anywhere in Europe. It is also consistent with official statistics: there are an estimated 25 million people of Russian nationality living in other successor states of the Soviet Union. This encourages Russians to think of CIS countries as the near abroad.

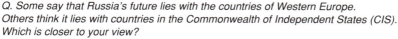

*Q. Some say that Russia's future lies with the countries of Western Europe. Others think it lies with countries in the Commonwealth of Independent States (CIS). Which is closer to your view?*

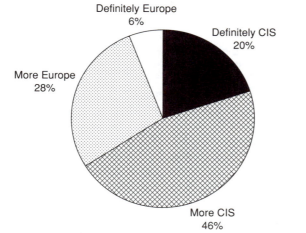

*Figure 19.2* Where Russia's future lies.
Source: Centre for the Study of Public Policy, New Russia Barometer, 2008.

The minority view of a third of Russians preferring a future linked with Europe is subject to pressures from the dominant majority. Russian is the lingua franca within the Commonwealth of Independent States and the Internet provides a populous Cyrillic 'ghetto' within which contacts can be maintained across eight time zones (Rose, 2006a). Being Russian is often a comparative advantage in dealings with less populous and less prosperous countries in the near abroad. The Russian-speaking population of the region is large, with a population of more than a quarter of a billion. Thus it can sustain economic and political activities on a massive scale.

The framework of Russian life encourages most people to focus on national concerns and the near abroad. The 'nearest' countries are not the most European of the former Soviet republics but those to the east. When NRB surveys ask about former republics with which Russia should maintain close ties, 66 per cent favour doing so with Kazakhstan and 61 per cent with Kyrgyzstan as against an average of 55 per cent with the three Baltic republics. Russia's only contiguous land borders are with Estonia, Latvia and Finland.

The contrast between how Russians view the world and how Central and East Europeans do so is evident in the extent to which Russians qualify their endorsement of democracy in reply to an NEB question asking whether democracy is always preferable; under some circumstances an authoritarian government is better; or it makes no difference how a country is governed. In new EU member states an average of 57 per cent say that democracy is always preferable; in Russia only 25 per cent are so strongly committed to democracy. The largest group of Russians is not indifferent to forms of government: 41 per cent think that in some circumstances an authoritarian government is preferable compared to 18 per cent in new EU member states. The 34 per cent of Russians who think that it makes no difference how a country is governed outnumber the quarter who have an unqualified commitment to democratic governance.

*Post-Soviet Muslims.* A geopolitical division of the world into the West versus Islam leaves open which side Russia is on. The Soviet Union had upwards of 40 million people of Muslim origin and in the Russian Federation today there are more than 10 million subjects of Muslim parentage, albeit of diverse and geographically scattered ethnicities and of varying degrees of assimilation to a dominant Russian culture. The break-up of the Soviet Union has given fresh significance to the perennial debate about identities. Insofar as religion is a source of political division, then the CIS must also be divided into countries that are Slavic and Russian Orthodox; Christian but not Russian Orthodox or Slavic (e.g., Armenia, Georgia, Moldova); and those that are predominantly Muslim.

In predicting a clash of civilizations, Samuel P. Huntington (1996: 214) argued: 'Whatever their political or religious opinions, Muslims agree that a basic difference exists between their culture and Western culture'. However, many Islamic specialists dismiss this view as an oversimplification: 'To say that someone is Muslim tells us little regarding that person's views on politics' (Brumberg, 2002: 109). Insofar as this is the case, there may be a clash of civilizations within countries, including the Russian Federation, a point underscored by the continuing resurgence of armed conflict between Russian forces and Chechens, who are also Muslims.

It is an open question what proportion of Muslims socialized into the Soviet system hold views more like the majority of their fellow citizens or are more oriented toward Mecca or Moscow. Evidence to answer this question is at hand from a 2001 sample survey in Kazakhstan and Kyrgyzstan (see Rose, 2002a). A consequence of Soviet rule was the displacement of both Islam and Orthodox Christianity by a materialist ideology emphasizing progress and re-inforced by an influx of Russians directed to settle in Central Asia in order to develop the region far from the prying and threatening eyes of Europe.

Broadbrush generalizations that place Kazakhstan and Kyrgyzstan in a single 'civilizational' category ignore the fact that neither is homogeneous in religion or ethnicity. In the last Soviet census of 1989, Kazakhs constituted only two-fifths of the republic's population; they were matched in number by ethnic Russians. In the last Soviet census in Kyrgyzstan, the titular nationality was just over half the population, Russians one-fifth, and Uzbeks the third largest group. In the Kazakhstan survey, 40 per cent say they are Muslim; 38 per cent Russian Orthodox; 16 per cent have no religion; and the remainder are scattered. In Kyrgyzstan, 75 per cent say they are Muslims; 16 per cent, Orthodox; only 4 per cent, none; and the rest are a miscellany.

Nominal identification with a religion is not evidence of commitment to its beliefs and practices. Mosque attendance is not an adequate measure of commitment to Islam, especially for women. Therefore, nominal Muslims were asked whether they followed the rules prescribed by their religion, wording that is particularly relevant to political action. In both countries, only one-fifth of Muslims say they constantly try to follow religious rules; three-fifths say they sometimes do so; and one-sixth do not bother with religious practices at all. Among the Russian Orthodox background, in Kazakhstan 37 per cent ignore religious rules while 56 per cent try to follow religious precepts some of the time and the rest try to do so regularly. In Kyrgyzstan 24 per cent of the nominally Orthodox are indifferent to religious precepts, 64 per cent say they sometimes follow these religious precepts, and 12 per cent try to do so all the time. Thus, strong commitment to religion is confined to a minority of Muslims and Russian Orthodox identifiers.

Neither Kazakhstan nor Kyrgyzstan is a rule-of-law democracy. On the basis of Freedom House evaluations, Kazakhstan is an unaccountable autocracy. Its 2007 election was competitive but unfair; the government party won all the seats in parliament; and OSCE monitors reported widespread irregularities in voting. Kyrgyzstan is a plebiscitarian autocracy in which the surprise result of the 2005 election led the president to resign and go into exile. The 2007 election resulted in three different parties winning seats in parliament but OSCE observers said the conduct of the election failed to meet its standards.

Autocratic rule appears to support Huntington's assertion that Muslims favour undemocratic, rule. The NEB question asking whether individuals prefer rule by a strong leader governing without any semblance of representative institutions is thus very relevant. Asking this question in Central Asia not only makes it possible to test the extent to which Muslims actually do prefer autocratic rule, but also whether they are more likely to do so than Russians.

Huntington's claim that Muslims invariably favour autocratic rule is rejected by the evidence. Even though elections and parliament are limited in their capacity to hold governors to account, a majority in both Kazakhstan and Kyrgyzstan want to keep them rather than have a strong-man rule without any institutions of accountability (Figure 19.3). Differences of opinion among Muslims show that it is unjustified to project onto all members of a given group the views of nominal representatives, whether presidents or imams. Detailed analysis shows that differences of opinion about strongman rule among nominal Muslims do not reflect differences in religious commitment.

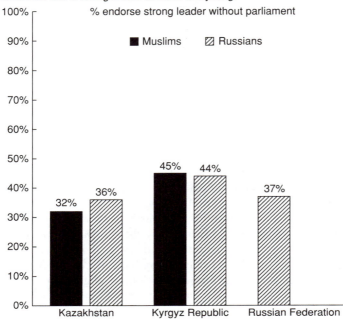

*Q. We would like it better if the parliament was dissolved, free elections were abolished and a strong leader decided everything.*

*Figure 19.3* Post-Soviet Muslims reject autocratic rule.
Sources: Kazakhstan: national sample, 1,890 interviews, 26 October–3 December 2001; Kyrgyzstan: national sample, 1,964 interviews, 16 October–27 November 2001; Russia: New Russia Barometer, 2005. In Central Asia, Russians defined as respondents saying they were nominally Russian Orthodox; in Russian Federation, all respondents.

There is no substantial difference in the percentage of more and less observant Muslims rejecting strong-man rule.

Comparing the views of Muslims and Russians in Central Asia reinforces the need to understand divisions within nominal ethnic, religious or 'civilizational' groups and, equally important, the existence of similarities that cross-cut groups. Within Kazakhstan and within Kyrgyzstan there is no significant difference in the way in which Russians and Muslims divide: the majority rejecting and the minority endorsing strong-man rule is much the same among both groups.

When the views of peoples in Central Asia are compared with NRB data from the Russian Federation, Muslims appear as much in favour of representative institutions as are Russians. The civilization that matters in post-Soviet states is not Islam; the chief influences are secular values, whether the legacy of Sovietization or values shared with Europe. However, this does not mean that there is a convergence between post-Soviet countries and Europe, for the divergence of institutional developments between CEE and post-Soviet countries means that both Russians and Muslims have learned to adapt to very different types of political regimes.

# 20 Post-transformation issues

A stable state is not a static state.

(Richard Rose)

Although transformation has ended, the problems of post-transformation societies continue. Entrance to the European Union was a major milestone in the progress of societies that were once Communist – but it is not the end of the journey. New EU member states do not need foreigners to tell them that there is a need to improve standards of governance and to make up for the economic growth and much else that was lost under Communism. However, the population resources and the geographical location of these Central and East European states means that independence is not the same as being able to ignore neighbouring countries. All 10 must adapt to being a part of a new system of interdependence in which the focal point is not Moscow but Brussels.

The situation of successor states of the Soviet Union is more problematic. None is a democracy. Plebiscitarian autocracies face the periodic risk that something goes 'wrong' with an election that was meant to confirm rulers in power. Unaccountable autocracies are less vulnerable to surprises at election time but they remain vulnerable to struggles for power and succession within the elites and such disputes must be settled without the assurance of orderliness that the party-state provided. The markets that have emerged are still hamstrung by bureaucratic regulations and prices not only refer to what consumers pay in shops but also what must be paid 'under the table' to get things done. Resource-rich countries have seen their revenues balloon with the rise in energy prices, but they have yet to demonstrate the understanding and skills to invest this vast windfall in ways that compensate for their Soviet legacy. Formal independence from Moscow is paralleled by informal interdependence that reflects geographical location and the disparity in size between the Russian Federation and other post-Soviet states. It also reflects the desire of Russia's leaders to dominate this network as part of a larger strategy of recovering a world role by exploiting its energy resources.

## I EU expansion increases heterogeneity

When six countries joined together to create the European Community in 1957 to advance their common interest in preventing the recurrence of war and depression their goals were not unique to France, Germany, Italy and the Benelux countries. But the intensity of recent experiences, combined with common borders that could encourage trade as well as military invasion, meant that they had much more in common than Scandinavian countries or such 'off-shore' Europeans as Britain. For a decade and a half the European Community remained an association of six countries.

What was once labelled the Common Market has greatly enlarged its membership as well as its functions to become the 27-country European Union of today. In 1973 there was enlargement to the west: the United Kingdom, Ireland and Denmark became members. Between 1981 and 1986 enlargement to the Mediterranean added three countries that had recently been dictatorships, Greece, Portugal and Spain. Nordic enlargement to Finland and Sweden plus Austria, brought EU membership up to 15 states in 1995. A massive step to the east was taken in 2004 with the admission of eight post-Communist countries – the Czech Republic, Estonia, Hungary, Latvia, Lithuania, Poland, Slovakia and Slovenia, plus the Republic of Cyprus and Malta – and an opening to the Balkans followed with the admission of Bulgaria and Romania in 2007.

Although the admission of post-Communist countries was unprecedented in scale, the fact that they had recently been dictatorships was not. Of the 27 member states, only seven have had a continuous record of democratic government since before the Second World War. Three of Europe's six founder countries had been Nazi or Fascist before 1945 and Malta and Cyprus were British colonies until the 1960s. Enlargement to the Mediterranean brought in three countries that had had dictatorships into the 1970s. The logic of admitting Greece, Portugal and Spain – locking new democratic governments into a league of European democracies – was subsequently used to justify the admission of post-Communist states with worse political legacies than the new Mediterranean democracies. Admitting countries with diverse economic characteristics is consistent with the idea that a single market involves the exchange of goods and services between economies with different comparative advantages.

The success of the European Union in attracting new members has virtually eliminated the difference between 'Europe' as a geographical category and a treaty-based institution. However, expansion has greatly increased the heterogeneity of the new Europe in terms of history, geography and culture. Today, EU members have 23 different national languages. Some differences, for example, the contrast between Northern and Southern Europe, predate the fall of the Berlin Wall. EU expansion since has added differences between the legacies of Eastern and Western Europe and restored Central European lands to a key position within the continent.

The territorial span of the EU results in geography uniting *and* dividing members from each other. Most post-Communist states have close ties with some old member states. For example, Nordic countries are close to the three Baltic states and Germany has a long common border with Poland. Austria shares borders with four new EU member states and has a history of a common Habsburg sovereign. Britain's maritime empire has left it a vanishing legacy of imperial ties with Ireland, Malta and Cyprus and a pull toward Anglophone countries on other continents.

The expansion of the European Union has been accompanied by an increasing disparity in the Gross Domestic Product per capita of member states, a gap opened by enlargement in the Mediterranean. The enlargement of 2004–7 has widened that gap. The disparities are gross when measured in euros or American dollars and remain large even after adjusting for national differences in purchasing power. The GDP average in the 10 new EU members is just over half that of the oldest 15 EU member states (Figure 20.1). Only Slovenia and the Czech Republic have a higher GDP per capita than Portugal, the poorest of the older EU members. The poorest new member state,

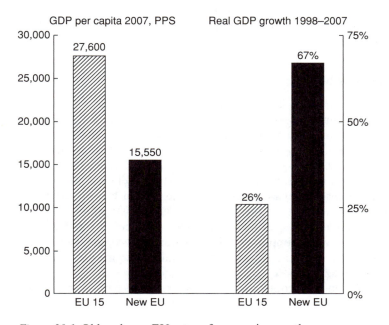

*Figure 20.1* Old and new EU rates of economic growth.
Source: Eurostat, Data Navigation Tree – General Economic Background http://epp.eurostat.ec.
europa.eu. Accessed 3 June 2008. Purchasing power standard (PPS) is an artificial reference currency
unit that eliminates price-level differences between countries.

Bulgaria, has a per capita income barely one-third the average of the older members.
When comparisons are made between the richest and the least well-off member states
of the 27-country EU, differences of more than 3 to 1 are found in the purchasing
power of their respective citizens. There are big differences in GDP among new member
states too. Slovenia and the Czech Republic have average living standards almost
double that of Romania and Bulgaria. While the EU has rhetoric endorsing social
cohesion through reducing differences in income, it has no legal authority to impose
the massive taxation that would be required to equalize income between member states
nor is there political support for redistributing income on a continental scale.

A snapshot comparing European economies at a single point in time is only
partially accurate. It cannot show the difference between the very high annual rate of
growth in post-transformation economies and the much lower rate of growth in the
15 older EU member states. Between 1997 and 2007 the 10 new EU states grew at an
average rate of 5.3 per cent compounded annually while the average for older members was 1.5 per cent. The disparity is even greater in the growth rate of the largest
new EU member state, Poland, which has averaged 4.2 per cent annually, and
Germany, which has averaged 1.5 per cent.

A booming market economy creates more opportunities for employment in the official
economy and for households to switch from do-it-yourself production to buying
goods and services that show up in the official national income accounts. New opportunities will raise national living standards not only in terms of income but also in
terms of health (see Chapter 9). However, given the size of the gap with more
established European economies and continued growth there, closing the gap will be

the work of a generation or more (see Chapter 3). The most and the least that countries can do to compensate for the costs of being part of the Communist bloc is to make rapid progress as new EU member states and most have been doing that.

## II  Improving standards of governance

Electoral accountability is demonstrated by citizens exercising their right to vote the government of the day out of office. By this standard, new member states of the European Union have shown a higher level of electoral accountability than old member states such as Britain or Sweden, since the difficulties of transformation and its aftermath have caused their governments to be voted out of office more frequently.

While electoral accountability is necessary, it is not a sufficient guarantee of democratic governance. This also requires adherence to the rule of law. When European Union member states are assessed on this criterion, a very different pattern emerges. The Transparency International Index confirms the evidence of the New Europe Barometer: the perception of corruption remains a major problem in new EU member states. However, it shows that some old EU member states also have major problems with corruption (Figure 20.2).

The extent of corruption in Europe today is not the result of a division between old and new EU member states. Instead, there is a substantial overlap in the extent to which the two groups of countries are perceived as corrupt. Greece, the lowest ranked of the old EU 15, is rated by Transparency International below seven of the 10 new post-Communist member states. Furthermore, Slovenia and Estonia have ratings as high or higher than Mediterranean countries.

The extent of corruption shows a deficit in democratic governance within Europe that can hardly be altered by electoral reforms. The Republic of Italy has tried doing that and has yet to succeed. Corruption is due to systemic political and administrative malfeasance that distorts decisions taken at the top of government departments about spending millions or more on building roads and hospitals, procuring military equipment and granting licences and privileges that are worth large sums to those so favoured.

The fact that old EU member states such as Italy and Greece are credited with a higher level of corruption in government than Transparency International assigns to some Middle Eastern and African countries shows that institutions of the European Union have a weak capacity to enforce 'Copenhagen-type' standards of governance on member states. The EU has sought to do this when admitting Bulgaria and Romania; it declared that after entry each country should reduce the role of corruption in governance and organized crime. However, now that both countries are within the EU, its Council of Ministers finds it difficult to invoke sanctions against these countries when it has not done so against old member states that are also deficient in adhering to the rule of law. In addition to locking in democracy and access to the single Europe market, EU enlargement risks locking in standards of governance in some new member states that are even worse than the low standards that it has been powerless to improve in Italy and Greece.

## III  The emerging European public space

The geography of Central and Eastern Europe is such that even in their most nationalistic periods, public space was trans-national. Prior to the First World War most

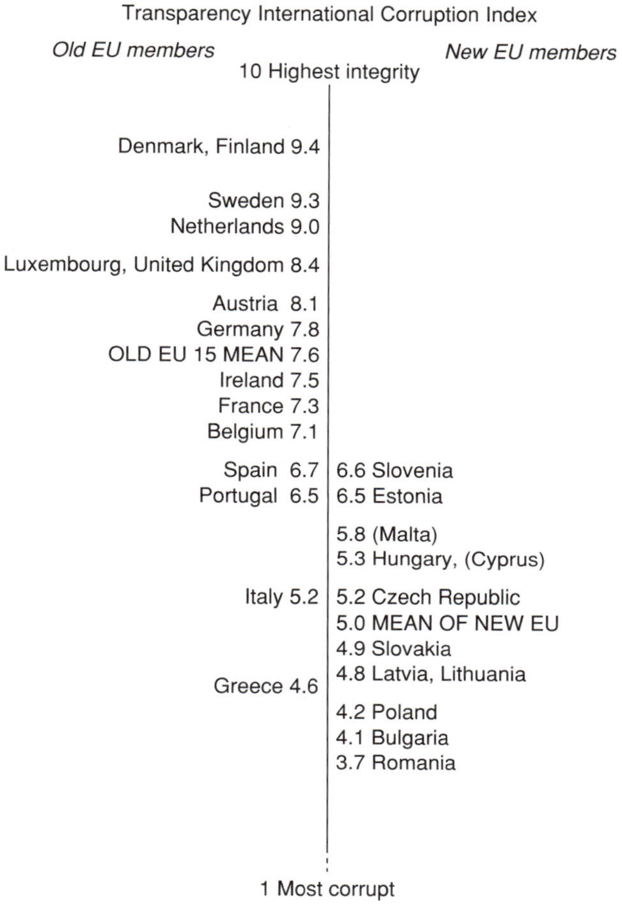

Transparency International Corruption Index

*Old EU members*                                    *New EU members*

10 Highest integrity

Denmark, Finland 9.4

Sweden 9.3
Netherlands 9.0

Luxembourg, United Kingdom 8.4

Austria  8.1
Germany 7.8
OLD EU 15 MEAN 7.6
Ireland 7.5
France 7.3
Belgium 7.1

Spain  6.7 | 6.6 Slovenia
Portugal  6.5 | 6.5 Estonia

5.8 (Malta)
5.3 Hungary, (Cyprus)

Italy 5.2 | 5.2 Czech Republic
5.0 MEAN OF NEW EU
4.9 Slovakia
4.8 Latvia, Lithuania
Greece 4.6 |

4.2 Poland
4.1 Bulgaria
3.7 Romania

1 Most corrupt

*Figure 20.2* Corruption ratings of EU member states.
Source: Transparency International, TI Corruption Perceptions Index 2007, www.transparency.org.
Accessed 20 May 2008.

people governed from Budapest were not Hungarians and most people in the Austrian portion of the Habsburg Empire were not Austrians. The Czechoslovak Republic was established with large minorities of Germans and Prague was closer to Dresden than to Vienna. There was a significant Hungarian minority in Slovakia and Bratislava was much closer to Vienna than to Prague. The Second World War re-oriented political space. Governments in Eastern Europe were forced to look to the capital of a Eurasian space, Moscow, while West European governments looked to Brussels, the home of both the European Union and of NATO.

The 2004–7 enlargement has turned the European Union from a set of West European countries to a Union with a public space extending from the Atlantic Ocean to the Black Sea. Its longest waterway is no longer the Rhine but the Danube and the centre of population of the EU has shifted from Western to Central Europe. Concurrently, there has been a demand to open up a trans-national European public space for the popular discussion of European Union policies that increasingly affect what happens to citizens across the continent.

To communicate about policies across national boundaries requires a widely accessible technology, a common language and an understanding of the interests of different nations. Communication across Europe today has never been easier, cheaper or faster. The Internet provides the technology for instant communication across the continent of Europe at little or no cost.

The enlargement of Europe has resulted in 23 diverse languages now being official EU languages. However, efficient communication between people with many different national languages requires a lingua franca, a common language spoken by people who lack a common home language. EU citizens have 'voted with their mouths' in favour of having a language that can be used across the continent to order meals on holiday and goods on the Internet and to learn what is needed to pass an examination or to use a piece of household equipment that may be manufactured in China rather than Europe. The language chosen is English. Today, EFL (that is, English as a Foreign Language) is used by more Europeans than use English as their native language.

More than half of Europe meets at least one criterion for transnational communication. A Europe-wide survey in 2003 found that 35 per cent of Europeans age 15 or above were able to use the Internet to communicate across the continent in English (Figure 20.3). Although Soviet-oriented-education distorted language education, nonetheless more than half of Estonian and Slovenian adults claim the ability to communicate in English, a higher proportion than in France and Italy. The chief influences on being able to communicate on the Internet in English are youthfulness, education and a country's Gross Domestic Product. Since education and national income levels continue to rise and the turnover of generations gradually increases the percentage of national populations fluent in both mediums, the number of adults able to communicate in European public space is steadily increasing so that in the foreseeable future half or more of Europeans will be able to do so (Rose, 2008b: 465).

Knowing a language is a necessary but not a sufficient condition of understanding what you are talking about. Whether the subject is physics or football, meaningful communication also requires a shared understanding of the subject matter. This is particularly the case in politics, where trans-national communication often involves differing and sometimes competing national interests. Even if interests are compatible, they are framed in very different political contexts. Since the EU is about agreeing political bargains, understanding other countries is important in order to advance one's own interests.

Understanding confers a measure of 'soft power', that is, the ability to get others to do what you want. If one partner in a political dialogue has a better understanding of the issues at hand and of the interests of those who are involved in bargaining that person has the advantage of soft power. Knowledge of a foreign language is one indication of understanding differences in national interests that can provide soft power in trans-national bargaining. This definition of soft power is the opposite of that of Harvard professor Joseph Nye, who has characterized the international use of English as evidence of the attractiveness of America's view of the world, and thus a form of soft power. Nye does not take into account that the use of English rather than American as the 'dialect' of discourse has significant implications about political outlooks. Compare the contents of *The Economist* and *Time* magazine or the *Financial*

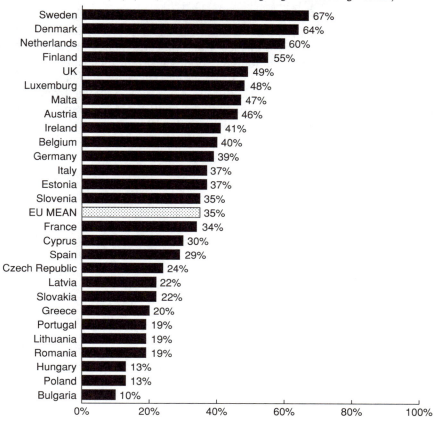

*(% population 15 or over knowing English **and** using Internet)*

*Figure 20.3* Ability to participate in European public space.
Source: European Foundation for Quality of Life Survey, 2003. www.eurofound.europa.eu Number
of respondents: 25,261 people in 27 EU countries. EU average is weighted to take size of national
population into account.

*Times* with the *Wall Street Journal*. Moreover, English can be learned for personal or
national advantage. Europeans have noted that not studying what foreigners say and
think can result in a very limited understanding of foreign nations, as the unilateral-
ist foreign policy of George W. Bush has shown.

Citizens of new EU member states have multiple advantages in participating in
European public space. First, like citizens in every small nation with a distinctive language, they have a strong incentive to learn a lingua franca for purposes of study, work
and leisure. Second, having been forced to cope with Moscow in Russian they have
learned how to cultivate the soft power of understanding other governments in hopes
of advancing their own national interests. Third, participation in European affairs offers
far wider opportunities than do activities within nations with populations of less than
5 or 10 million people. Finally, distance is no barrier to trans-national communication since Berlin, Vienna and even Brussels are closer to the national capitals of new
EU member states than is Moscow.

Discussing common problems with other Europeans does not guarantee political satisfaction, since every political bargain involves compromises and can produce losers as well as winners. Governments of small European states, and every CEE country except Poland falls into this category, do not expect to be decisive in deliberations. The aim is make their voices heard in such a way that when decisions are made, their soft power in understanding and communication will produce benefits.

Participation in the seemingly endless discussions that characterize the European Union is time-consuming and often tedious. But for countries excluded from European discourse for many decades, it is proof that the biggest goal of transformation has been achieved. Central and East Europeans are now integrated as full participants in the European political process. As Winston Churchill once remarked, 'jaw, jaw' is better than 'war, war', and the peoples of Central and Eastern Europe have seen more than enough of war.

# Appendix A  Collecting data

## An insider's approach

A wise man's question is half the answer.

(Old East European proverb)

Every modern society needs a feedback of information between governors and governed. In democracies it is provided by elections, markets and official statistics. However, regimes with a totalitarian vocation suppress feedback. The commanders of a command economy were not interested in popular demands but in imposing their goals from the top down. Instead of feedback, they relied upon ideology to produce statistics about what was happening. In Karl Deutsch's (1963: 111) words, the regime used its power to favour 'the priority of output over intake, the ability to talk instead of listen; the ability to afford not to learn'. Their power to control data was buried by the fall of the Berlin Wall.

At the start of transformation, policymakers faced what the Organization for Economic Cooperation and Development (OECD, 1991: 21) referred to as 'people problems'. Because of the Communist corruption of sources of information, basic data about what people were doing were lacking. The need for valid evidence of individual behaviour was particularly great, because so much of the economic activity that people relied on to cope with everyday life was outside the scope of official statistics. The weakness of representative institutions gave additional importance to evidence of public opinion.

Fortunately, there was at hand a familiar and tested means of finding out what individuals do and think, the nationwide sample survey. At the beginning of the great depression, Paul Lazarsfeld *et al.* (1933) pioneered the use of sample surveys to study the impact of unemployment in Austria. After becoming a political refugee, Lazarsfeld *et al.* (1944) conducted the first survey study of voting behaviour in the United States in 1940. Much microeconomic information about labour-force participation, earnings and consumption comes from sample surveys. Because survey data are more immediately available, they can be more up to date than census data, which are years old when published. While sampling fluctuations create a margin of error in all surveys, there are substantial errors of undercounting and estimation in macroeconomic statistics and censuses too.

In Communist times, individuals had expressed their views obliquely, by *anekdoty* (jokes) or in privately circulated *samizdat* publications (Lewis, 2008; Shlapentokh, 2001: Chapter 10). The collapse of Communist regimes has made it possible to turn anecdotes into data by asking people what they are doing and thinking. At least five different approaches can be found in surveys of public opinion in transformation societies.

1   Media surveys of current events are the most visible, but the information that can be conveyed in a headline or a sound bite is slight and the popularity ratings of personalities are of only ephemeral significance. The media lack the time and inclination to analyze surveys in depth.

2   A sponsor survey asks questions of utilitarian use to the organization paying for it. Market research for commercial products is a familiar example. Organizations such as the European Commission and the United States government ask people what they think of the European Union or of Washington.

3   Many Western social scientists rely on a destination model, asking about attitudes toward idealized features of a democratic system and a market economy. Destination surveys measure how near or far the values of a population are from goals defined in Western terms. Distinctive features of the Communist legacy are left out.

4   Anthropologists favour studies that emphasize the persistence of behaviour and attitudes in informal contexts. Although devoid of generalizability, ethnographic studies serve as a reminder that attitudes and habits formed in the old regime can and do persist.

5   A transformation model combines concern with current conditions, evaluations of the past and expectations of the future. In a stable democracy the differences between these three periods of time are limited. However, in societies in transformation there are fundamental differences in the context of time and space (Rose, 2007). This model is the foundation of New Europe Barometer surveys, which monitor trends across time and across national boundaries.

*Design of the New Europe Barometer*. A survey is only reliable if it represents the population it seeks to describe. Interviews must be conducted face-to-face with a representative sample of the population nationwide. In each country, an established survey institute draws a multi-stage random probability sample stratified by regions, urban and rural population, and small administrative districts (e.g., census tracts, wards or villages) that can serve as primary sampling units. Within each primary sampling unit an average of 10 interviews is conducted. Interviewers go to randomly selected addresses and within a household the respondent is chosen randomly according to the next member to have a birthday or from a Kish matrix, named after the Hungarian-born University of Michigan leader in developing methods for randomizing the selection of respondents. Technical calculations show that interviewing 1,000 adults is normally sufficient to provide data that can be reliably generalized to a national population. In Russia 1,600 to 2,000 persons are normally interviewed. In Estonia, Latvia and Lithuania special sampling procedures are used to ensure the representation of both the Russian and the Baltic populations Details of samples are at www.abdn.ac.uk/cspp/NEBsurveys.shtml. Altogether, the surveys constituting the data base for this book include replies from more than 120,000 respondents.

Questionnaires do not write themselves. I spent 1991 flying and faxing between Sofia, Prague, Poznan, Moscow and Vienna in dialogue with social scientists who wanted to know what was happening in their own society and had created institutes capable of undertaking nationwide sample surveys. Designing the first questionnaire for use with Bulgarians, Czechs and Slovaks ensured the collection of comparable data about common problems of people in post-Communist societies. I then analyzed the replies intensively in order to identify meaningful indicators that could be generalized across post-Communist societies (Rose, 1991). Additional measures were developed in questionnaires for lengthy surveys that autumn in Poland and what was by January 1992 the Russian Federation. The first multi-country NEB survey, in collaboration with the Paul Lazarsfeld Society, Vienna, went in the field in autumn, 1991. The design and authority over all questionnaires has rested with myself.

Whereas designing a sample is a technical task, designing a questionnaire is as much an art as a science. The New Europe Barometer operates on the principle of the Heineken's beer advertisement: it reaches the parts that others do not reach, especially public-policy concerns not reported in official statistics (see www.abdn.ac.uk/cspp/ NEBsurveys.shtml for the English text of questionnaires.) The NEB questionnaire asks people to assess economic changes in terms of their everyday experience. It is much easier for people to do this than make choices between abstractions such as capitalism and socialism. Questions are posed about what people are doing to make ends meet and the answers are empirical and quantifiable. To dismiss data about the household production of food as 'soft' implies that currencies such as the Lithuanian *litas*, the Polish *zloty* or the Romanian *lei* are 'hard' and constant measures of value. In a society in which prices change erratically and unevenly between categories of goods, the official rate of inflation is subject to a wide margin of error. Converting national currencies into US dollars requires heroic assumptions about unstable prices and unstable exchange rates between that currency and American dollars.

In politics the NEB approach has been realist: it gives priority to competition between regimes past, present and future and to the evaluation of what government does rather than what people would like government to do. Only after the secure establishment of a democracy can competition between parties become the primary concern. An idealist focus on democracy as the destination is inappropriate to understand change, since the starting point for democratization is one or another type of undemocratic regime. In post-Communist countries, adults had lived through one, two or even three undemocratic alternatives. Instead of the repressive legacy of Communism making people shy about answering political questions, in reaction to the past, people were ready to voice their opinions (Rose, 2007a).

In addition to questions of particular concern in this book, every national survey collects a great deal of data about age, education, gender, income and other social and demographic characteristics that make it possible to produce spin off publications on such topics as anti-modern as well as modern sources of income in Russia (Rose and McAllister, 1996), the conditions of female pensioners in the Baltic states (Rose, 1995e), alternative measures of poverty in Romania (Rose, 1994a) and a host of publications on health (e.g. Rose, 2000a).

Face-to-face interviews last long enough to cover a multiplicity of topics; thus it is possible to introduce fresh questions as well as repeat trend questions critical for monitoring the effects of transformation and its aftermath. In the early years NEB surveys asked about topics of particular relevance to moving from a command to a market economy, such as queuing and privatization. Official statistics of an unexpected and dramatic decline in life expectancy in Russia led to collaboration with medical scientists in the University of London on studies of health. While official statistics focus on causes of death, NEB surveys provide statistics about the behaviour of healthy as well as unhealthy persons. The eruption of interest in the idea of social capital gave extra value to questions on social-capital networks that had been in NEB surveys since 1991. It also stimulated innovative questions relevant to post-Communist societies and other countries where trust and bureaucratic integrity are problematic. Questions of specific national concern are sometimes asked too, for example, language use in the Baltic states and experience of electoral corruption in a survey in Ukraine in 2005.

*Comparing people*s. Historical and cultural approaches assume unique characteristics of countries and categoric differences between them, thus implying a great deal of commonality in views among everyone interviewed in a national survey. Social science theories emphasize what is common in many countries; everyone interviewed shared the experience of having lived in a Communist party-state. But such theories also emphasize that within a country, differences in class, education, gender or age can cause differences in the way in which people respond to transformation.

The NEB paradigm is simple: Under what circumstances and to what extent do common experiences produce similar or different responses within and across post-Communist societies? Paradoxically, divisions within countries can create similarities across national boundaries. For example, in every society there are differences in age, gender or education. To measure the extent to which divisions within nations are similar across countries, we employ the NEB mean, calculated by averaging replies from each country and weighting each equally. This makes it possible to identify how much or how little people in a particular country, whether prosperous Slovenia or post-Communist Russia, differ from the average. While there are invariably differences between national means, they are usually much less than differences between people within a country.

Since 1991 the Centre for the Study of Public Policy and its collaborators have organized more than 100 surveys in 20 different countries of Central and Eastern Europe and successor states of the Soviet Union (see Table A.1). To provide a benchmark for comparison with Western Europe, surveys were conducted in Austria in 1991 and 1998 and in West Germany as well as East Germany in 1993. The experience of designing

*Table A.1* CSPP Barometer surveys by country and year

| | 1991 | '92 | '93 | '94 | '95 | '96 | '98 | 2000 | '01 | '03 | '04 | '05 | '07 | '08 |
|---|---|---|---|---|---|---|---|---|---|---|---|---|---|---|
| *New European Union countries* | | | | | | | | | | | | | | |
| Bulgaria | 2x | x | x | | x | | x | | x | | x | x | | |
| Czech Republic | 2x | x | x | | x | | x | | x | | x | | | |
| Estonia | | | x | | x | x | | x | x | | x | | | |
| Hungary | x | x | x | | x | | x | | x | | x | | | |
| Latvia | | | x | | x | x | | x | x | | x | | | |
| Lithuania | | | x | | x | x | | x | x | | x | | | |
| Poland | 2x | x | x | | x | | x | | x | | x | | | |
| Romania | x | x | x | | x | | x | | x | | x | x | | |
| Slovakia | 2x | x | x | | x | | x | | x | | x | | | |
| Slovenia | x | x | x | | x | | x | | x | | x | | | |
| *Post-Soviet countries* | | | | | | | | | | | | | | |
| Belarus | | x | x | | x | | x | x | | | x | | | |
| Russia | | x | x | x | x | 2x | x | 2x | x | 2x | x | x | 2x | x |
| Ukraine | | x | x | | x | | x | x | | | | x | | |

(When two surveys have been done in a country in a year, this is shown as 2x)

Plus surveys in Moldova, 2001, 2002; Croatia, 1992, 1993, 1995, 1996, 1998, 2002, 2005; Serbia, 1998, 2000, 2002, 2005; Bosnia-Herzegovina, 2004, 2005. In Western Europe: Austria, 1991, 1998; East Germany, 1993; West Germany, 1993.

a questionnaire for countries that had not had a regime change was instructive; it made clear which specific features of the Communist experience were not relevant to countries the other side of the Iron Curtain. Relevant NEB questions have been adapted for use with collaborators in Turkey and in the Republic of Korea, each of which has experienced a change of regime within the memory of most adults while free of a legacy of Communist totalitarianism. A number of questions have also been adapted by Michael Bratton and colleagues in the Afrobarometer, in the Living in Transition survey of the European Bank for Reconstruction and Development, and by the World Values Survey.

In this book survey results are presented in two complementary forms. Results from the 10 Central and East European countries that are now European Union member countries – Bulgaria, the Czech Republic, Estonia, Hungary, Latvia, Lithuania, Poland, Romania, Slovakia and Slovenia – are often pooled under the heading of New Europe Barometer. They can be contrasted and compared with results from the New Russia Barometer. The rich trove of NRB data is drawn on to highlight what are often differences with new EU member states. In addition, Ukraine and Belarus data are reported along with NRB data; together, the three are referred to as post-Soviet states. All statistics have been calculated afresh and for that reason may differ marginally from previously published figures because of modifications in such things as the treatment of missing data or minor adjustments in coding.

A minimum of six nationwide surveys have been conducted to date in each NEB country, and often more. In addition, 17 surveys have been conducted to date in Russia. Bilingual surveys of the Baltic and Russian populations of Estonia, Latvia and Lithuania have been separately organized by the Centre for the Study of Public Policy (CSPP). All the New Russia Barometer surveys have been designed by the CSPP in collaboration with what was originally known as VCIOM and is now the Levada Centre, Moscow. Differences in politics and in funding research have meant that groups of countries were not always interviewed in the same year. For example, the first round of NEB surveys in Central and Eastern Europe occurred before the break-up of the Soviet Union and of Czechoslovakia. A consequence of NEB surveys running in the winter months is that fieldwork in November and January in different countries appears to be a year apart. To avoid such distortions, each round of the multinational NEB survey is referred to by the year in which it started; the exact dates of fieldwork for all surveys are given at the CSPP website. In Russia, separate Duma and presidential elections have resulted in two surveys being held in some years: these are differentiated by the year in question having an a or b suffix.

*The research network*. To undertake this research has required collaboration across more than 20 countries. In societies undergoing transformation, many social scientists set up institutes that were not only independent of government but also of public universities that were themselves in the throes of transformation. The tasks of translating an NEB questionnaire into the national language, drawing a national sample, training and fielding interviewers nationwide, verifying interviews and turning individual respondents into a computerized data base were undertaken by institutes that had an established reputation in the country in which fieldwork was done.

Comparative survey research requires co-ordination if survey questionnaires are to be comparable and answers collected in many languages integrated for comparative analysis in a multinational data set. It is also the responsibility of co-ordinating institutes to raise the funds necessary to conduct surveys across up to a dozen countries and extending over more than a decade. The NEB was launched as a collaborative effort of the Centre for the Study of Public Policy and the Paul Lazarsfeld Society, Vienna, under the imaginative direction of Dr Heinz Kienzl. The New Russia Barometer and Baltic surveys have always been the responsibility of the Centre for the Study of Public Policy, where Evgeny Tikhomirov and then Dr Neil Munro have provided technical assistance. After the 1998 NEB round, all Barometer surveys became the responsibility of the CSPP; the Lazarsfeld Society has concentrated on the successor states of Yugoslavia. In view of political developments, the term NEB has been maintained for the 10 new EU member states.

For many years the CSPP has had to invest a part of its own budget to meet a significant fraction of the cost of co-ordinating surveys. At times it has had to draw on internal funds to finance fieldwork as well. Where funding was sufficient to employ staff to undertake the time-consuming task of turning working research files into a form suitable for secondary analysis, along with appropriate multilingual documentation, surveys have been deposited at the Data Archive, Colchester, England.

# Appendix B    Acknowledgements and references

Better a hundred friends than a hundred roubles.

(Russian proverb)

## Acknowledgements

The persistence of the New Europe Barometer over two decades has been made possible by the Centre for the Study of Public Policy's position as a research department within a university and the University of Aberdeen has provided a congenial setting for preparing this book. Two other institutions have been recurringly helpful over the years, the Paul Lazarsfeld Gesellschaft, Vienna, and the Wissenschaftszentrum für Sozialforschung Berlin. In addition, I have benefited from collaborating with Sir Michael Marmot and colleagues at the University College London Medical School on studies of life as well as death in post-Communist countries.

The Austrian Ministry of Science and the Austrian National Bank were of primary importance in the launch of the New Europe Barometer and funded the first five multinational rounds. The British Economic and Social Research Council (ESRC) has been a major funder of the Barometer research programme since the mid-1990s. Immediately, the book has benefited from ESRC grant RES-062-23-0341 to understand regime support in Russia from the start of transformation to its current status as a diarchy of President Medvedev and Prime Minister Putin. Funding has also come from not-for-profit and government research agencies in the United Kingdom, France, Germany, Hungary, Sweden and the United States, and from intergovernmental agencies such as the World Bank, the European Commission and UN agencies. All of these organizations have respected my academic independence in deciding which questions to ask and how to interpret the replies; therefore, I am solely responsible for what this book contains.

In the Communist era there was a dearth of empirical evidence about how ordinary people were living and what they were actually thinking. The chief sources of information were official documents and what could be read between their lines and anecdotes. Transformation revealed the anti-modern nature of much quantified evidence and created an immediate need for up-to-date information about how people were coping. Hence, when the New Europe Barometer was launched in 1991, I gave first priority to disseminating the results to people living in societies in transformation and to policymakers trying to deal with its consequences. A multiplicity of media has been employed ranging from television appearances in Tallinn and Riga to World Bank reports in Washington, DC. Publication of six books with university presses followed and more than 100 journal articles and reports in Russian, French and German as well as English in journals and books of political science, public administration, economics, sociology, social policy, geography, information technology and medicine.

Two resources have been particularly valuable in achieving rapid dissemination. The *Studies in Public Policy* (*SPP*) series of the Centre for the Study of Public Policy has put in print within eight weeks of completion more than 250 papers drawing on NEB surveys and related studies by researchers on four continents (www.abdn.ac.uk/cspp/catalog12_0.shtml). *SPP* reports of Barometer surveys include complete frequency distributions for every survey cited in Table A.1. The World Wide Web has also been utilized to disseminate information about research in progress to visitors from more than 75 countries. Two websites – *www.RussiaVotes.org* and *www.BalticVoices.org* – provide extensive documentation of Barometer surveys. Unfortunately, to date proposals have been rejected on both sides of the Atlantic to fund on-line access to NEB data in ways that policymakers, the media and interested citizens as well as academics can use.

## Introduction: Transformation and its aftermath

For the background to New Europe Barometer surveys, see Rose (2006b: Chapter 1) and for the New Russia Barometer, Rose (2008c). For the author's own background, see Rose (1997).

## 1 The Iron Curtain falls

For a schematic account of the transformations of twentieth-century Europe, see the opening chapters of *What Is Europe?* (Rose, 1996). An extraordinary sociological study of the *Public and Private Life of the Soviet People* was written by Vladimir Shlapentokh (1989), using materials he had collected before and after being expelled from his post at Moscow State University (see also Shlapentokh, 2001). A classic economic analysis is Janos Kornai's (1992) *The Socialist System*, a political economy analysis of the party-state's attempt to command the economy. For an account of how Kornai's thinking evolved from a youth in hiding in Nazi-occupied Budapest to a Harvard professorship see Kornai (2006).

My interpretation of the consequences of the collapse of the Soviet Union – 'Escaping from Absolute Dissatisfaction: A Trial-and-Error Model of Change in Eastern Europe' (Rose, 1992) – was written only a few months after that event. The underlying theory of trial-and-error search as the means of reducing dissatisfaction and finding satisfaction comes from the work of Herbert Simon (see e.g., 1978). A model of popular choices between political regimes as a choice of the lesser evil, 'the Churchill hypothesis', can be found in *Democracy and Its Alternatives* (Rose, Mishler and Haerpfer, 1998). It is extended in a comparison of realist versus idealist theories of 'Political Support for Incomplete Democracies' (Mishler and Rose, 2001).

## 2 Living in an anti-modern society

The concept of a modern society employed in this chapter is based on the writings of Max Weber (1947). Once I began to make visits and observe what life was actually like in Russia, Bulgaria, Czechoslovakia, East Germany and Poland, Weber's ideas helped me to identify what was missing in Communist-style modernization. The concept of an anti-modern society has been developed from reading, travel and discussions with friends who had the misfortune to be subject to that system for too much of their lives. The ideas were first set out in 'Russia as an Hour-Glass Society: A Constitution without Citizens' (Rose, 1995), and have subsequently been developed in articles and in chapters of books.

## 3 Making progress and falling behind

The logic of analyzing the rate of progress within a nation and comparing results cross-nationally to see whether a country is catching up or falling behind is set out in 'Making Progress and Catching Up' (Rose, 1995a). The methodology is applied systematically to the analysis of infant mortality, female participation in the labour force, the proportion of the population in work and education in a major report for the European Centre for Social Welfare Policy and Research (Rose, 1994). The copious trend data in that report compare rates of change across countries in Western Europe, Eastern Europe and republics of the Soviet Union. Statistics on a large variety of social conditions in all post-Communist countries are available from UNICEF's Innocenti Research Centre (annual). A more detailed discussion of topics in the chapter can be found in 'The Long and the Short of Transformation in Central Europe' (Rose, 1999a). Relevant evidence can also be found in 'Evaluating Benefits: The Views of Russian Employees' (Rose, 1996a).

## 4 The need for patience

In Western Europe, Albert Hirschman's book on *Exit, Voice and Loyalty* (1970) described alternative responses to unsatisfactory situations. The book for Eastern Europe was different: Sartre's *Huis Clos* (No Exit). The concept of patience was developed in order to describe how people who were weaponless endured their subordination to a Communist regime with a totalitarian vocation. It is a reflection of the unduly optimistic view of social scientists that problems can be resolved rather than suffered that the concept of patience receives little attention in academe compared. The ideas in this chapter were initially set out in 'How Patient Are People in Post-Communist Societies?' in *World Affairs* (Rose, 1997a).

## 5 The need for a civil economy

The basic ideas in this chapter were set out in 'Eastern Europe's Need for a Civil Economy' (Rose, 1992a). It was written to call attention to a topic that conventional economics textbooks left out, the role of political and civil-society institutions in creating and sustaining markets. Fortunately, it struck a chord among economists confronting post-Communist countries, for a committee including the President of the Bundesbank, the Chief Economist of the European Bank for Reconstruction and Development, the editor of *The Economist* and City of London bankers awarded it the $25,000 Robert Marjolin Prize in International Economics. The illustrations from the Soviet era draw particularly on ethnographic writings about the multiple economies of the Soviet Union (Grossman, 1977; Katsenelinboigen, 1977) and on my own experience of working across the region at the time of transformation. For

a technical discussion of the accounts of command economies, see Marer *et al.*
(1992).

## 6 Getting enough to eat

The collectivization of agriculture was a tribute to the importance of ideology and power
in Communist party-states. It was carried out with brutality and great loss of life
and sustained for upwards of half a century in the face of evident shortcomings in
producing food, with all this implied for poor diet and ill-health. It also had major
political consequences, forcing the Soviet Union to import food from the United States.
Given the fundamental need for food to avoid the loss of life through malnutrition,
the early NEB questionnaires paid particular attention to collecting data about how
or whether people were feeding themselves. This chapter draws particularly on Rose
and Tikhomirov (1993), 'Who Grows Food in Russia and Eastern Europe', published
in *Post-Soviet Geography* with updated data from New Russia Barometer surveys.

## 7 Social capital when government fails

Like Molière's Monsieur Jourdain, I had been writing about social capital long before
it became a catchword in the mid-1990s. The original impetus came from observing
social-capital networks being mobilized to carry on a triangular civil war involving
Catholics, Protestants and British forces in Northern Ireland from 1969 onwards.
Examining how people coped with rising unemployment in the 1970s led me to the
literature of multiple economies in the Soviet Union, as referenced in Chapter 5. Once
social capital gained international recognition, I had the good fortune to become involved
in a workshop organized by Ismail Serageldin, then a vice president of the World Bank.
It provided a cash grant to design a special-purpose social capital questionnaire for
Russia (Rose, 1998a) as well as intellectual capital from a wide-ranging discussion with
distinguished economists and policymakers as well as social scientists (see Dasgupta
and Serageldin, 2000). This chapter draws principally on 'Uses of Social Capital in
Russia: Modern, Pre-modern and Anti-modern' (Rose, 2000) and 'When Government
Fails' (Rose, 2001). For a sceptical view of the relationship between social trust and
democratic values, a major concern of many social scientists, see 'What Does Social
Capital Add to Democratic Values?' (Rose and Weller, 2003), 'What Are the Political
Consequences of Trust?' (Mishler and Rose, 2005) and 'How Much Does Social Capital
Add to Individual Health?' (Rose, 2000a). For additional publications and updates,
see *www.abdn.ac.uk/socialcapital*.

## 8 Juggling multiple economies

My introduction to the world of multiple economies came in the early 1980s, when
rising unemployment meant that many households were suffering a loss of cash
income. It was fashionable to suggest that people were supplementing their unemployment
benefits by working for cash-in-hand in the shadow economy. However, such anec-
dote-based generalizations ignore the fact that when money is tight the demand for
such work falls while the time available to produce goods and services at home
increases. Hence, my first publication on getting by in three economies concerned Britain
(Rose, 1985). A trip to Japan, where public expenditure on welfare services was then

half that of European countries but welfare was as high or higher, led me to develop a three-economy model of total welfare in the family (Rose, 1986). Thus, before the Berlin Wall fell I had a model to account for how people could maintain their basic welfare notwithstanding the upheavals consequent to transformation. The first application to societies in transformation (Rose, 1993a) emphasized both the advantages for individuals of multiple economies and the obstacles this created for the development of large-scale enterprises necessary to generate growth in the national economy. Subsequent articles explored poverty, destitution and income measures (e.g., Rose, 1994a). The concept of resilience was developed in an article on Ukraine (Rose, 1995c). The cross-cultural problems that multiple economies pose for social scientists and policymakers as well as ordinary people are set out in Rose (2002).

## 9  Stresses and opportunities: The impact on health

Although surveys about life in Communist countries were few, there were data about death. Hence, at the beginning of transformation I undertook a systematic analysis of long-term trends in official statistics of infant mortality and life expectancy extending back to 1949 and earlier (Rose, 1994). Concurrently, epidemiologists were focusing on post-1989 mortality statistics in transformation societies. Aggregate mortality statistics use data about the dead to draw inferences about the living, while NEB surveys dealt directly with the living. In 1996 I began publishing articles on post-Communist health with clinically trained epidemiologists in a team led by Sir Michael Marmot and his colleagues at the University College London Medical School (Bobak *et al.*, 1998, 2003; Gilmore, McKee and Rose, 2002; McKee *et al.*, 1998; Murphy *et al.*, 2006; Nicholson *et al.*, 2005; Perlman *et al.*, 2003; Pomerleau *et al.*, 2004). New Europe Barometer surveys make it possible to avoid problems of ecological inference, which, at the extreme, would treat those who did not commit suicide in the anomic conditions of transformation as deviant cases (Rose, 2003). We have examined causes of variations in health within a society and, with multi-level modelling, variations in health between societies. This chapter draws particularly on Rose and Bobak (2007), which was prepared with the assistance of a grant from the British Economic and Social Research Council, RES-000-22-2429.

## 10  Freedom as a fundamental gain

Growing up in a segregated American city and knowing many people who had fled persecution and war in Europe made me aware from youth that freedom could not be taken for granted. Being active in the American Civil Liberties Union under McCarthyism and attending Isaiah Berlin's inaugural lecture on two concepts of liberty (1958) re-inforced my commitment to freedom. Participation in the councils of the International Political Science Association, a dependency of UNESCO, gave me firsthand contact with representatives of unfree social science in Brezhnev's Moscow, Ceausescu's Bucharest and Mugabe's Zimbabwe. It also made me aware of the mote-and-beam approach that some Western liberals used when dealing with Communist-bloc countries. The immediate inspiration for the freedom index came from the impromptu remarks of Marietta Nettl, who, after coming to Britain from Budapest after the Second World War, needed two decades before she would say what she thought in front of strangers, and Professor Ivana Markova FBA, who prized freedom more than a homeland under Soviet occupation. This paper is a revision of 'Freedom as a Fundamental Value', *International Social Science Journal* (1995c).

## 11  Democratization backwards

To anyone knowing the history of twentieth-century Europe, it was premature to interpret the collapse of the Communist bloc as heralding the democratization of successor states (Rose, 1996: Chapter 1). The challenge facing leaders of post-Communist regimes – democratization without the rule of law – is set out in detail in Rose and Shin (2001). Transformation did start a process of regime change – but regimes could and did go in different directions. The fullest discussion of the varied forms of undemocratic regimes, with particular emphasis on the difference between totalitarian and non-totalitarian regimes, is in Linz (2000). My own typology is developed with relevance to Russia in Rose, Mishler and Munro (2006); with relevance to democratic governance within the European Union in Rose (2008) and more broadly in Rose (2009). In doing this work I have benefited from acting as a consultant both to Freedom House and Transparency International.

## 12  The impact of a ready-made German state

Berliners – East and West – took the Wall as a fact of life; after all, by the late 1980s it had lasted more than twice as long as Hitler's 'Thousand Year' Reich. Frequent trips to East Berlin to partake of the legacy of an older German *Kultur* (and to Dresden five years before Vladimir Putin arrived as a KGB agent) made me very conscious of the divergence of the two Germanies. In autumn 1989, the Wall fell. East Germans were no longer the leading country in the Communist bloc; they were awkward and poor relations of West Germans. This chapter traces the consequences – for both groups of Germans – of being re-united within the framework of the 'iron cage' of the Rechtsstaat. It draws on a study of the same title originally presented at Humboldt University at a conference marking the fifth anniversary of German re-unification (Rose and Haerpfer, 1996) and a related analysis of what accounts for different responses among Germans (Rose and Page, 1996). The Anglo-German Foundation, London, and the Hans-Boeckler Stiftung, Dusseldorf, provided financial support for the German surveys reported here, which were organized in collaboration with the Wissenschaftszentrum Berlin (Rose, Zapf and Seifert, 1993).

## 13  Ex-Communists in post-Communist societies

Writing my doctoral thesis on the relation of socialist principles to the foreign policy of the 1945–51 British Labour government made me well aware of the gap between the ideology that a party may proclaim and what their leaders and voters actually think and do. Writing many books on parties in Western nations created an understanding of the non-ideological reasons why people participate in parties. This chapter extends this sceptical approach to the comparison of the political values of Communist Party members with those of non-members. The chapter draws on an article originally published in *Political Quarterly* (Rose, 1996b). Since then, its conclusions have frequently been tested by including Communist Party membership as an independent variable in regression analyses of the determinants of political attitudes. Past association with that Party consistently fails to be of statistical significance or has only a slight effect.

## 14 Parties without civil society

The starting point for analyzing the relation between parties and society is Lipset and Rokkan's (1967) model of the twentieth-century development of party systems in Western Europe. I applied this multidimensional framework to first- and second-wave democracies in Rose and Urwin (1969). The Communist purging of civil-society institutions made that framework problematic in its application to transformation societies. First findings from the New Europe Barometer were presented in 'Mobilizing Demobilized Voters in Post-Communist Societies' (Rose, 1995d); 'Negative and Positive Partisanship in Post-Communist Countries' (Rose and Mishler, 1998); in subsequent articles and books on Russian elections (White, Rose and McAllister, 1997; Rose and Munro, 2002); and in *Parties and Elections in New European Democracies* (Rose and Munro, 2009). The work has been followed up by a 28-country comparative analysis of participation in civil society in Eastern and Western Europe (Rose, 2006).

## 15 A floating system of parties

The extent to which electoral support was institutionalized in democratic party systems in the quarter-century after the Second World War was very striking (Rose and Urwin, 1970). The decades since have been marked by challenges to incumbent parties (Rose and Mackie, 1983), an increase in parties that split or merge (Rose and Mackie, 1988) and voters floating between established parties and on occasion new parties emerging (see e.g., Rose and McAllister, 1990). The transformation of party competition in post-Communist countries has been of a different order of magnitude. The idea of a floating party system was developed in the context of Duma elections in the 1990s (Rose, 2000b). The data on parties used in this chapter, along with more extensive analysis, can be found in Rose and Munro (2009).

## 16 Voters without trust

Distrust of politicians can be found throughout the world, but the causes and consequences of distrust have differed between free societies and unfree Communist-bloc countries. The party-state's claim to represent workers was shown to be hollow by the results of the first free elections in 1990. Notwithstanding this, citizens must endorse a party in order to cast a valid vote, and most electors do. This chapter draws on a series of articles written on the causes and consequences of political trust, with William Mishler, over a decade (see especially Mishler and Rose, 1997; Mishler and Rose, 2007). The importance of scepticism in evaluating regimes in transformation is set out in Rose and Mishler (1994). The discussion of political values without parties draws on a comparative analysis of attitudes toward individual and collective welfare values (Rose and Makkai, 1995).

## 17 Learning to support new regimes

The challenge of transformation is to understand what is happening at the moment. Since it can take a scholar years to achieve this, by the time a book is published the 'present' that is described therein may be past. There is the additional risk that those who subsequently read the book will assume that what they learn about the past has not been affected by what has happened since the author collected the evidence and ideas set out there. Trend analysis integrates evidence from the past and the present. The logic of Barometer surveys is to monitor trends in popular attitudes in order to see how much or how little transformation has altered attitudes and behaviour from 1991 to its twenty-first-century aftermath. For people living in a society that has been transformed, learning about change is more than academic; it is a necessity. This chapter draws on more than 100 surveys undertaken since 1991 to show what has happened. It draws on a model of political learning set out in detail in *Russia Transformed* (Rose, Mishler and Munro, 2006) and in shorter form in an article in the *Journal of Democracy* (Rose, 2007) and in the *Journal of Communist Studies and Transition Politics* (Rose, Mishler and Munro, 2008).

## 18  Adapting to Russia-style normality

For a social scientist, visits to the Soviet Union in the Brezhnev era were a reminder of the difference between societies with markets and freedom and societies without. They challenged a Westerner to learn the norms that Russians took for granted in going about such daily routines as getting something to eat or hailing a taxi. The transformation of Russia made many of these practices obsolete, but it also required people to adapt to new norms. But what were these norms? The point was made evident when I rang a friend in Moscow a month after the shoot-out at the parliament building in October 1993 and asked in intentionally vague terms how things were. The reply was '*Normalno*' (Rose, 1994b). The New Russia Barometer began including questions that explicitly addressed what Russians mean by normality. This chapter updates and expands an earlier analysis published in *Demokratizatsiya* (Rose, 2008a).

## 19  An evolving Europe

New Europe Barometer surveys have tracked the journey of Central and Eastern Europeans escaping from absolute dissatisfaction to membership in an enlarged European Union. *What Is Europe?* (Rose, 1996) marked the distance that needed to be travelled as a consequence of a twentieth-century legacy of undemocratic regimes. It also demonstrated that this was no disqualification to democratization in countries such as the Federal Republic of Germany. The extent to which democratic governance had been achieved in the eyes of citizens is reported in 'Evaluating Democratic Governance' (Rose, 2008). The different direction in which Russia is heading has been tracked in a series of articles and books over more than half a dozen years, most recently *Russia Transformed* (Rose, Mishler and Munro, 2006) and 'Do Russians See Their Future in Europe or the CIS?' (Rose and Munro, 2008). The analysis of post-Soviet Muslims draws on an article originally published in *Journal of Democracy* (Rose, 2002a).

## 20  Post-transformation issues

The successful establishment of democratic and market institutions in Central and Eastern Europe is altering the answers that can be given to the question *What Is Europe?* (cf. Rose, 1996). The overarching institutions of Europe now embrace 27 countries of increasing heterogeneity. Differences in rates of economic growth are starting to reduce differences in average national income between new and old member states. The fact that low standards of democratic governance in some CEE countries are matched by some older member states of the EU increases the need to raise European standards of governance (Rose, 2008; Transparency International). The expansion of EU membership has also added 10 diverse new voices to an increasingly multinational discussion, with consequences explored in 'Political Communication in a European Public Space' (Rose, 2008b).

# References

Ash, Timothy N., 1992. *The Food Balance in the Former Soviet Union*. Edinburgh: Heriot-Watt University Centre for Economic Reform and Transformation.

Barber, Lionel, Buckley, Neil and Belton, Catherine, 2008. 'Laying down the Law', *Financial Times*, 25 March.

Berlin, Isaiah, 1958. *Two Concepts of Liberty: An Inaugural Lecture*. Oxford: Clarendon Press.

Beyme, Klaus von, 1990. 'Transition to Democracy – or *Anschluss?*', *Government and Opposition* 25, 170–190.

Blasi, Joseph R., Kroumova, Maya and Kruse, Douglas, 1997. *Kremlin Capitalism: Privatizing the Russian Economy*. Ithaca, NY: Cornell University Press.

Bobak, Martin, Murphy, Michael, Rose, Richard and Marmot, Michael, 2003. 'Determinants of Adult Mortality in Russia: Estimates from Sibling Data', *Epidemiology* 14, 5, 603–611.

Bobak, M., Pikhart, H., Hertzman, C., Rose, R. and Marmot, M., 1998. 'Socioeconomic Factors, Perceived Control and Self-Reported Health in Russia', *Social Science and Medicine* 47, 269–279.

Breslauer, George W., 1978. 'On the Adaptability of Soviet Welfare-State Authoritarianism'. In Karl W. Ryavec, ed., *Soviet Society and the Communist Party*. Amherst: University of Massachusetts Press, pp. 3–25.

Breslauer, George, 2001. 'Personalism versus Proceduralism: Boris Yeltsin and the Institutional Fragility of the Russian System'. In V. E. Bonnell and G. W. Breslauer, eds., *Russia in the New Century*. Boulder, CO: Westview Press, 35–58.

Brumberg, Daniel, 2002. 'Islamists and the Politics of Consensus', *Journal of Democracy*, 13, 3, 109–115.

Bryce, James A., 1921. *Modern Democracies* (2 vols). London: Macmillan.

Camdessus, Michel, 1994. 'Camdessus Expresses Confidence in Russian Economic Reform', *IMF Survey*, 4 April, 97–98.

Carnaghan, Ellen, 2007. *Out of Order: Russian Political Values in an Imperfect World*. State College: Pennsylvania State University Press.

Centre for the Study of Public Policy. *www.abdn.ac.uk/cspp*. Aberdeen: University of Aberdeen.

Churchill, Winston, 1947. 'Debate', House of Commons *Hansard*. London: HMSO, 11 November, col. 206.

Cockerham, William C., 1999. *Health and Social Change in Russia and Eastern Europe*. London: Routledge.

Cockerham, William, 2007. *Social Causes of Health and Disease*. Cambridge: Polity Press.

Coleman, James, 1990. *Foundations of Social Theory*. Cambridge, MA: Harvard University Press.

Dahl, Robert A., 1971. *Polyarchy: Participation and Opposition*. New Haven, CT: Yale University Press.

Dasgupta, Partha and Serageldin, Ismail, eds., 2000. *Social Capital: A Multi-faceted Perspective*. Washington, DC: World Bank.

Deacon, Bob, 1993. 'Developments in East European Social Policy'. In Catherine Jones, ed., *New Perspectives on the Welfare State in Europe*. London: Routledge, 177–197.

Deutsch, Karl W., 1963. *The Nerves of Government*. New York: Free Press.

Durkheim, Emile, 1952. *Suicide: A Study in Sociology*. London: Routledge, 1952.

EBRD (European Bank for Reconstruction and Development), annual. *Transition Report*, updated at www.ebrd.com. London: European Bank for Reconstruction and Development.

Fish, M. Steven, 1995. *Democracy from Scratch: Opposition and Regime in the New Russian Revolution*. Princeton, NJ: Princeton University Press.

Flora, Peter and Alber, Jens, 1981. 'Modernization, Democratization and the Development of Welfare States in Western Europe'. In Flora and A. J. Heidenheimer, eds., *The Development of Welfare States in Europe and America*. New Brunswick, NJ: Transaction, 37–80.

Freddi, Giorgio, 1986. 'Bureaucratic Rationalities and the Prospect for Party Government'. In F. G. Castles and Rudolf Wildenmann, eds., *Visions and Realities of Party Government*. Berlin: Walter de Gruyter, 143–178.

Freedom House, 2007. *www.freedomhouse.org*.

Freeland, Chrystia, 2000. *Sale of the Century: The Inside Story of the Second Russian Revolution*. London: Little, Brown.

Fukuyama, Francis, 1995. *Trust: The Social Virtues and the Creation of Prosperity*. New York: Free Press.

Furtak, Robert K., ed., 1990. *Elections in Socialist States*. New York: Harvester Wheatsheaf, 20–52.

Galbreath, David J. and Rose, Richard, 2008. 'Fair Treatment in a Divided Society: A Bottom-up Assessment of Bureaucratic Encounters in Latvia', *Governance* 21, 1, 53–73.

Galeski, B., 1987. 'Sociological Problems of the Occupation of a Farmer'. In T. Shanin, ed., *Peasants and Peasant Societies*. Oxford: Oxford University Press.

Garton Ash, Timothy, 1990. *The Uses of Adversity*. Cambridge: Granta Books.

Gerber, Theodore P. and Hout, Michael, 1998. 'More Shock than Therapy: Market Transition, Employment and Income in Russia, 1991–1995', *American Journal of Sociology* 101, 1, 1–50.

Gilmore, Anna, McKee, M. and Rose, R., 2002. 'Determinants of Inequalities in Self-Perceived Health in Ukraine', *Social Science and Medicine* 55, 2177–2188.

Goble, Paul A., 1995. 'Chechnya and Its Consequences', *Post-Soviet Affairs*, 11, 1, 23–27.

Grossman, Gregory, 1977. 'The Second Economy of the USSR', *Problems of Communism* 26, 5, 25–40.

Gurr, Ted R., 1970. *Why Men Rebel*. Princeton, NJ: Princeton University Press.

Hankiss, Elemer, 1990. *East European Alternatives*. Oxford: Clarendon Press.

Heller, Mikhail, 1988. *Cogs in the Soviet Wheel: The Formation of Soviet Man*. London: Collins Harvill.

Hirschman, Albert O., 1970. *Exit, Voice and Loyalty*. Cambridge, MA: Harvard University Press.

Hough, Jerry F., 1977. *The Soviet Union and Social Science Theory*. Cambridge, MA: Harvard University Press.

Huntington, Samuel P., 1991. *The Third Wave: Democratization in the Late Twentieth Century*. Norman: University of Oklahoma Press.

Huntington, Samuel P., 1996. *The Clash of Civilizations and the Remaking of World Order*. New York: Simon and Schuster.

Huntington, Samuel P., 1996. 'Democracy for the Long Haul', *Journal of Democracy* 7, 2, 3–13.

Inglehart, Ronald, 1997. *Modernization and Postmodernization: Cultural, Economic and Political Change in 41 Societies*. Princeton, NJ: Princeton University Press.

International Child Development Centre, 1997. *Children at Risk in Central and Eastern Europe*. Florence: ICDC/UNICEF Regional Monitoring Report No. 4.

Johnson, Juliet, 2001. 'Path Contingency in Postcommunist Transformations', *Comparative Politics* 33, 3, 253–274.

Jowitt, Kenneth, 1992. *New World Disorder: The Leninist Extinction*. Berkeley: University of California Press.

Karl, Terry Lynn, 2000. 'Electoralism'. In Richard Rose, ed., *The International Encyclopedia of Elections*. Washington, DC: CQ Press, 96–97.

Katsenelinboigen, A., 1977. 'Coloured Markets in the Soviet Union', *Soviet Studies* 29, 1, 62–85.

King, David, 1997. *The Commissar Vanishes: The Falsification of Photographs and Art in Stalin's Russia*. Edinburgh: Canongate.

Kis, Janos, 1998. 'Between Reform and Revolution', *East European Politics and Society* 12, 2, 300–333.

Klebnikov, Paul, 2000. *Godfather of the Kremlin: Boris Berezovsky and the Looting of Russia*. New York: Harcourt, Brace.

Koestler, Arthur, 1940. *Darkness at Noon*. New York: Bantam Books edition, 1968.

Kornai, Janos, 1992. *The Socialist System: The Political Economy of Communism*. Princeton, NJ: Princeton University Press.

Kornai, Janos, 2006. *By Force of Thought: Irregular Memories of an Intellectual Journey*. Cambridge, MA: MIT Press.

Lavigne, Marie, 1995. *The Economics of Transition: From Socialist Economy to Market Economy*. London: Macmillan.

Lazarsfeld, Paul, Berelson, Bernard and Gaudet, Hazel, 1944. *The People's Choice*. New York: Duell, Sloan and Pearce.

Lazarsfeld, Paul, Jahoda, Marie and Zeisel, Hans, 1933. *Die Arbeitslosen von Marienthal*. Leipzig: S. Hirzel Verlag.

Lewis, Ben, 2008. *Hammer and Tickle*. London: Weidenfeld and Nicolson.

Linz, Juan J., 1990. 'Transitions to Democracy', *The Washington Quarterly*, Summer, 143–164.

Linz, Juan, 1997. 'Some Thoughts on the Victory and Future of Democracy'. In A. Hadenius, ed., *Democracy's Victory and Crisis*. New York: Cambridge University Press, 404–426.

Linz, Juan J., 2000. *Totalitarian and Authoritarian Regimes*. Boulder, CO: Lynne Rienner Publishers.

Lipset, S. M. and Rokkan, Stein, eds., 1967. *Party Systems and Voter Alignments*. New York: Free Press.

Lomax, Bill, 1995. 'Impediments to Democratization in Post-Communist East-Central Europe'. In Gordon Wightman, ed., *Party Formation in East-Central Europe*. Aldershot: Edward Elgar, 179–201.

Lopez-Claros, Augusto and Zadornov, Mikhail M., 2002. 'Economic Reforms: Steady as She Goes', *The Washington Quarterly* 25, 1, 105–116.

McKee, Martin, Bobak, M., Rose, R., Shkolnikov, V., Chenet, L. and Leon, D., 1998. 'Patterns of Smoking in Russia', *Tobacco Control* 7, 22–26.

Mainwaring, Scott and Scully, Tim, eds. 1995. *Building Democratic Institutions: Party Systems in Latin America*. Stanford, CA: Stanford University Press.

Marer, Paul, Arvay, Janos, O'Connor, John, Schrenk, Martin and Swanson, Daniel, 1992. *Historically Planned Economies: A Guide to the Data*. Washington, DC: World Bank.

Marshall, T. H., 1950. *Citizenship and Social Class*. Cambridge: Cambridge University Press.

Miller, Arthur H. and Klobucar, Thomas F., 2000. 'The Development of Party Identification in Post-Soviet Societies', *American Journal of Political Science* 44, 4, 667–685.

Mishler, William and Rose, Richard, 1997. 'Trust, Distrust and Skepticism: Popular Evaluations of Civil and Political Institutions in Post-Communist Societies', *Journal of Politics* 59, 2, 418–451.

Mishler, William and Rose, Richard, 2001. 'Political Support for Incomplete Democracies: Realist vs. Idealist Theories and Measures', *International Political Science Review* 22, 4, 303–320.

Mishler, William and Rose, Richard, 2002. 'Learning and Re-Learning Regime Support: The Dynamics of Post-Communist Regimes', *European Journal of Political Research* 41, 1, 5–36.

Mishler, William and Rose, Richard, 2005. 'What Are the Political Consequences of Trust? A Test of Cultural and Institutional Theories in Russia', *Comparative Political Studies*, 38, 9, 1050–1078.

Mishler, William and Rose, Richard, 2007. 'Generation, Age and Time: The Dynamics of Political Learning through Russia's Transformation', *American Journal of Political Science* 51, 4, 822–834.

Munro, Neil, 2006. 'Russia's Persistent Communist Legacy: Nostalgia, Reaction, and Reactionary Expectations', *Post-Soviet Affairs* 22, 4, 289–313.

Murphy, Michael, Bobak, M., Nicholson, A., Rose, R. and Marmot, M., 2006. 'The Widening Trend in Mortality by Educational Level in Russia, 1980–2001', *American Journal of Public Health* 96, 1293–1299.

Nicholson, Amanda, Bobak, M., Murphy, M., Rose, R. and Marmot, M., 2005. 'Socioeconomic Influences on Self-Rated Health in Russian Men and Women – A Life Course Approach', *Social Science and Medicine* 61, 2345–2354.

Nodia, Ghia, 1996. 'How Different Are Postcommunist Transitions?', *Journal of Democracy* 7, 4, 15–29.

North, Douglass C., forthcoming. 'Norms, Politics, Institutions and Economic Reform', *Business Economics*.

Nye, Joseph S., 2004. *Soft Power: The Means to Success in World Politics*. New York: Public Affairs Press.

OECD, 1991. *Statistics for a Market Economy*. Paris: OECD.

Olson, David M., 1993. 'Political Parties and Party Systems in Regime Transformation: Inner Transition in the New Democracies of Central Europe', *American Review of Politics* 13 (Winter), 619–658.

Perlman, Francesca, Bobak, M., Steptoe, A., Rose, R. and Marmot, M., 2003. 'Do Health Control Beliefs Predict Behaviour in Russians?', *Preventive Medicine* 37, 73–81.

Polanyi, Karl F., 1957. *The Great Transformation*. Boston, MA: Beacon Press.

Pomerleau, J., Gilmore, A., McKee, M., Rose, R. and Haerpfer, C., 2004. 'Prevalence of Smoking in Eight Countries of the Former Soviet Union', *Addiction* 99, 12, 1577–1585.

Pryor, Frederic L., 1992. *The Red and the Green: The Rise and Fall of Collectivized Agriculture in Marxist Regimes*. London: George Allen & Unwin.

Putin, Vladimir, with N. Gevorkyan, N. Timakova and A. Kolesnikov, 2000. *First Person*. London: Hutchinson.

Putnam, Robert, with Robert Leonardi and Raffaella Y. Nanetti, 1993. *Making Democracy Work*. Princeton, NJ: Princeton University Press.

Putnam, Robert, 1997. 'Democracy in America at Century's End'. In Axel Hadenius, ed., *Democracy's Victory and Crisis*. New York: Cambridge University Press, 27–70.

Reddaway, Peter and Glinski, Dmitri, 2001. *The Tragedy of Russia's Reforms: Market Bolshevism against Democracy*. Washington, DC: United States Institute of Peace Press.

Roberts, Andrew, 2004. 'The State of Socialism: A Note on Terminology', *Slavic Review* 63, 2, 349–368.

Rose, Richard, 1969. 'Dynamic Tendencies in the Authority of Regimes', *World Politics* 21, 4, 612–628.

Rose, Richard, 1980. 'Misperceiving Public Expenditure: Feelings about "Cuts"'. In C. H. Levine and I. Rubin, eds., *Fiscal Stress and Public Policy*. Beverly Hills, CA: Sage, 203–230.

Rose, Richard, 1985. 'Getting by in Three Economies: The Resources of the Official, Unofficial and Domestic Economies'. In Jan-Erik Lane, ed., *State and Market*. London: Sage, 103–141.

Rose, Richard, 1986. 'Common Goals but Different Roles: The State's Contribution to the Welfare Mix'. In R. Rose and Rei Shiratori, eds., *The Welfare State East and West*. New York: Oxford University Press, 13–39.

Rose, Richard, 1991. *Between State and Market: Key Indicators of Transition in Eastern Europe*. Glasgow Centre for the Study of Public Policy *Studies in Public Policy* 196.

Rose, Richard, 1992. 'Escaping from Absolute Dissatisfaction: A Trial-and-Error Model of Change in Eastern Europe', *Journal of Theoretical Politics* 4, 4, 371–93.

Rose, Richard, 1992a. 'Eastern Europe's Need for a Civil Economy'. In Richard O'Brien, ed., *Finance and the International Economy*, 6. Oxford: Oxford University Press, 4–16.

Rose, Richard, 1993. 'Bringing Freedom Back In: Rethinking Priorities of the Welfare State'. In Catherine Jones, ed., *New Perspectives on the Welfare State in Europe*. London: Routledge, 221–241.

Rose, Richard, 1993a. 'Contradictions between Micro and Macro-Economic Goals in Post-communist Societies', *Europe-Asia Studies* 45, 3, 419–444.

Rose, Richard, 1994. *Comparing Welfare across Time and Space*. Vienna: European Centre for Social Welfare Policy and Research, Eurosocial Report 49.

Rose, Richard, 1994a. 'Who Needs Social Protection in Eastern Europe?'. In Stein Ringen and Claire Wallace, eds., *Societies in Transition: East-Central Europe Today*. Aldershot: Avebury, 175–220.

Rose, Richard, 1994b. 'Getting by without Government: Everyday Life in Russia', *Daedalus*, 123, 3, 41–62.

Rose, Richard, 1995. 'Russia as an Hour-Glass Society: A Constitution without Citizens', *East European Constitutional Review* 4, 3, 34–42.

Rose, Richard, 1995a. 'Making Progress and Catching Up: Comparative Analysis for Social Policymaking', *International Social Science Journal* 143, 113–126.

Rose, Richard, 1995b. 'Adaptation, Resilience and Destitution: Alternative Responses to Transition in the Ukraine', *Problems of Post-Communism* 42, 6, 52–61.

Rose, Richard, 1995c. 'Freedom as a Fundamental Value', *International Social Science Journal* 145, 457–471.

Rose, Richard, 1995d. 'Mobilizing Demobilized Voters in Post-Communist Societies', *Party Politics* 1, 4, 549–563.

Rose, Richard, 1995e. *Pensioners, Gender and Poverty in the Baltic States*. Washington, DC: World Bank Discussion Paper IDP-151.

Rose, Richard, 1996. *What Is Europe? A Dynamic Perspective*. New York and London: Longman.

Rose, Richard, 1996a. 'Evaluating Benefits: The Views of Russian Employees'. In Douglas Lippoldt, ed., *Social Benefits and the Russian Enterprise: A Time of Transition*. Paris: OECD, 39–60.

Rose, Richard, 1996b. 'Ex-Communists in Post-Communist Societies', *Political Quarterly* 67, 1, 14–25.

Rose, Richard, 1997. 'The Art of Writing about Politics'. In Hans Daalder, ed., *Comparative European Politics: The Story of a Profession*. London and Washington, DC: Pinter, 127–139.

Rose, Richard, 1997a. 'How Patient Are People in Post-Communist Societies?', *World Affairs* 159, 3, 130–144.

Rose, Richard, 1998. 'What Is the Demand for Price Stability in Post-Communist Countries?', *Problems of Post-Communism* 45, 2, 43–50.

Rose, Richard, 1998a. *Getting Things Done with Social Capital: New Russia Barometer VII*. Glasgow: Centre for the Study of Public Policy *Studies in Public Policy* No. 303.

Rose, Richard, 1999. 'Living in an Antimodern Society', *East European Constitutional Review* 8, 1–2, 68–75.

Rose, Richard, 1999a. 'The Long and the Short of the Transformation in Central Europe'. In R. Andorka, T. Kolosi, R. Rose and G. Vukovich, eds., *A Society Transformed: Hungary in Time–Space Perspective*. Budapest: Central European University Press, 179–204.

Rose, Richard, 2000. 'Uses of Social Capital in Russia: Modern, Pre-modern and Anti-modern', *Post-Soviet Affairs* 16, 1, 33–57.

Rose, Richard, 2000a. 'How Much Does Social Capital Add to Individual Health? A Survey Study of Russians', *Social Science and Medicine* 51, 9, 1421–1435.

Rose, Richard, 2000b. 'A Supply-Side View of Russia's Elections', *East European Constitutional Review* 9, 1–2, 53–59.

Rose, Richard, 2001. 'When Government Fails: Social Capital in an Antimodern Russia'. In B. Edwards, M. W. Foley and Mario Diani, eds., *Beyond Tocqueville: Civil Society and Social Capital in Comparative Perspective*. Hanover, NH: University Press of New England, 56–69.

Rose, Richard, 2002. 'Economies in Transformation: A Multidimensional Approach to a Cross-Cultural Problem', *East European Constitutional Review* 11, 4/12, 1, 62–70.

Rose, Richard, 2002a. 'How Muslims View Democracy: The View from Central Asia', *Journal of Democracy* 13, 4, 102–111.

Rose, Richard, 2003. 'Social Shocks, Social Confidence and Health'. In Judyth Twigg and Kate Schecter, eds., *Social Cohesion and Social Capital in Russia.* Armonk, NY: M. E. Sharpe, 98–117.

Rose, Richard, 2006. *Participation in Civil Society.* Dublin: First European Quality of Life Survey: European Foundation for the Improvement of Living and Working Conditions.

Rose, Richard, 2006a. *Internet Diffusion Not Divide: A Proximity Model of Internet Take Off in Russia.* Oxford: Oxford Internet Institute Research Report No. 10.

Rose, Richard, 2006b. *Diverging Paths of Post-Communist Countries: New Europe Barometer Trends since 1991.* Aberdeen: Centre for the Study of Public Policy *Studies in Public Policy* No. 418.

Rose, Richard, 2007. 'Learning to Support New Regimes in Europe', *Journal of Democracy* 18, 3, 111–125.

Rose, Richard, 2007a. 'Going Public with Private Opinions: Are Post-Communist Citizens Afraid to Say What They Think?', *Journal of Elections and Public Opinion* 17, 2, 123–142.

Rose, Richard, 2008. 'Evaluating Democratic Governance: A Bottom-up Approach to European Union Enlargement', *Democratization* 15, 2, 251–271.

Rose, Richard, 2008a. 'Is Russia Becoming a Normal Society?', *Demokratizatsiya* 16, 1, 75–86.

Rose, Richard, 2008b. 'Political Communication in a European Public Space', *Journal of Common Market Studies* 46, 3, 451–475.

Rose, Richard, 2008c. *New Russia Barometer Trends since 1992.* Aberdeen: Centre for the Study of Public Policy *Studies in Public Policy* No. 450.

Rose, Richard, 2009. 'Democratic and Undemocratic States'. In C. W. Haerpfer, P. Bernhagen, R. Inglehart and C. Welzel, eds., *Democratization.* Oxford: Oxford University Press.

Rose, Richard and Bobak, Martin, 2007. *Stresses and Opportunities of Post-Communist Transformation: The Impact on Health.* Aberdeen: Centre for the Study of Public Policy *Studies in Public Policy* No. 434.

Rose, Richard and Haerpfer, Christian, 1996. 'The Impact of a Ready-Made State' [in German]. In Helmut Wiesenthal, ed., *Vergleichende Perspektiven auf die Transformation Ostdeutschlands.* Frankfurt am Main: Campus, 105–140 and in English *German Politics* 6, 1, 1997, 100–121.

Rose, Richard and Haerpfer, Christian, 1998. 'Making Good Use of Multinational Surveys in Post-Communist Countries'. In Rachel Walker and Marcia Freed Taylor, eds., *Information Dissemination and Access in Russia and Eastern Europe.* Amsterdam: IOS Press, 178–187.

Rose, Richard and McAllister, Ian, 1990. *The Loyalty of Voters.* London: Sage.

Rose, Richard and McAllister, Ian, 1996. 'Is Money the Measure of Welfare in Russia?', *Review of Income and Wealth* 42, 1, 75–90.

Rose, Richard and Mackie, Thomas T., 1983. 'Incumbency in Government: Liability or Asset?'. In H. Daalder and P. Mair, eds., *West European Party Systems.* London: Sage, 115–137.

Rose, Richard and Mackie, Thomas T., 1988. 'Do Parties Persist or Fail? The Big Trade-Off Facing Organizations'. In Kay Lawson and Peter Merkl, eds., *When Parties Fail.* Princeton, NJ: Princeton University Press, 533–558.

Rose, Richard and Makkai, Toni, 1995. 'Consensus or Dissensus in Welfare Values in Post-Communist Societies?', *European Journal of Political Research* 28, 2, 203–224.

Rose, Richard, and Mishler, William, 1994. 'Mass Reaction to Regime Change in Eastern Europe: Polarization or Leaders and Laggards', *British Journal of Political Science* 24, 2, 159–182.

Rose, Richard and Mishler, William, 1998. 'Negative and Positive Partisanship in Post-Communist Countries', *Electoral Studies* 17, 2, 217–234.

Rose, Richard and Mishler, William, 2008. *A Supply-and-Demand Model of Party System Institutionalization.* Aberdeen: Centre for the Study of Public Policy *Studies in Public Policy* No. 445.

Rose, Richard, Mishler, William and Haerpfer, Christian, 1998. *Democracy and Its Alternatives: Understanding Post-Communist Societies.* Oxford: Polity Press and Baltimore, MD: Johns Hopkins University Press.

Rose, Richard, Mishler, William and Munro, Neil, 2006. *Russia Transformed: Developing Popular Support for a New Regime*. Cambridge: Cambridge University Press.

Rose, Richard, Mishler, William and Munro, Neil, 2008. 'Time Matters: Adapting to Transformation', *Journal of Communist and Post-Communist Studies* 24, 1, 90–114.

Rose, Richard and Munro, Neil, 2002. *Elections without Order: Russia's Challenge to Vladimir Putin*. New York: Cambridge University Press.

Rose, Richard and Munro, Neil, 2003. *Elections and Parties in New European Democracies*. Washington, DC: CQ Press.

Rose, Richard and Munro, Neil, 2008. 'Do Russians See Their Future in Europe or the CIS?', *Europe-Asia Studies* 60, 1, 49–66.

Rose, Richard and Munro, Neil, 2003. *Parties and Elections in New European Democracies*. Colchester: ECPR Press.

Rose, Richard and Page, Edward, 1996. 'German Responses to Regime Change: Culture, Economy or Context?', *West European Politics* 19, 1, 1–27.

Rose, Richard and Shin, Doh Chull, 2001. 'Democratization Backwards: The Problem of Third-Wave Democracies', *British Journal of Political Science* 31, 2, 331–354.

Rose, Richard, Shin, Doh Chull and Munro, Neil, 1999. 'Tensions between the Democratic Ideal and Reality: South Korea'. In Pippa Norris, ed., *Critical Citizens*. Oxford: Oxford University Press, 146–165.

Rose, Richard and Tikhomirov, Evgeny, 1993. 'Who Grows Food in Russia and Eastern Europe?', *Post-Soviet Geography* 34, 2, 111–126.

Rose, Richard and Urwin, Derek, 1969. 'Social Cohesion, Political Parties and Strains in Regimes', *Comparative Political Studies* 2, 1, 7–67.

Rose, Richard and Urwin, Derek, 1970. 'Persistence and Change in Western Party Systems since 1945', *Political Studies* 18, 3, 287–319.

Rose, Richard and Weller, Craig, 2003. 'What Does Social Capital Add to Democratic Values?'. In Gabriel Badescu and Eric Uslaner, eds., *Social Capital and the Transition to Democracy*. London and New York: Routledge, 200–218.

Rose, Richard, Zapf, Wolfgang and Seifert, Wolfgang, 1993. *Germans in Comparative Perspective*. Glasgow: Centre for the Study of Public Policy *Studies in Public Policy* No. 218.

Schedler, Andreas, ed., 2006. *Electoral Authoritarianism: The Dynamics of Unfree Competition*. Boulder, CO: Lynne Rienner.

Schmitter, Philippe C., 1995. 'Corporatism'. In S. M. Lipset, ed., *The Encyclopedia of Democracy* (vol. 1). Washington, DC: Congressional Quarterly, 308–310.

Schumpeter, Joseph A., 1946. 'The American Economy in the Interwar Years', *American Economic Review* 36, supplement, 1–10.

Schumpeter, Joseph A., 1952. *Capitalism, Socialism and Democracy*. 4th edn. London: George Allen & Unwin.

Shanin, Teodor, 1990. *Defining Peasants*. Oxford: Basil Blackwell.

Shi, Tianjian, 1997. *Political Participation in Beijing*. Cambridge, MA: Harvard University Press.

Shin, Doh Chull and Rose, Richard, 1997. *Koreans Evaluate Democracy: A New Korea Barometer Survey*. Glasgow: Centre for the Study of Public Policy *Studies in Public Policy* No. 292.

Shlapentokh, Vladimir, 1989. *Public and Private Life of the Soviet People*. New York: Oxford University Press.

Shlapentokh, Vladimir, 2001. *A Normal Totalitarian Society: How the Soviet Union Functioned and How It Collapsed*. Armonk, NY: M. E. Sharpe.

Simon, Herbert A., 1978. 'Rationality as Process and as Product of Thought', *American Economic Review* 68, 2, 1–16.

Simon, Herbert A., 1979. 'Rational Decision-Making in Business Organizations', *American Economic Review* 69, 4, 493–513.

Simon, Janos, 1996. *Popular Conceptions of Democracy in Postcommunist Europe*. Glasgow: Centre for the Study of Public Policy *Studies in Public Policy* No. 273.

Sirc, Ljubo, 1989. *Between Hitler and Tito: Nazi Occupation and Communist Oppression.* London: Andre Deutsch.

Summers, Lawrence H., 1991. 'Lessons of Reform for the Baltics'. Indianapolis: Paper to Hudson Institute Conference, 29 October.

Syme, S. L., 1989. 'Control and Health: a Personal Perspective'. In A. Steptoe and A. Appels, eds., *Stress, Personal Control and Health.* New York: John Wiley, 3–18.

Transparency International, annual. *www.transparency.org.*

Tworzecki, Hubert, 2003. *Learning to Choose: Electoral Politics in East-Central Europe.* Stanford, CA: Stanford University Press.

UNICEF (annual). *Innocenti Social Monitor.* Florence: Innocenti Research Centre MONEE project.

Webb, Beatrice and Webb, Sidney, 1937. *Soviet Communism: A New Civilization.* 2nd edn. London: Printed for trade union subscribers.

Webb, W. J., 1992. 'The Polish General Election of 1991', *Electoral Studies* 11, 2, 166–170.

Weber, Max, 1947. *The Theory of Social and Economic Organization.* Glencoe, IL: Free Press.

Weber, Max, 1948. *From Max Weber.* Edited by H. H. Gerth and C. Wright Mills. London: Routledge.

Weber, Max, 1968. *Economy and Society.* Edited by Guenther Roth and Claus Wittich. Berkeley: University of California Press, 1968.

Weber, Max, 1973. *Wirtschaft und Gesellschaft.* 5th edn. Tübingen: J. C. B. Mohr.

Wedel, Janine R., 1986. *The Private Poland.* New York: Facts on File.

Wedel, Janine R., ed., 1992. *The Unplanned Society: Poland during and after Communism.* New York: Columbia University Press.

Wedel, Janine, 1998. *Collision and Collusion.* New York: St. Martin's Press.

White, Stephen, 1979. *Political Culture and Soviet Politics.* London: Macmillan.

White, Stephen, ed., 1990. 'Elections in Eastern Europe', a special issue of *Electoral Studies* 9, 4, 275–366.

White, Stephen, Rose, Richard and McAllister, Ian, 1997. *How Russia Votes.* Chatham, NJ: Chatham House.

Wiles, P. J. D., 1983. 'Soviet Inflation, 1982', *Jahrbuch der Wirtschaft Osteuropas* 8, 2.

Winiecki, Jan, 1988. *The Distorted World of Soviet-Type Economics.* London: Routledge.

Yurchak, Alexei, 2006. *Everything Was Forever, Until It Was No More.* Princeton, NJ: Princeton University Press.

Z, 1990. 'To the Stalin Mausoleum', *Daedalus* 119, 1, 295–344.

Zaslavsky, V. and Brym, Robert, 1978. 'The Functions of Elections in the USSR', *Soviet Studies* 30, 362–371.

# Index